CIVILIZATIONS

OF ANCIENT IRAQ

CIVILIZATIONS
OF ANCIENT IRAQ

Benjamin R. Foster
Karen Polinger Foster

PRINCETON UNIVERSITY PRESS   *Princeton & Oxford*

Frontispiece. Tablet of the *Epic of Gilgamesh*, Yale Babylonian Collection (see figure 22).

Copyright © 2009 by Princeton University Press

Published by Princeton University Press, 41 William Street, Princeton, New Jersey 08540

In the United Kingdom: Princeton University Press, 6 Oxford Street, Woodstock, Oxfordshire OX20 1TW

press.princeton.edu

All Rights Reserved

Second printing, and first paperback printing, 2011
Paperback ISBN 978-0-691-14997-4

The Library of Congress has cataloged the cloth edition of this book as follows

Foster, Benjamin R. (Benjamin Read)
  Civilizations of ancient Iraq / Benjamin R. Foster,
Karen Polinger Foster.
    p.   cm.
  Includes bibliographical references and index.
  ISBN 978-0-691-13722-3 (hardcover : alk. paper)
  1. Civilization, Assyro-Babylonian. 2. Assyria—Antiquities.
3. Babylonia—Antiquities. 4. Babylonia—Social life and
customs. 5. Iraq—History—To 634. I. Foster, Karen
Polinger, 1950. II. Title.
  DS7.7.F67 2009
  935—dc22   2008048067

British Library Cataloging-in-Publication Data is available

This book has been composed in Adobe Garamond

Printed on acid-free paper. ∞

Printed in the United States of America

10 9 8 7 6 5 4 3 2

CONTENTS

Illustrations ix

Preface xi

1. IN THE BEGINNING
   Of Tigris and Euphrates 1
   The First Villages 7
   From the Foothills to the Plains 12

2. THE BIRTHPLACE OF CIVILIZATION
   The First Cities 15
   From City to State 27
   Sumerians Abroad 29
   Setting Words on Clay 30
   The Uruk Phenomenon 33

3. EARLY CITY-STATES
   New Polities 35
   Ur and the Royal Graves 36
   When Kingship Came down from Heaven 39
   Shuruppak, City of Wisdom 40
   A Tale of Two Cities 42

4. KINGS OF THE FOUR QUARTERS OF THE WORLD
   The First Empire 51
   Naram-Sin: When Kingship Went up to Heaven 55
   A Golden Age of Sumerian Culture 61
   Management and Crisis 67

5. THE AGE OF HAMMURABI
   The Amorites 71
   Rim-Sin, King of Larsa 73

124200

Shamshi-Adad, King of Upper Mesopotamia   74
Hammurabi, King of Babylon   76
Arts of the Table and Bedroom   81
The *Epic of Gilgamesh*   83
The End of Amorite Rule   85

6. BABYLONIA IN THE FAMILY OF NATIONS

The Kassites   87
Kassite Statecraft and Society   90
The Club of Great Powers   93
Science and Literature   94
The Hurrians   99
The End of Kassite Rule   100

7. THE ASSYRIAN ACHIEVEMENT

The Rise of Assur   105
The Middle Assyrian Empire   109
The Neo-Assyrian Empire   113
Assurnasirpal II and Nimrud   115
Sennacherib and Nineveh   119
The Library of Assurbanipal   123
The Fall of Assyria   126

8. THE GLORY OF BABYLON

The Last Babylonian Empire   129
Nabonidus, King of Babylon   132
Learning and Memory in Babylonia   134
Works and Days   140
The Persian Empire   142

9. MESOPOTAMIA BETWEEN TWO WORLDS

Alexander the Great and the Seleucids   147
Antiochus I Soter, King of Asia   149
The Realm and Its Economy   152
The Culture of Hellenistic Babylonia   154
The Rise of Parthia   156
Mithridates I and the Reunification of Iraq   158
Parthian Iraq   160

Roman Armies in Iraq   164
The End of Mesopotamian Civilization   166

10. SASSANIAN IRAQ

The Sassanian Empire and Religious Pluralism   168
By the Waters of Babylon: Judaism in Iraq   173
Christianity in Iraq   176
Sassanian Society, Statecraft, and Economy   178
Arab Settlement in Iraq   180
Sassanian Art   182
Shapur I and Shapur II   184
The Sassanians and Byzantium   187
Prelude to Conquest   189

EPILOGUE   DISCOVERY AND DESTRUCTION
              OF ANCIENT IRAQ

Exploration and Decipherment   191
Archaeology Past and Present   198
The Nation of Iraq and Cultural Heritage   201
The Gulf War and Cultural Destruction   205
The Iraq War and Cultural Devastation   206

Notes   211
Bibliography   231
Index   283

ILLUSTRATIONS

Maps

Map 1. From Rome to the Indus   2
Map 2. Ancient Iraq   3

Figures

Frontispiece. Tablet of the *Epic of Gilgamesh*, Yale Babylonian
    Collection
Figure 1. Halaf ware bowl from Arpachiyah, Iraq Museum   11
Figure 2. Cone mosaics from Uruk, Vorderasiatisches
    Museum   20
Figure 3. Uruk Head, Iraq Museum   23
Figure 4. Uruk Vase, Iraq Museum   24, 25
Figure 5. Drawings of cylinder seal impressions from various
    sites, periods, and museums   26
Figure 6. Inlaid harp from Ur, Iraq Museum   38
Figure 7. Stele of the Vultures from Lagash, Louvre   44
Figure 8. Statue of Enmetena from Ur, Iraq Museum   46
Figure 9. Victory Stele of Naram-Sin from Susa, Louvre   57
Figure 10. Ziggurat at Ur   63
Figure 11. Law Code of Hammurabi from Susa, Louvre   78
Figure 12. Molded brick façade from Uruk, Vorderasiatisches
    Museum   89
Figure 13. Glass goblet from Tell al-Rimah, Iraq Museum   101
Figure 14. Tablet and envelope from Kanesh, Yale Babylonian
    Collection   107
Figure 15. Relief from the throne room of Assurnasirpal at
    Nimrud, British Museum   117

Figure 16. Relief from Court VI of Sennacherib at Nineveh, British Museum 122

Figure 17. Ivory furniture panel from Nimrud, Iraq Museum 127

Figure 18. Limestone tablet from Sippar, British Museum 136

Figure 19. Silver tetradrachm of Antiochus I Soter, private collection 150

Figure 20. Temple complex, Hatra 162

Figure 21. Royal bust from Kish, Field Museum of Natural History 185

Figure 22. Tablet of the *Epic of Gilgamesh*, Yale Babylonian Collection 199

PREFACE

Iraq is one of the birthplaces of human civilization. This land saw the first towns and cities, the first states and empires. Here writing was invented, and with it the world's oldest poetry and prose and the beginnings of mathematics, astronomy, and law. Here too are found pioneering achievements in pyrotechnology, as well as important innovations in art and architecture. From Iraq comes rich documentation for nearly every aspect of human endeavor and activity millennia ago, from the administration of production, surplus, and the environment to religious belief and practice, even haute cuisine recipes and passionate love songs.

This book offers a brief historical and cultural survey of Iraq from earliest times to the Muslim conquest in 637, drawing together political, social, economic, artistic, and intellectual sources, both primary and secondary. The Epilogue offers an introduction to the history of archaeology in this region, set in the broader context of the development of archaeology as a scientific discipline. This section also focuses on the discovery, management, preservation, and destruction of the cultural heritage of Iraq.

The figures not only illustrate significant works of art and architecture in a representative choice of media and subjects, but also afford a basis for understanding cultural property issues in the aftermath of the looting of the Iraq Museum in April 2003 and in view of the ongoing devastation of Iraqi archaeological sites and trafficking in antiquities. The figure captions, taken as a whole, constitute a short essay on these matters, complementing the art-historical discussions in the text.

Some chapters are substantial revisions of work that initially appeared in *Iraq Beyond the Headlines: History, Archaeology, and War*, co-authored by both of us in 2005 with Patty Gerstenblith, whose publisher, World Scientific, permitted us to reshape the book into its present form.

Over the years, questions posed by students and audiences in our courses and public lectures have greatly contributed to the sharpening of our theses and our selection of material. Portions of the book originated in the McKee-May Academic Lectures in Greenwich, Connecticut, given by Benjamin R. Foster in the winter of 2003 at the invitation of Jennifer Vietor Evans.

The book has also much benefited from discussions with colleagues during several conferences and panels on current issues, among them "A Future for Our Past: An International Symposium for Redefining the Concept of Cultural Heritage and Its Protection," held in Istanbul in June 2004; a series of programs entitled "Iraq Beyond the Headlines," held at Yale University in April 2003, October 2003, October 2004, and February 2008; "Iraq: At the Brink of Civil War?" held at Yale University in April 2006; and "The Future of the Global Past: An International Symposium on Cultural Property, Antiquities Issues, and Archaeological Ethics," held at Yale University in April 2007.

For references, images, information, thought-provoking comments, and eyewitness accounts, we are particularly grateful to Roger Atwood, Zainab Bahrani, Matthew Bogdanos, Annie Caubet, Dominique Charpin, Dominique Collon, John Darnell, Amira Edan, Joanne Farchakh, Bassam Frangieh, Patty Gerstenblith, Dimitri Gutas, McGuire Gibson, Nawala al-Mutawalli, Susanne Paulus, Gül Pulhan, John Russell, Catherine Sease, Alice Slotsky, Matthew Stolper, Margarete Van Ess, and Donny George Youkhana.

In the production of the illustrations and maps, we thank especially Yale Photographic Services, Peter W. Johnson, and those publishers still holding copyrights on the images reproduced here. Robert Tempio of the Princeton University Press has enthusiastically supported this project from the start.

CIVILIZATIONS

OF ANCIENT IRAQ

1. In the Beginning

Marduk created wild animals, the living
creatures of the open country.
He created and put in place Tigris and
Euphrates rivers,
He pronounced their names with favor.

Marduk, Creator of the World

Of Tigris and Euphrates

Ancient Iraq is the gift of two rivers. The Euphrates rises on the
Anatolian plateau in Turkey, flows southwest into Syria and then
turns southeast across Iraq, emptying into the Gulf. Its broad,
shallow channel makes it an ideal source for irrigation water, and
in many stretches the Euphrates is easily navigable. As the river
moves across the southern alluvial plains and approaches the Gulf,
it merges with the Tigris, amidst a network of smaller rivers, lakes,
and marshes. To a Babylonian poet, the Euphrates seemed a mighty
canal, divinely made:

O River, creator of all things,
When the great gods dug your bed,
They set well-being along your banks.[1]

The Tigris, though it too rises on the Anatolian plateau, passes
through more rugged terrain, at one point disappearing into a

1

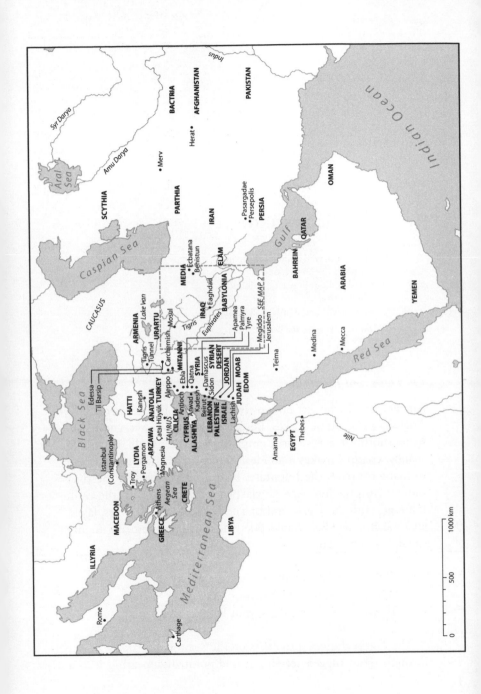

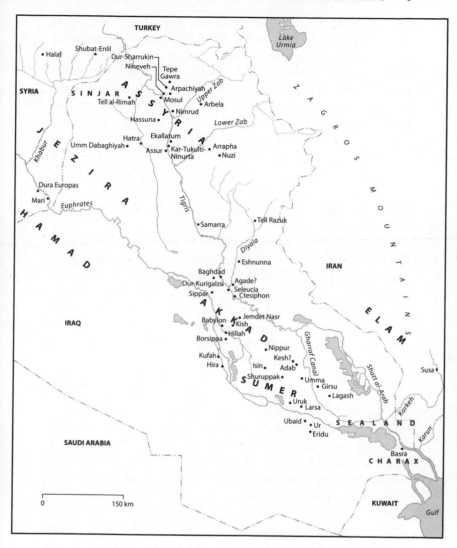

Map 1. *(left)* From Rome to the Indus (after Collon 1995)

Map 2. *(above)* Ancient Iraq (after Lloyd 1978)

natural tunnel. A Sumerian poet mythologized the volcanic origin of the Tigris headlands as an epic battle between a hero-god and a personified, erupting volcano that "gashed the earth's body . . . bathed the sky in blood . . . and till today black cinders are in the fields."[2] Both rivers flood when the snows melt in the highlands, but the Tigris often does so in violent, destructive onslaughts of water, swelled by its three main tributaries—the Upper and Lower Zab and the Diyala—pouring down from deep gorges in the Zagros Mountains. By contrast, the two principal tributaries of the Euphrates—the Khabur and Balikh, which join it in northeastern Syria—enclose a swath of fine agricultural land known as the Jezira, whose productivity is augmented by sufficient annual rainfall for crops.

The rivers of Iraq have determined its history in three crucial ways. The Euphrates was an important route of communication with Syria, central Turkey, and the Mediterranean; the Tigris and its tributaries afforded links with eastern Turkey and the Iranian plateau. Above all, both rivers made possible human life on the plains, annually renewing the soil with flood-borne silts and bringing the water that farmers needed to till their fields and herdsmen to sustain their flocks.[3]

During the Pliocene and early Pleistocene epochs, the earth's great tectonic plates began shaping the main geographical features of Iraq. As the Arabian and African plates moved slowly northward, they encountered the more intransigent Iranian and Turkish plates and were forced to grind beneath them, resulting in the uplift of the Zagros on Iraq's eastern border and the Anatolian ranges and plateau on its northern border. Where the Arabian plate thrust under the Iranian plate, subduction pressures also formed the trough of the Gulf and the alluvial plains of Iraq's river systems. Ongoing tectonic activity accounts for the Middle East's frequent earthquakes and numerous volcanoes.

Over the eons, Iraq's major hydrological and environmental changes have been brought about primarily by worldwide cooling and warming trends, which have caused the waters of the Gulf to fall and rise, respectively. At the height of the last Ice Age, the Gulf was a plain through which the ancestral Tigris and Euphrates meandered. As the glaciers melted, the Gulf reached approximately its current level, with temperature fluctuations over the millennia causing repeated advances and retreats of the coastline. Studies of pollen preserved in the sediments of ancient lakes have shed considerable light on the region's climate and vegetation, from the last glaciation to early historical times. Millennia of dry cold seem to have given way to a warmer, moister period about ten thousand years ago, which in turn ended in renewed desiccation, producing the desert and steppe we recognize as salient features of Iraq's present landscape. Grazing, agriculture, and the deforestation of the Zagros woodlands have affected the region's ecosystems as well.[4]

Today, as in historical antiquity, forbidding deserts stretch to the west of the plains of Iraq for hundreds of kilometers. To the east and north, the foothills ascend swiftly to mountains with peaks "sharp-tipped as a spear point," as an Assyrian writer put it.[5] To the south is the Gulf. Small wonder, then, that the people of ancient Iraq thought that the alluvial plains were the center of the inhabited world, ringed by deserts, mountains, and seas. For them, all that lay beyond was foreign and strange, the source of exotic materials and strange beasts, the abode of brutish folk. The farthest reaches the plains dwellers knew were the "Upper and Lower Seas," the Mediterranean and the Gulf.[6]

No one knows what the earliest names for the region signify. Kengir or Sumer (biblical Shinar) referred to the southern half of the alluvial plains, while the northern half was called Wari, later Akkad. After about 1700 B.C.E., Sumer and Akkad together constituted what came to be known as Babylonia. A thousand years later, the southern marshes were called the Sealand, later Chaldea. The region north of Baghdad, along the Tigris, was known as Assyria. The word Subir was sometimes used to refer to northern Mesopotamia as a whole.[7]

The modern name Iraq was first regularly used after the Muslim conquest of 637. Though it appears to be an Arabic word, its meaning and etymology are obscure. The various proposals by medieval Arab geographers show only that they were making them up. One of the most widely accepted explanations is that it means "arable land along a major river," vaguely corresponding to English "alluvium," but this may have been reasoned backwards from the reality of Iraq itself.[8]

The ancient Greek term Mesopotamia, now generally understood to mean "Land Between Rivers," has also been used to refer
to Iraq, especially by European scholars and twentieth-century
colonial administrators. Mesopotamia originally denoted the land
enclosed by the big bend of the Middle Euphrates River, east of
modern Aleppo in Syria, but it soon came to mean the expanse of
plains and uplands between the Tigris and Euphrates, from the
Gulf to the Anatolian plateau.[9] Many writers today use the term
Mesopotamia when discussing the region before the Muslim conquest, and Iraq thereafter. Although this may be a convenient historical distinction, others prefer not to separate the pre-Islamic
and Islamic past of Iraq. In this book, we use Mesopotamia and
Iraq interchangeably.

To visitors from parts of the earth with more temperate cli-
mates and more varied scenery, the hot, featureless plains of
southern Iraq may seem a place inhospitable to the development
of civilization. Nor are there splendid ruins to admire or reflect
on, such as might evoke a glorious past. In fact, the only hints on
the landscape attesting to the remote antiquity of human habitation are mounds covered with potsherds, broken bricks, and other
debris, sometimes lying amongst faint outlines of walls and dwellings, all that remain of once bustling cities and towns, home to a
vibrant and long-lived literate culture. This early Victorian traveler's experience still rings true:

> He has left the land where nature is still lovely, where, in his
> mind's eye, he can rebuild the temple or the theatre. . . . He
> is now at a loss to give any form to the rude heaps upon
> which he is gazing. . . . The scene around is worthy of the
> ruin he is contemplating; desolation meets desolation; a
> feeling of awe succeeds to wonder; for there is nothing to
> relieve the mind, to lead to hope, or to tell of what has
> gone by.[10]

The ancient visitor would have had a very different view, largely
because the Tigris and Euphrates, like other restless waterways, are
prone to carving out new courses, sometimes shifting their river-
beds by many kilometers. Today in southern Iraq, the Euphrates

flows far to the east of its course in historical antiquity, so that what were once riverside or canalside cities, towns, and villages became the "rude heaps" of remote deserts. As a result, many of the important ancient cities in southern Iraq were left unmolested and uninhabited for thousands of years. Unhampered by modern development, archaeologists have been able to investigate these sites in depth, recovering most of what we know about the history and culture of ancient Iraq. In more recent times, these isolated fields of ruins have fallen easy prey to large-scale looting and destruction. Much of their vast and rich historical record is now lost forever. In the north, where the river channels are more stable, ancient settlements and cities often underlie modern ones, making them more difficult to excavate, but less vulnerable to looters. We return to these matters in the Epilogue.

Still, one may well ask, why was civilization born on these alluvial plains, so far in advance of all other places in the world? There are at once many answers and no answer to this simple question. Intensive archaeological research in Iraq and in neighboring lands has given us numerous responses, and we may draw these proposals and theories together into a narrative that seems reasonable and convincing in its outline, even if specifics remain frustratingly elusive. At the same time, there is no answer, for we often describe events and changes without really knowing how or why they came about, and refer to people about whom we know very little. New discoveries and reinterpretations of old ones give us fascinating evidence to work into the story, but ultimately leave the reader wishing to know more than we can say at present.

The First Villages

Of the many ways to describe human beings of former times and how they lived, one long popular has been with reference to their technology. We may speak of the Old Stone Age (Paleolithic) and New Stone Age (Neolithic), implying that people mostly used stone tools, or the Bronze Age, when people mostly used bronze weapons. Or we may focus on religious belief, referring to pagan, Christian, or pre-Islamic societies. In older books, one wrote of races: Oriental and Occidental peoples, the "great white race," the Indo-Europeans, the Semites. Since the 1960s, anthropologists and archaeologists have used a more inclusive system referring to modes of subsistence, that is, by what means people obtained the food they needed to survive.[11]

For almost its entire history, the human race subsisted by hunting game and gathering naturally occurring plants. This mode was so successful and so undemanding as a way of life that it ensured human survival for hundreds of thousands of years. To judge from present-day hunting cultures, hunters need exercise their skill only two or three days out of seven to provide sufficient meat for their community. They kill and collect only what they need to live, and do not reduce their resources for sport or entertainment. Hunter-gatherer populations, moreover, tend to remain fairly stable. They usually have small families; their children, especially girls, mature late; and some groups even abandon infants to control population.[12]

About ten thousand years ago, peoples in the Middle East evolved a radically different subsistence pattern based on agriculture and the management of domesticated animals. Some historians refer to this momentous development as a revolution, thereby implying sweeping change.[13] But the change was abrupt only in comparison with the manner in which people had interacted with the natural world for all the preceding millennia. We see the transition vividly in Iraq and also, at about the same time, in Iran, Turkey, Syria, Israel, and Palestine.[14] How and why did it occur, and what did it mean for the human race?

Archaeological work in the foothills of the Zagros has shown that people began settling in small villages in areas where certain wild grains, such as barley, and wild animals, such as sheep and goats, occurred naturally and plentifully. Gradually, people came to realize that these resources could be managed by controlling their reproduction to obtain specific desirable traits. This selection process, termed the domestication of plants and animals, caused permanent genetic and associated morphological changes in the species involved. Barley, for example, was selected for preferred strains, such as those with softer husks and larger ears of grain;

animals were bred for quality of wool or milk, or for fattiness or yield of meat. Within the village confines, plots were sown and animals penned, though in some seasons the animals might be herded to better, more distant pastures. Although we may now be able to describe in some detail the transition from hunting and gathering to pastoral and village life, we still cannot explain why this occurred when it did.[15]

The domestication of plants and animals brought with it substantial changes in social outlook, behavior, and organization. The hunter attacked or trapped, whereas the farmer and herdsman nurtured. The self-narrative of the hunter was aggressive and dramatic, that of the farmer and herdsman reliant and protective. For much of the year, agricultural work was systematic and unrelenting: preparing the soil, sowing, watering, weeding, driving off pests, harvesting, threshing, and storing. This pattern of life brought with it an ethos of working in rhythm with the seasons for family and community, of saving against future want, and of hopeful dependence on uncontrollable forces and events. Agricultural success resulted in larger families, because even small children could be useful in fieldwork and herding. And with earlier physical maturity came steady, even exponential, population growth.[16]

In response to agricultural and pastoral needs, new technologies developed for producing such items as ground-stone tools, wooden implements, baskets, and textiles. New materials also appeared, among them obsidian from the volcanic areas of eastern and central Turkey. It is not clear how obsidian, prized for sharp blades, reached the early farming villages of Iraq, whether brought by traders or acquired though expeditions, but its presence attests to well-established, long-distance networks.[17]

The most important innovation was pottery. Prior to about 6500 B.C.E., containers had been made of skins, bitumen-coated baskets, gypsum or lime plaster, and stone. The earliest ceramic vessels were lightly fired, but the development of more efficient kilns resulted in the production of nonporous, durable wares adaptable to a wide range of uses.[18] These included the storage, transport, preparation, and cooking of a variety of solids and liquids, from grain and cheese to beer. The discovery of fermentation created beverages that altered mood and behavior; drinking thus acquired social and ritual functions, as Sumerian drinking songs celebrate:

> When I make my way around a round of beer,
> When I feel grand, when I feel grand,
> Drinking beer in a merry mood,
> Imbibing fruit of the field in a light-hearted state,
> With a joyful heart and a happy inside . . .[19]

Because fired clay is a nearly indestructible material, the shapes and decorations of pottery vessels usually afford the best evidence we have for the creativity and aesthetic sensibilities of ancient peoples. In Iraq, as elsewhere, major pottery types are frequently named after the sites at which they were first discovered, or which seem to have been centers of production. The Hassuna ware of the mid-seventh millennium from northern Iraq tends to be decorated with herringbone and other patterns incised with a pointed tool. The Samarra and Halaf wares that followed, from northern and central Iraq, are more finely made, with painted patterns on a buff ground. The interiors of Samarra bowls often feature stylized horned animals circling round, drawn in dark brown with verve and assurance. Halaf pottery of the mid-sixth millennium is the first polychrome ware known, characterized by sophisticated geometric designs in red, black, and white, possibly inspired by textiles. Vessels such as the bowl pictured here (figure 1) were likely made by specialized potters based in certain villages, whereas simpler pots were probably made locally.[20]

So it was, in this period of change ten thousand years ago, in the foothills of Iraq, that small villages sprang up, their mud-brick houses consisting of a few rooms and an open area, pens for animals and storage bins for foods, the settlements surrounded by an agricultural hinterland extending perhaps several hours' walk.[21] So forceful was this new trajectory of human life that in a few places beyond Iraq, such as Çatal Hüyük in central Turkey, good-sized towns appeared, with comparatively large populations and elaborately embellished structures, apparently serving some religious

Figure 1. Halaf ware bowl from Arpachiyah, diameter 33 cm, Iraq Museum, Baghdad. (Strommenger 1962: pl. II) *For most periods of ancient Iraq, pottery provides the chronological framework essential for understanding the successive levels of occupation of a site. During the course of an archaeological excavation, hundreds of thousands of potsherds are collected and recorded. The smallest fragment may be as valuable as an intact vessel for enriching our knowledge of techniques, artistic developments, and interconnections. When the Iraq Museum storerooms were ransacked in April 2003, the excavated pottery and other artifacts awaiting study and final publication were thrown into disorder or stolen.*

purpose.[22] But this was exceptional. Most villages comprised a few dozen houses, all of the same size and plan, suggesting an egalitarian society, with communal as well as individual storage facilities. Perhaps resources of fields and flocks were also managed communally.

From the Foothills to the Plains

A second important transition, several thousand years after the development of agriculture, was the movement of farmers and stockbreeders down from the foothills onto the plains of Iraq. No one knows precisely when this occurred, for the earliest lowland settlements may be buried deep in the modern alluvium and thus archaeologically inaccessible. Why move to the plains? One theory is population pressure, but no evidence has been produced from the foothills to suggest that the population had become too large to be sustained there. The important point is that once human beings had mastered agricultural and pastoral skills, they could live in areas where the wild ancestors of the domesticated plants and animals they had come to depend on did not naturally occur. In bringing the new species of plants and animals with them, humans caused permanent changes in the ecology of the plains.[23]

In Iraq, the lowlands presented challenges that were not easily met. The dearth of rainfall in the south required irrigation for the cultivation of cereal crops. In principle, irrigation need only be a matter of digging a ditch to bring water to a field. In practice, irrigation involved community participation in the construction and maintenance of a network of ditches, as well as decisions about who was to receive how much water, where, and when. The water situation in southern Iraq was further complicated by the fact that the rivers flood in the early spring, at sowing time, and reach their low point in the hot season, at growing time, when water is most needed. Despite these challenges, people settled first in small villages dispersed across the alluvial plains, especially in the south, then in increasing numbers along natural watercourses, allowing us to trace those now vanished or shifted thanks to patterns of habitation. Furthermore, we can see in the relative sizes of the villages an emerging hierarchy among them.[24]

The settlement of farmers on the alluvial plains of Iraq was thus a success, the first stage in a story of human activity there that continues to the present day. We need not imagine, of course, that the plains lay empty before people began to till the soil. Hunter-gatherers had long pursued the abundant game, such as gazelle,

and the marsh creatures, such as turtles, birds, and fish, that this
hospitable Sumerian fisherman invites into his traps:

> Let your acquaintances come,
> Let those precious to you come,
> Let your father and grandfather come, . . .
> Let your wife and children come, . . .
> Let the group around your doorway come,
> Do not leave anyone around you out, not a single one![25]

But with the advent of agriculture and stockbreeding, the land
was changed forever. These two modes coexisted well, and might
be carried on by members of the same family. Flocks of sheep and
goats grazed widely on the grassy plains and on the first springtime shoots of the grain crops, increasing the already high yields
of the fields by causing the grain to put out a thicker second
growth and by fertilizing the soil.[26] In summer, when the grass
withered in the heat, the animals might be moved to higher pastures or fed on stored grain and the leftovers from milling and
brewing. To judge from later periods, for which written sources
are available, the main products of the time were wool, wheat,
and barley. The diet was supplemented by the fruit of the date
palm, plentiful river fish, sheep and goats, and wild game.

From about 5900 to 4300 B.C.E., this lowland peasant culture,
termed by archaeologists the Ubaid, diffused throughout Iraq and
far beyond, into the Anatolian plateau and the steppes of northern Syria.[27] Differences in water resources led to variations in how
northern and southern Iraq developed. In the north, where agriculture could be sustained by rainfall and wells, there was less intensive fieldwork than in the irrigated south, and the potential
existed for a greater area under cultivation. But if the south had
smaller plots, those irrigated fields had much higher productivity
per hectare. And because the population was concentrated in the
south, extensive areas of the north may not have been cultivated
at all, even during later periods. Southern settlements followed
the natural watercourses needed for irrigation and transportation;
northern villages tended to be spread across the landscape, wherever wells could be dug.[28]

Material culture, south and north, befitted a peasant way of life: simple tools, practical vessels. In general, Ubaid ceramics are modestly decorated, often, in the later phases, with dark painted patterns rapidly applied, showing none of the glossy polychromy of Halaf ware (figure 1). We see the spread of Ubaid culture through finding its pottery, including some locally made imitations, from the Mediterranean to Oman.[29]

What these peoples called themselves, what languages they spoke, what social institutions, spiritual life, and traditions they had, we know not. The platforms, niched façades, and interior fittings of some Ubaid shrines became standard elements of later temples, which suggests a certain measure of continuity. Because both shrines and houses often had a tripartite plan (a central room flanked by rows of rooms), and because the plastic arts that have come down to us are primarily exaggerated representations of the female body, we surmise that Ubaid religious belief and practice focused on the forces most important to their way of life, especially fertility, procreation, and the safety of the home hearth.[30]

Four aspects of the Ubaid culture impress the modern observer: its longevity of 1,600 years, or more, indicating that a viable way of life had been successfully transplanted to the alluvial plains of Iraq and beyond; its wide extent, compared to later cultures; its overall uniformity throughout Iraq, notwithstanding regional phases and variations; and its striking absence of weapons and fortifications, implying peaceful coexistence. People might have continued to live in this mode indefinitely had not something extraordinary happened.

2. The Birthplace of Civilization

> This fastness, thrusting high above the azure plain around,
> This city Kullab, sprouting tall from earth to sky,
> This Uruk, whose very name gleams like the rainbow,
> Radiating across heaven with its multicolored glow,
> Standing bright against the sky, like the shining curve
>   of the new moon.
>
> *Enmerkar and Ensuhgiranna*

The First Cities

Little in the material remains of the long-lived Ubaid culture hints at what was about to take place in southern Iraq: the appearance at Uruk and elsewhere of the first cities known anywhere in the world. Why did this happen here? A later Babylonian poem honoring the god Marduk as creator of the world saw the process as sudden and dramatic:

> No holy house, no house for the gods, had been built in a
>   sacred place,
> No reed had come forth, no tree had been created,
> No brick had been laid, no brick mold had been created,
> No house had been built, no city had been created, . . .
> The world was marsh and canebrake. . . .
> Then Marduk built Uruk, he created Eanna.[1]

An archaeologist of the future, studying the development of urban life in Manhattan from 1600 to 1900 might reasonably conclude that the enormous changes seen in the material culture of the island began with the advent of new peoples, then took off with incredible rapidity; as hunter-gatherers gave way to farmers, a town grew to a metropolis, all within a 300-year period. This is what an older generation of scholars concluded about Iraq. Wont to explain any significant cultural innovation by invasion or migration, they believed that the impulse that led from villages to huge, walled cities had to have been the result of an influx of settlers, whom they suggested came by sea or down from the mountains. They named the newcomers the Sumerians, and spoke confidently of their arrival about 3600 B.C.E. and their swift transformation of the plains of southern Iraq, just as Europeans had done in Manhattan over an equivalent span of time.

Truth to tell, this Sumerian immigration was imagined; there is no visible break in material culture between the modest Ubaid centers and the gigantic city of Uruk. New ceramic methods and pottery types do appear, such as the use of a low flywheel and a small handmade bowl with a beveled rim, probably mass-produced in molds, but these emerged in response to developing needs, not as imports from abroad. Nor do foreign goods, techniques, or styles suddenly appear in any other media.[2] Instead, there seems to have been a quickening, an intensification of the earlier way of life, a realization of its potentials for following a powerful, dynamic, fundamentally different trajectory. If modern Manhattan had been created within three centuries by the indigenous peoples living there in 1600, that would be the better analogy for what occurred at Uruk.

Why this happened in southern Iraq, ahead of anywhere else in the world, is one of the most fascinating unsolved riddles of antiquity. We can watch the process unfold and measure certain aspects of it, however, thanks to the painstaking excavations of Uruk and other early cities. Furthermore, as we shall see later in this chapter, archaeologists have identified artifacts of the Uruk culture across a vast area, from Syria to eastern Iran, whence it spread rapidly and intrusively, with the result that aspects of it, such as domestic architecture, are better known abroad than at Uruk itself. For a few centuries, it seems, the Sumerian city of Uruk was the greatest city on earth.

Uruk is a place that has been occupied under the same name—biblical Erech, modern Warka—for over five thousand years. As described in the *Epic of Gilgamesh*,

> One square mile of city, one square mile of gardens,
> One square mile of clay pits, a half square mile of Ishtar's dwelling,
> Three and a half square miles is the measure of Uruk![3]

Excavations have concentrated on a series of major public buildings in the center of the walled city, probably temples, that must have been visible from far across the plain, while most of Iraq was still a peasant culture. About 3600 B.C.E., a large edifice was erected using limestone laboriously transported from some 80 kilometers away across open desert. Other impressive buildings soon joined it on Uruk's skyline.

One of these was constructed atop an irregularly shaped platform nearly 12 meters high, oriented to the points of the compass. Accessible by a ramp and staircase and dubbed the White Temple because it was coated with gypsum plaster, it was probably a sanctuary dedicated to An, the sky god. Like its Ubaid predecessors, it had a tripartite plan, with an altar at one end and niched walls. Close by was another complex, likely the Eanna temple, dedicated to the goddess Inanna, which included several sanctuaries as well as housing, possibly for officiants.[4]

Mesopotamian religious thought was pluralistic, accepting the existence of innumerable gods but preferring one or a small group for local or personal devotion. The gods were everywhere, yet at the same time present in specific symbols or images kept in certain cities and their shrines. A common tactic in wartime was to abduct the cult statues, thereby depriving the enemy city of its divine residents and protectors.[5]

The temple complexes came to resemble palaces, with reception rooms, bedrooms, dining halls, and gardens for the pleasure of their divine householders, families, and courtiers. They were entertained with music, taken on journeys, and served lavish repasts.[6]

In a Neo-Babylonian temple, in which a single divine meal might be enough to feed a hundred people, the menu included the following delicacies:

> Excellent bread, mighty oxen, fine fatted rams, geese, ducks, wild fowl, pigeons, dormice, offerings of fish, cultivated fruit in enormous quantities, the pride of orchards, apples, figs, pomegranates, grapes, dates, imported dates, raisins, abundant vegetables, the yield of the garden, fine mixed beer, honey, ghee, refined oil, best-quality milk, sweet emmer beer, fine wine, the finest of grain and vine of all mountains and lands.[7]

Though immortal and omnipotent, the gods were usually visualized in human form as male and female, motivated by such human needs and drives as hunger and thirst, sexual desire, ambition, and rivalry. The principal deities had individual personalities and characteristics. The Mesopotamians feared, rather than loved, their gods and goddesses, deeming them as capricious and self-absorbed as their autocratic rulers. The pantheon was organized in various ways: by devising genealogies and generations; by attributing to particular gods the control of different regions of the earth or universe; and by identifying deities with natural phenomena, such as storms, or with realms of nature, such as trees, mountains, or livestock, or with human institutions, such as agriculture, husbandry, and handicrafts.[8] Over the millennia, we see in divine iconography both constant and evolving elements in the gods' emblems, accoutrements, and settings. Our difficulty in identifying the imagery is further complicated by the general lack of captions and by the frequent disparity between pictorial and textual sources for the gods and their activities.[9]

Of the major deities worshiped at Uruk, An was remote from human affairs, whereas Inanna was very much involved in them. The Sumerian goddess of fertility, love, and procreation, Inanna was early on identified with the Semitic Ishtar, goddess of combat and love. According to a Sumerian myth, Enki, the god of intelligence and wisdom, gave Inanna contradiction as her responsibility in the universe, as opposed to the less complex roles assigned to the other gods:

> You are to twist the straight thread, you are to straighten
>   the twisted thread,
> You pile up boasts like burial mounds, you sow words that
>   grow up lush,
> You destroy what cannot be destroyed, you set up what
>   cannot be set up,
> You take the cover off the drum for laments, you put the
>   cover on the drum for happy songs,
> Your eye never wearies of your admirers.[10]

Inanna was at once a girl falling in love for the first time and a bloodthirsty warrior cutting off heads. She reigned over tender domestic moments and over carnage in war. The goddess was alluring and passionate, but brought misery where there was happiness, and joy where there was woe.

Describing Inanna was perennially inspirational for writers.[11] For this Sumerian poet, she was a pelting rainstorm:

> When you have spewed your venom on the land like a
>   dragon,
> When you roar like thunder at the earth, nothing that
>   grows can withstand you![12]

A Babylonian poet pictured her at home, aglow with erotic thoughts as her parents welcome her lover:

> When you came in, my father was glad to see you,
> My mother, Ningal, made a nice fuss over you,
> She offered rubbing oil from the best dish (and said):
> "When you come in, may the door bolt welcome you"
>   (but I say to myself):
> Let the door fly open, all by itself!
> You door bolt, you piece of wood, what do you know?
> What would you know of my lover's 'coming in'?
> Yes, I'm in love, I'm in love![13]

Figure 2. Cone mosaics from Uruk, cone diameter ca. 2 cm, Vorderasiatisches Museum, Berlin. (Moortgat 1967: pl. 2) *The excavations of Uruk carried out by the German Oriental Society, beginning over a century ago, were among the first to apply scrupulous archaeological methods to the stratigraphically complex sites of ancient Iraq. Under the antiquities law of the day, a share of the finds from Uruk went to Berlin, including some of the cone mosaics, a temple façade (figure 12), and other monuments. Thus far, Uruk has been spared the extensive looting carried out elsewhere in southern Iraq since the Iraq War began, owing to the protection afforded it by the leaders of the tribes whose men have been employed by the German archaeologists for generations.*

Here she is according to another Babylonian poet:

> Raising loud battle cries, teeth chattering in fear,
> Coiffing, playing with hair are yours, O Ishtar, . . .
> Opening the loins to the lover's urge,
> Twin babies, founding a family, then watching it grow are
>   yours, O Ishtar.[14]

Eanna, her sanctuary at Uruk, had a monumental entrance, whose double staircase and massive columns, over 2 meters in diameter, were decorated with mosaics made from tens of thousands of baked-clay or gypsum cones, painted black, red, or white and set into wet plaster (figure 2). Their various geometric patterns, reminding us in color and effect of Halaf designs (figure 1), and perhaps likewise originating in textiles, may have had symbolic meanings or been purely decorative. Also in the Eanna precinct were cone mosaics made of naturally colored stones. Elsewhere in southern Iraq, we find the same kind of temple architecture, similarly adorned with cone mosaics or their painted imitations. To the Sumerians, their great temples glistened in the sun and moonlight with sublime splendor:

> Like full-grown fresh fruit, marvelous, superb in its beauty,
> This shrine, come down from highest heaven, built for the
> sacrificed steer,
> Eanna is a seven-cornered house that sends aloft at night
> seven rays of fire![15]

The countless resources and man-hours of labor that went into creating and adorning these structures had to have been drawn from other activities and compensated in some way. But whose organizational and creative genius planned and constructed these remarkable buildings?

Another approach to understanding the Uruk phenomenon has entailed surveying the surrounding countryside to map and index the settlements there by size, historical period, and distribution. From these surveys we learn that throughout the region a more pronounced hierarchy of settlements developed during the mid-fourth millennium B.C.E. Some villages grew into towns and cities, with smaller settlements subordinate to or dependent on them. Quantitatively, Uruk is extraordinary: a city eventually enclosed by nearly 10 kilometers of walls, drawing into itself the neighboring towns and villages, so as to leave a kind of empty corona of surrounding land; a city many times larger than any other settlement observed in Iraq at the time. Thus evidence from within Uruk and from its rural hinterlands converges to suggest a unique agglomeration that transcended the millennial limitations of its environment, but had grown out of that environment, carrying further than anyplace else the changes that were occurring more tentatively elsewhere in Iraq and in southwestern Iran.[16]

We may also consider Uruk from an art-historical perspective. A critical development was the world's first art made to represent specific, identifiable persons and deities. And we often see in art of the Uruk period the earliest forms of what would become standard, long-lived aspects of iconography in ancient Iraq. A small stone statue of a ruler of Uruk, for example, shows a serious, pensive leader, whose full beard, close-fitting cap, and hands held before him recur for millennia in royal imagery.[17]

The most spectacular works were found in a later temple treasury in the Eanna precinct, evidently retained as heirlooms from this period. One is a life-size alabaster mask of a female face, known as the Uruk Head (figure 3). Drill holes in its sides enabled it to be attached, perhaps to a statue of wood or some other perishable material. Originally, the piece probably had shell and lapis lazuli or obsidian eyes and lapis eyebrows, and the hair may have been a sheet of gold or copper, chased with fine grooves. The features, especially the expressive mouth, are modeled with exquisite sensitivity, one of the earliest naturalistic renderings of a face, though whether divine or human we cannot tell. Perhaps she was meant to be Inanna herself.[18]

There was also an alabaster chalice, known as the Uruk Vase, whose reliefs offer one of the earliest and most complete cult scenes we have, depicting people bringing offerings to Inanna (figure 4). Because stone vase fragments with similar imagery have been found elsewhere, we may suppose that these vessels played an important role in ritual. The two lower bands, or registers, represent the managed fertility of fields and herds, over which Inanna presided. In the upper register, an elaborately garbed ruler and his attendant approach the goddess. She and her attendants are accompanied by poles, each adorned with a scarf or headdress, knotted at the top, her oldest cult symbol. Near Inanna appear two vessels of the same chalice type, the first instance we have of self-referenced objects. There may well have been such an identical pair at Uruk, for a small fragment in the Berlin Museum, purchased on the antiquities market years before the Uruk Vase was excavated, proved to be a perfect match to it. The Uruk vase was repaired in antiquity with thin strips of copper, testimony to the esteem in which the vessel was held. Above Inanna's head, a small section was replaced, but the restorer did not carve the goddess's headdress, nor quite match the rim molding, so perhaps this

Figure 3. Uruk Head, alabaster, height 20 cm, Iraq Museum, Baghdad. (Moortgat 1967: pl. 26) *Five months after the Uruk Head vanished from the Iraq Museum, it was recovered, wrapped in rags, from a shallow pit in a suburban Baghdad garden. The asking price had been $25,000.*

mended a later breakage. When the vase was reassembled in modern times, most of the copper strips were removed; tiny holes show where they were.[19]

Another innovation of this period was the cylinder seal, replacing the simple stamp seal used previously. Small cylinders of soft or hard stones or other materials were engraved with representational imagery and geometric patterns, then rolled across the clay nodules used to seal the door locks of storerooms and warehouses,

Figure 4. (*left and above*) Uruk Vase, alabaster, height 105 cm, Iraq Museum, Baghdad. (Zervos 1935: 62; Roaf 1990: 61) *Curators debated the wisdom of moving the Uruk Vase to safety in the winter of 2003, deciding that it was too fragile to transport. During the looting, the vase disintegrated along old breakage lines; the fragments were brought back to the museum during the amnesty on such returns. The tender stone suffered some abrasion and chipping, but the vase has been restored once more.*

as well as packages of goods and the tops of containers. In due course, seals were also used in connection with record-keeping. Since their purpose was to signify authority and ownership, each one was unique, affording us much insight into the development of art in ancient Iraq across the millennia.[20] From the Uruk period, we have over two thousand seals or their impressions. The seals depict naturalistically modeled people and animals, miniature counterparts to those seen on larger works, but the impressions are restricted to geometric designs. No one knows why this should be so.[21]

Figure 5. Drawings of cylinder seal impressions from various sites, periods, and museums, average seal height 3 cm. (Roaf 1990: 73) *When the looters broke into one of the basement magazines of the Iraq Museum, they took more than five thousand seals, all from known archaeological contexts. In the dark and confusion, the thieves dropped the keys to the nearby cabinets before they could open them. The cabinets housed thousands more seals, as well as a collection of ancient and Islamic gold and silver coins. Some of the stolen seals have now appeared in the United States, Europe, and Iraq's neighboring countries; the majority are said to be in the possession of dealers in Beirut.*

Figure 5 illustrates six representative cylinder seals from different periods, shown for clarity as drawings based on their impressions. The first is a marble seal found near Uruk, on which we recognize the same cult symbol of Inanna and theme of fertility of fields and herds as on the Uruk Vase (figure 4). Below that is a green calcite seal contemporaneous with the Royal Graves at Ur (see chapter 3), whose bottom register depicts a dense row of animal combats in which a nude hero participates, and whose upper register is filled with a similarly crowded banquet scene. The third on the left is a rock crystal seal of the Akkadian period (see chapter 4), inscribed with the owner's name and a pair of combatants (hero/bull and bull-man/lion), whose sophisticated use of negative space is one of the hallmarks of that era.

The owner of the hematite seal at the top right offers a prayer to a god, the writing framed by a protective goddess and the king, both in attitudes typical of the age of Hammurabi (see chapter 5, also figure 11). The naturalistic stag and tree on the middle-right seal, a chalcedony cylinder of the Middle Assyrian period (see chapter 7), belonged to a man whose ownership inscription passes behind the tree in an interesting integration of text and image. The last, the property of a scribe, is a carnelian seal with a so-called winged genius figure throttling two ostriches, iconography frequently seen in Neo-Assyrian art (see chapter 7, also figure 15).

The builders of Uruk experimented with a new kind of small, standardized brick, with the expansion of modular architectural units into large structures, and with various methods of bonding brick fabric to make these large structures more stable.[22] The agricultural planners of Uruk may have increased productivity by using a novel concept of field management, laying out long strips with their narrow side by a watercourse, reaching as far out into the countryside as subsidiary water could be brought.[23] Later Sumerian mathematicians worked theoretical problems involving extreme cases of such fields.[24] In short, in every aspect of the Uruk culture one can point to experimentation and innovation.

From City to State

No longer was southern Iraq a place of small farmers and modest villages, but an ordered, hierarchical land dominated by an urban elite, with the will and the means to mobilize vast human and material resources in its service. How, then, was this stratified society achieved, and how did this elite maintain its dominance over the rest of the population, which greatly outnumbered it?

To answer these questions, we turn to social and economic theory. A particularly persuasive hypothesis is based on the presumed capacity of the southern plains to produce an agricultural and livestock surplus sufficient to form the basis for wealth, power, and prestige.[25] Decisions about how to deploy this staple surplus, as economic historians term it, may well lie at the heart of the new social stratification. In such redistribution systems, as they are called, some people produce raw materials for food and clothing and others decide what is to be done with these goods and oversee their distribution to nonproducers. In ancient Iraq, these distributions were in both raw form, as barley, wool, vegetable oils, and animal fats, and prepared form, as bread, textiles, and fermented beverages.[26] This system would presuppose, in the case of a city like Uruk, extensive capability for the management of people, sophisticated storage and accounting techniques, and important facilities for the mass production of prepared food, as well as organized ways of distributing it. One would expect, and in fact we find, mass production in other sectors of the economy too, such as the numerous standardized vessels for the preparation and distribution of food, accounting for the bevel-rimmed bowls mentioned above, or agricultural implements fitted speedily with teeth of clay, rather than with labor-intensive flint or costly metal.[27]

Many writers on early economy believe that a redistribution system could not effectively have been imposed on a population by brute force; rather, there must have been some ideological basis impelling people of like rank within a stratified social order to act on their beliefs. If so, the great investment in monumental structures at Uruk, which dominated the city and plain, indicates that religion provided what theoreticians call the noneconomic means of regulating production and distribution.[28] One does not have to look far in ancient Mesopotamian literature to find the notions that the temple was the "linking point of heaven and earth,"[29] that human beings were created to serve the gods, like so many workers or drones, and that human rulers were the vicegerents of the gods on earth, the stewards of their households, the shepherds of their human flocks:

> Their labor shall be labor for the gods:
> To maintain the boundary ditch for all time,
> To set pickaxe and workbasket in their hands,
> To make the great dwellings of the gods,

> Worthy to be their sublime sanctuary,
> To add field to field.[30]

Although to some modern scholars, these metaphors were excogitated to shore up an existing social order, to others they bespeak deeply held, motivating beliefs.

Sumerians Abroad

One of the recent surprises of Uruk-period archaeology has been the discovery of distant settlements that were unmistakably colonies of the city of Uruk; previously, southern Iraq had been thought to be a self-contained world. Overlooking the Euphrates in Syria, for example, three small cities were founded on virgin soil. Their fortifications, planned residential quarters, monumental buildings, and material culture are clearly related to those of Uruk, down to the kind of brick used and the bowls with beveled rims. Even farther up the Euphrates, we find cone mosaics at several sites in Turkey. The colonists had in mind a specific pattern or model of how urban settlements should look and operate, and enough manpower at their disposal to create thriving cities. The colonies were not long-lived undertakings, however, lasting perhaps two centuries before being abandoned and never thereafter occupied.

Archaeologists have begun to trace a network of comparable settlements from the Mediterranean to Iran, some primary in the sense that they seem closely related to the culture of Uruk, others secondary in the sense that they may have been founded by other colonies, or reflect an admixture of Uruk and local traditions. These colonies and outposts tended to follow natural water or land routes, and seem to be situated at key points along them. Most were short-lived, destroyed by violence or abandoned.[31]

What was the purpose of these far-flung colonies? One answer has been the desire of the Uruk state to secure resources not available in southern Iraq, such as metals, timber, and stone. But this seems an inadequate explanation for many of the settlements, as for example those on the Euphrates in Syria, which had no special resources. Nor, of course, is it necessary to colonize to conduct trade. Other suggestions include an attempt to control as much territory as possible, or to resettle excess population from Uruk, or to deal with some sort of social change or discontent. From the perspective of four millennia, the discovery of sixteenth- and seventeenth-century English settlements in Holland and Massachusetts might be equally perplexing, and the explanations no less creative.

In short, we cannot yet understand why Uruk culture and influence suddenly spread throughout the Middle East, even as far as Egypt. There, the appearance of brick, niched architecture, cylinder seals, and cone mosaics suggests that there may have been overland and maritime connections between the Uruk colonies in north Syria, or the mid-Euphrates, and the western Nile Delta.[32] Some archaeologists contend that cultural diffusion exclusively from Uruk is too simple an explanation, pointing to a similar expansion apparently taking place in Iran at about the same time, centered in the city of Susa, which might have had independent connections with Upper Egypt via the Gulf and the Red Sea. They also argue that the multiple, independent, cultural and economic dynamics of northern Iraq, Syria, and Turkey need to be brought into an inclusive portrayal of what was happening in the region at the end of the fourth millennium.[33] Owing to modern political conditions, the archaeological spotlight has shifted from Iraq and Iran to Syria and Turkey, where ever more traces of the Uruk culture are coming to light, as well as abundant evidence for local cultures, some sharing traits with Uruk, some not. Thus we can expect in the immediate future both more evidence and a wealth of conflicting theories and explanations for the growth and outward expansion of the Uruk culture.

Setting Words on Clay

The invention of writing was the most lasting and portentous achievement of the Uruk culture. Writing, like other great discoveries, has been invented more than once, in different places, but the world's earliest writing is found at Uruk. Furthermore, it stands at the beginning of one of the longest traditions of its use: writing in cuneiform, as the script is called, continued for over three thousand years, until early in the Christian era (see chapter 9).[34]

Speculations on the origins of writing abound, from late antiquity to modern times. These fall into two main categories, the first a belief that God gave people writing, and the second that drawing pictures evolved to writing words and sounds. With respect to medieval Christian and Jewish traditions of the divine origins of writing, it is interesting to note that the Sumerians themselves, who associated many human institutions with divine planning, considered writing a human invention:

> Because the messenger's mouth was too overburdened, he
>   could not repeat it,
> The lord of Kullab [part of Uruk] smoothed some clay, set
>   words on it as on a tablet.
> Before that time, there had been no setting words on clay.[35]

The pictographic theory has been the more popular and pervasive, and is still found in many current books. Uruk has given us firm evidence to reject it. We understand now that from the start, writing at Uruk used both abstract symbols and representational images, though predominantly the latter. Furthermore, as the system developed, several principles were at work, including purely arbitrary, nonpictorial, symbolic techniques, in which signs were combined with other signs, inscribed within each other, reversed, inverted, or tilted, or had certain parts of them emphasized with hatched lines. Even the earliest writing was complex, employing about 1,900 characters, and was probably known only to a few. Its adepts enjoyed a new kind of power and status:

> The scribal art is a good lot, one of wealth and plenty,
> When you are a youngster, you suffer, when you are
>   mature, you prosper.[36]

Writing seems therefore to have been invented as a deliberate, brilliantly conceived, intellectual effort to represent *language*, not ideas or images, in symbolic form, across space and time.[37] It was not invented in isolation, but appeared at Uruk in the social, economic, artistic, and technological context we have outlined above.[38] Uruk seems to have been a city in which the power of symbolism was appreciated and exploited to an exceptional degree. Nor did writing appear without precedents, for other symbolic systems of recording information already existed.

One of the most ingenious of these involved clay tokens or counters that stood for quantities of certain commodities. These counters were enclosed in clay envelopes to record quantities of goods in separate transactions, and sometimes seals were rolled across the surface of the envelope to indicate the authority or identity behind the transaction. To reconstruct the transaction, one had to break open the envelope and count the tokens. Record-keepers then hit on the idea of marking the outside of the envelope to show what counters were enclosed. This mode of recording information had important limitations, not least of which was that there was not yet an independent concept of number.[39] As a result, separate forms and types of counters were required for each commodity, and the symbol for a given quantity of one commodity might stand for a different quantity of another. Thus a circle could mean ten if counting sheep but eighteen if counting measures of land surface, and there was no symbol that denoted the number ten per se. In addition, it was not possible to convey basic information about the transaction—income, outgo, balance—nor was there any way to indicate its relationship to time. Some of these problems may have been dealt with by grouping envelopes of tokens in containers referring to specific matters.[40]

Symbolic manipulation of tokens enclosed in clay envelopes was for a short time contemporaneous with writing, as documented by excavations at Susa, then abandoned, though it remained a folk practice in Iraq as late as the 1930s.[41] Its influences on the invention of writing include the shape of some of the signs for numerals, the possibility that some counters were scored or marked rather the way later signs were, the practice of marking the outside of the clay envelope to show what and how many counters were enclosed within it, and the fact that later rectilinear cuneiform tablets were in reality flattened spheres, such that the surface of a tablet was regarded as continuous both horizontally and vertically. Perhaps we can define the relationship between tokens and writing most succinctly by saying that although both systems were invented in response to some of the same needs, tokens limited human expression to the tangible, whereas writing offered infinite scope for recorded language and thought. Writing did not evolve from tokens, however, but was devised by someone conversant with them and well aware of their limitations.

Some 5,800 clay tablets, dating to the end of the fourth millennium, have been discovered in the heart of the Uruk temple complexes, as well as at a few other sites, including several Uruk colonies and outposts. Some tablets are inscribed with numerals; others bear signs. There are also perforated labels, as if for bales or containers of goods, with numerals and signs, as well as small tablets, ruled off in columns and cases, that show administrators at work accounting for staples, of both livestock and field crops. A particularly interesting group of tablets consists of systematic lists of written signs, such as the signs for offices and professions, as well as different kinds of oxen, fish, birds, pigs, and objects of clay, metal, and wood. These are the earliest speculative and associative documents of the human race, forming the basis for later encyclopedic collections.[42]

The Uruk Phenomenon

Surveying the culture of Uruk as a whole, we find that it contained within itself many of the fundamental social, political, spiritual, and material elements of the later cultures that would develop in southern Iraq, not to mention the tendency to expand beyond the alluvial plains whenever circumstances permitted. The more we learn, the more we see this period as the real beginning of Mesopotamian civilization, which was to last until the early Christian era.

Yet, so far as we can tell, later Mesopotamian tradition had no specific memory of the Uruk culture. The Sumerians did believe that in some past age they had brought civilization to the rest of the world:

> O great land, territory without limit,
> Illumined by a light that will never be dimmed,
> Which gave to all peoples their powers to produce and
> create,

> To the farthest reaches of the horizon,
> Your powers to produce and create are sublime
>   and beyond understanding,
> Your heart is full of mysteries too deep to solve.[43]

But there was no direct recollection of the primacy of Uruk, her expansion and colonies, her innovative and accomplished use of symbols, her teeming thousands of workers serving their gods and rulers.

3. Early City-States

You enter the house blind, you come out seeing. What is it?
A school.

Sumerian riddle

There is commerce in a city,
But fishermen caught the food.

Sumerian proverb

New Polities

By the end of the fourth millennium, Uruk's influence and colonies had contracted or vanished, leaving a cultural vacuum soon filled by local polities, from the Mediterranean to the Gulf. We see the inner workings of one such polity through the discovery of the archives from a fortified building at Jemdet Nasr in northern Babylonia. The grand scale of this building suggests that it was the seat of some major institution. The cuneiform tablets found scattered throughout the rooms tell us further that it controlled a manor of perhaps more than 2,200 hectares, whose exploitation its administrators planned with care. They proceeded on the operative principle that the land should be divided into two main categories, using a consistent proportion of 2:1. Two-thirds of the total arable land sustained the manor and its chief personage (whether priest or king we do not know), and one-third, divided into five parcels of roughly equal size, supported its institutional staff.[1]

Also found in the archives were tablets bearing the impressions of seals. In some cases, they had been rolled across the clay, then the writing added, the opposite of later practice, in which seals were rolled over writing. A small group of tablets recorded choice foods, each document impressed with a great seal, on which appear the symbols of more than a dozen cities throughout Mesopotamia. These cities formed a recognized cultural community that used the Sumerian language for record-keeping and acknowledged a league or federation of allies, some politically and economically powerful, others consisting of little more than a temple, such as Kesh, an isolated sanctuary of the birth goddess. The choice foods may have been offerings for a sanctuary of primary importance to the league of cities, perhaps at Uruk. We do not know the formal basis for a city's inclusion, but we see evidence later at other cities, notably Ur and Shuruppak, that this or similar leagues remained a long-standing arrangement.[2]

Ur and the Royal Graves

A leading member of this league was Ur, home to a sanctuary of the moon god, called Nanna in Sumerian, Sin in Akkadian, that dominated the city. The written records of Ur, several centuries later than those of Jemdet Nasr, not only give us additional evidence for a league of cities, they show the pattern of management of agricultural land use typical of the irrigated zone for the rest of the third millennium: parcels of similar size set out in orderly blocks managed by individual cultivators and overseers, each of whom reported to a supervisor, with no trace of the grand scheme seen farther north.[3]

As important as its agricultural resources were for the city's wealth, nothing in these records could prepare us for the astonishing discovery of exceptionally rich tombs, known as the Royal Graves, within an extensive cemetery dating to the mid-third millennium B.C.E. Their meticulous excavation and publication have shed considerable light on the international contacts of the period, which brought gold, lapis lazuli, carnelian, and other luxury materials to Ur. Several of the Royal Graves reflect elaborate burial rituals, in which as many as seventy-four people went to their deaths in order to accompany the tomb's principal occupant into the netherworld. Members of the court—soldiers, servants, and musicians, dressed in their finest—descended the tomb's sloping passage, followed by men driving oxen or asses hitched to wagons. When all were in place, they drank poison. The animals were killed, the bodies of beasts and people positioned, and the grave-shafts filled with earth.[4]

It would seem that the ever more powerful kings of Ur intro-duced mass burial for certain deceased members of the ruling family. According to a Sumerian poem describing the funeral rites for Gilgamesh, legendary king of Uruk, he too was buried with his family and entourage:

> His beloved wife, his beloved children,
> His beloved senior wife and concubine,
> His beloved minstrel, cupbearer, . . .
> His beloved barber, . . .
> His beloved courtiers and palace attendants,
> His beloved personal effects,
> They were interred beside him, in palatial display, at Uruk.[5]

Among the grave goods at Ur were gold vessels and weapons, inlaid gaming boards, intricate jewelry, fine furniture, small stat-ues of exotic materials, and even a gold straw for drinking the beer of eternity. Nine or more harps, or lyres, were also recovered, carefully placed near or upon the musicians' bodies after they died. Like the rest, the harp pictured here (figure 6) has been re-constructed thanks to close examination of the impressions and hollows left by the wooden elements and strings of gut, fiber, or wire, which had long since disintegrated. As we see, the sound box and arms were decorated with sheet gold bands and shell, lapis, and red limestone inlays reminiscent of architectural mo-saic work. This harp has a gold bull's head on the front; other harp heads include gold-plated bulls with lapis beards, copper and silver cows, copper-alloy stags, and a copper-alloy horned deity. On all the instruments, the flat panel beneath the animal heads bears shell inlays of human and animal vignettes, possibly derived from songs or fables. Later texts discuss the tuning of

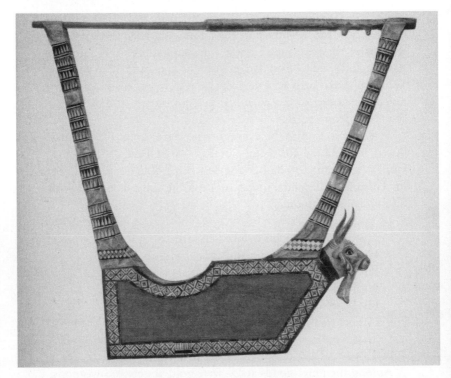

Figure 6. Inlaid harp from Ur, gold, shell, lapis lazuli, and other materials, height 1.2 m, Iraq Museum, Baghdad. (Woolley 1934: pl. 114) *In the spring of 2003, conservators were treating the harp, as well as a group of Assyrian ivories (see figure 17). The harp's gold bull's head had long since been taken to the Central Bank for safekeeping and replaced by a copy. When the looters burst into the workroom, they found the harp on a table and stripped its gold bands, damaging some of the fragile inlays. They also took the replica bull's head; the real one was unharmed in the flooding of the bank vaults during the fall of Baghdad.*

harps, hinting at a rich musical repertory performed on these splendid instruments.[6]

The sumptuous goods from the Royal Graves are remarkable not only for their exquisite workmanship and mastery of techniques, but also for their confident expression of royal power and prestige. The craftsmen used lavish amounts of lapis lazuli, for example, which had to be imported arduously from the mountains of Afghanistan, attesting to the ability of the kings of Ur to acquire this semiprecious stone. At the same time, venerable arts, such as mosaic and inlay work, were given new roles as vehicles for the earliest secular narratives we have, as seen for instance on the trapezoidal box known as the Standard of Ur, whose registers depict on one side a battle, on the other a royal victory banquet, complete with harp entertainment. Battle and feasting scenes occur too often, though, on seals (figure 5), plaques, and other work of the period for us to assign any specific historical significance to the imagery.[7]

When Kingship Came down from Heaven

Mesopotamian tradition was fascinated with royalty. According to a historical document called the Sumerian King List, kingship was a gift from the gods, first bestowed on the city of Kish, north of Sumer.[8] A legend preserved in later sources adds that the first king, Etana of Kish, yearned to establish a dynasty by passing his diadem on to a son, but the gods had not planned for a dynasty, perhaps intending to bestow kingship wherever they willed. After various adventures, Etana flies up to heaven, clutching dizzily to the body of an eagle, to seek from the goddess Ishtar a magic plant that would help him beget an heir. As he peers down anxiously, we have the earliest description of what the world might look like from the sky:

> When he had borne him aloft a third league,
> The eagle said to him, to Etana,
> "Look, my friend, how the land is now."
> "The sea has become a gardener's ditch!"[9]

Though the Kishites evidently saw descent from father to son as the natural devolvement of kingship, it is interesting that the Sumerian King List made special note of eight particularly successful kings of old, seven of whom were not of royal birth, the exception being a ruler of Uruk. This suggests that there may have been a separate tradition associating the earliest kingship with Uruk.[10]

Some traditions of the King List, perhaps originating in Sumer, appear resentful of the primacy of Kish, adding a section so that the list would start with Sumerian kings who ruled before the Flood "swept over." The antediluvian Sumerian kings had immensely long lives, tens of thousands of years each. Nonetheless, many ancient Mesopotamian historians, including those at Nippur, were satisfied with the tradition of placing the first kings at Kish, and they repeated it for generations.[11]

Kish was quite a different city from its Sumerian counterparts. For one, its inhabitants mainly spoke Kishite, a Semitic language belonging to the same linguistic family as Arabic and Hebrew and closely related to Akkadian. Sumerian, on the other hand, is not related to any other known language. If the Sumerians had taught the Kishites how to write, the Kishites taught the Sumerians how to rule. It was Kish, not Uruk or Ur, that may have produced the first king to establish an empire, as we shall see in chapter 4.[12]

By the mid-third millennium B.C.E., Iraq had become a land of cities ruled by kings allied for military, religious, or commercial purposes. At the same time, the Sumerians acknowledged the conflicting ambitions of these burgeoning cities. Were there too many kings for the plains? Was the arable land not sufficient to sustain them all in their grand projects? Was there, as some scholars maintain, a progressive desiccation or salinization of the region, owing to a gradual change in climate or to intensive irrigation, so that cities became increasingly competitive in the face of dwindling resources?[13]

Shuruppak, City of Wisdom

We gain insight into the intellectual, administrative, and commercial activities of the period through studying the tablets and seals found in one small city, Shuruppak, which belonged to the league headed by the king of Kish. For centuries, Sumerian had been the only written language in Iraq. When the Kishites began to write their own language, they spelled it using Sumerian signs, and they even interspersed Sumerian words that the reader was expected to translate as he went along. Kishite students thus had to master Sumerian first. For this, they went to Shuruppak, a city famed for its wisdom and said to have preserved writing from before the legendary Flood. There they worked through the demanding curriculum of the time, memorizing long lists of signs, words, and names, many of them of no practical value, graduating when they could copy out elaborate hymns to Sumerian deities, some written in a special, abstruse orthography. Proudly, they signed their names to their efforts: "Shumaba wrote this tablet."[14]

We know all this through the diligent excavations of the site, where the schoolboys' work was found buried in the remains of houses throughout the city. Perhaps the students had boarded with their teachers. When the tablets were discovered in the early twentieth century, scholars could not read them, nor understand the significance of hundreds of other Shuruppak tablets, but more than two generations later, new discoveries in Sumer shed light upon them. Nor could anyone then have imagined that excavations in the 1970s at the Syrian site of Ebla would yield tablets showing that the Kishites taught the Eblaites, perhaps through their nearer neighbors at Mari, how to write and keep records, using the signs and words they had learned in Sumer.[15]

The finds from Shuruppak also reveal that administrators did not always use the central suite of offices, in which numerous documents were kept, but often worked at home, writing vouchers, posting them to combined accounts, then carrying these forward into larger accounts, so that the original vouchers could still be traced.[16] From the activities recorded, we learn, among other things, that there was a staging area nearby, where contingents of men from Sumerian cities such as Adab and Umma, presumably allies and members of the league to which Shuruppak belonged, converged, probably for some military campaign, perhaps a foreshadowing of the end that was shortly to befall the city:

1,532 able-bodied men, 39 working boys, 41 serving women.
Total: 1,612 persons on rations (plus) 47 gone to Kish.[17]

In addition to tablets, numerous seal impressions were retrieved, many of them on the broken clay nodules that had been tossed aside when storeroom doors or consignments of goods were opened 4,400 years ago. Modern study of their find spots and correlations has reconstructed an interlocking network of officials and men of affairs who went about this city of perhaps 20,000 souls, on various business.[18]

In a pattern that was to remain true of life in Sumer thereafter, a wealthy elite bought and sold urban lots among themselves, perhaps to enlarge their dwellings or to collect rents. They drew up dated, witnessed sale contracts for this purpose, the first of their kind in history. Unfortunately, this group of documents was found by illegal diggers, so we know nothing of their context, probably some central registry office.[19]

Disaster struck. About 2400 B.C.E., an enemy force took Shuruppak by storm, burning the whole town and leaving it a desolate waste where, as the Sumerians put it, the owl was the only denizen, "bird of destroyed cities, the bird awake in times of slumber, the bird of heartfelt sorrow."[20] In reading the records of this ancient city we have therefore a snapshot, as it were, of the last year of its busy existence, before its inhabitants fell victim to the barbarities of warfare. Was the attacker one of the kings of Ur, mortal foe of the Kishite league, who later claimed to be king of Kish? This would have been possible only if he had conquered Kish and her allies.[21]

A Tale of Two Cities

In the years that followed, the Sumerian cities of Lagash and Umma, freed of their bond of alliance in the Kishite league, fought for generations over a strip of arable land lying between them. The records of their struggles give us our earliest example of an extensively documented conflict.[22] In a typical episode,

> Urlumma, ruler of Umma, diverted water into the boundary-channel of Ningirsu and the boundary-channel of Nanshe. He set fire to their monuments and smashed them, and destroyed the established chapels of the gods that were built on the boundary-levee called Namnunda-kigara. He recruited foreigners and transgressed the boundary-ditch of Ningirsu.[23]

The best-preserved monument of this war, known as the Stele of the Vultures, comes from Lagash. The piece commemorates in text and image a victory of Eannatum, ruler of Lagash, over Umma. On one side, Eannatum appears in each register, on foot or in his chariot, leading his troops on their march across enemy corpses, spearing the enemy, and libating on the battlefield. The stele takes its name from the scene at the top, in which vultures set upon the dead. The other side (figure 7) is dominated by a giant bearded figure, usually taken to be the god Ningirsu, who has entered the fray on behalf of his city, capturing the men of Umma in a net and smiting them with his mace. We have here one of the first pictorial narratives of an actual historical event, whose tale unrolls in successive registers, some of which even wrap around the side, as though impressed by enormous cylinder seals. In the millennium since the Uruk Vase (figure 4), Sumerian art had responded to a growing need to glorify city and ruler, but not at the expense of the gods, a challenge the Stele of the Vultures met with accomplished skill.[24]

Despite the war, Lagash prospered, owing to her fertile fields, vast flocks of sheep, and vital fishing industry. The use at Lagash and elsewhere of a new tool, a seeder plow with a funnel mounted on it, through which seed dropped into the furrows at regular intervals and at a consistent depth, enhanced productivity and allowed scribes to calculate precisely the cultivation expenses and ratio of return for a given plot of land. As a Sumerian manual of agriculture instructs,

> Make eight furrows per cubit of width, the grain will sit better in furrows closely spaced. When you have to work a field with a seeder plow, watch the man who drops in the seed. The grain should fall two fingers deep, he should put in one ounce of seed per cubit.[25]

Merchants from Lagash traveled as far as Mari, on the Euphrates, and Elam, in southwestern Iran, and they sailed down the Gulf to Dilmun, a place probably to be identified with the island of Bahrein.[26] Perhaps originally because of its verdant palm groves,

Figure 7. Stele of the Vultures from Lagash, limestone, height 1.8 m, Louvre, Paris. (Moortgat 1967: pl. 118) *Illicit digging at Lagash had begun decades before Ernest de Sarzec commenced excavations in 1877. During his seasons of work, many finds were stolen from the site. Of the seven fragments he unearthed of the Stele of the Vultures, broken in antiquity, one ended up in the British Museum, which in 1932 gave it to the Louvre, where the other six pieces had been since 1881. Today, the sites of Lagash and Umma, the two arch-rivals of the third millennium, have both been so extensively damaged by looters that nothing remains for future archaeologists.*

Dilmun was fabled as a kind of paradise in Sumerian poetry, a place where nothing unpleasant ever happened:

> No lion kills,
> No wolf snatches a lamb, . . .
> No old woman there says, "I am an old woman,"
> No old man there says, "I am an old man,"
> No young girl throws her bath water out into the city (street),
> No ferryman says, "It's night" (no more service).[27]

To the business-minded merchants from Lagash and other cities, though, Dilmun was an important trading center where their shiploads of grain, wool, cloth, silver, fat, and resin could be exchanged for copper and tin.

Once these metals reached Sumer, they were absorbed into the thriving pyrotechnical industries. Copper and tin were the essential components of bronze, the alloy of choice for both weapons and tools. Already in the Uruk period, metallurgists had mastered the lost-wax casting method, and Sumerian smiths could anneal and plate.[28] The Uruk period also saw the invention of the first artificial material, the fruit of much pyrotechnical experimentation. Faience, as we call it, was made by mixing silicates, sodium carbonate binding agents, and colorants, which coalesced at a high firing temperature into a glossy, smooth substance. The earliest faience, mainly blue ornaments, comes from northern Iraq, where it apparently substituted for lapis lazuli, but by the mid-third millennium, when the Sumerian elite were acquiring large amounts of lapis, as we saw in the Royal Graves, faience makers were exploring a wide range of uses for this versatile material. Their work led to the development of glass and glazed ceramics in the mid-second millennium (see figure 13).[29]

Diorite, a hard black stone obtained from Oman and Iran, was prized for royal sculpture, one of the earliest examples of which is a statue of Enmetena (figure 8). The piece represents the Lagash king as a votary, wearing the typical male dedicant's fleecelike skirt and clasping his hands before him in a traditional, respectful gesture. As access to Sumerian temples was probably increasingly

Figure 8. Statue of Enmetena from Ur, diorite, height 76 cm, Iraq Museum, Baghdad. (Moortgat 1967: pl. 87) *Taken from Lagash as a trophy of war in the mid-third millennium, this statue again found itself plundered in April 2003. It was quickly listed in print and electronically among some thirty stolen Mesopotamian works of particular artistic and cultural importance. In principle, this made it unsalable on the antiquities market. In June 2006, it was seized at Kennedy airport in New York. As of this writing, the piece is in the Iraqi Embassy in Washington, D.C.*

limited to temple personnel, votive statues of worshippers, both men and women, became popular. The figures, standing or seated, often with inscriptions, were placed on benches or tables in the temples, conveying to the deity in perpetuity the names and prayers of their donors. Their eyes generally have exaggerated lapis lazuli pupils, as if the figures were awestruck at the sight of the deity in whose presence they found themselves. Here, rather than a prayer, we have an inscription giving the name of the statue, "Enmetena whom the god Enlil loves," then a list of various temples Enmetena built, followed by a record of an important land transaction between the king and the Enlil temple. It is noteworthy that the statue was found at Ur, not Lagash, apparently taken from its home temple as booty during some Sumerian war. Stylistically, it is typical of Sumerian works made for cultic purposes, with its emphasis on the piety of the gesture, rather than on naturalistic anatomical proportions.[30]

We learn more about the affairs of this energetic state from a long series of inscriptions telling of the concerns and achievements of the Lagash rulers.[31] Some of the most fascinating come from the chancellery of an enigmatic sovereign called Uruinimgina (in older books, Urukagina), who used his high military rank to jockey aside the heir apparent to become ruler himself about 2350 B.C.E. He took the title of *lugal* or king, which rulers of Lagash did not normally use. Uruinimgina boasts that he changed long-standing practices of the city, instituting a new order in which the gods were paramount. Inspectors and fees were removed, and even the costs of burial were altered. From a provision concerning the human rights of people of subordinate status, we learn incidentally that there was a free economy:

> When the house of an important person adjoins the house of a subordinate, and the important person says to him, "I want to buy it from you"; whether he lets him buy it from him, saying to him, "Pay me the price I want, the cubic volume of my house in barley," or whether he does not let him buy it from him at all, the important man may not strike him in anger.[32]

We are fortunate in being able to see beyond the royal bombast to real events, thanks to the discovery of about 1,200 detailed administrative records of the time. What Uruinimgina actually did was to take control of teams of workers and other resources belonging to the temples, to reorganize them, and then proclaim that he and his family were managing all on behalf of the family of gods who ruled Lagash. To judge from the documents, his attempt at usurpation failed, for it seems that he soon had to retreat from some of his more extreme measures.[33] His strange, often incomprehensible proclamations of reform suggest to some an original and dynamic leader, to others a vainglorious tyrant, but in any case he is one of the first rulers of history we see as an individual personality.

Lugalzagesi, ruler of Umma and a contemporary of Uruinimgina, nursed and acted upon the Sumerian kings' perennial ambition to rule all of Sumer as one land. Early in his campaigns, he laid siege to Lagash and the city capitulated, finally ending their war. Lugalzagesi went farther and farther, telling us in a triumphal commemoration that he defeated cities throughout Sumer. He commissioned an inscribed stone vase in honor of each of these conquests, depositing more than fifty of them in the temple of the god Enlil in Nippur.[34]

Nippur was the main holy city of Sumer, and its principal temple, called Ekur ("Mountain House"), was home to Enlil, the chief god on earth. Why Nippur, which had never had aggressive political leadership, would have occupied such a prestigious cultic position, we are not sure. Later, the city was considered a center of learning, a reputation borne out by the archaeological discovery, in private houses, of thousands of tablets preserving works of Sumerian literature. Nippur was also where triumphant kings went to be crowned king of Sumer and Akkad.[35] It was natural, therefore, for Lugalzagesi to proclaim his victories at Nippur, and to ask Enlil to look with favor upon his sovereignty.

According to *Atrahasis*, the Babylonian story of the Flood, Enlil was an irascible god, so annoyed by the racket of the multiplying human race, which had been created to serve divine needs, that he sends in turn a plague, a famine, and a drought to wipe everybody out. Enki, the god of wisdom, helps his favorite human, Atrahasis, to circumvent each disaster. Furious, Enlil demands that the gods swear an oath not to tell any person of his next measure, the Flood. When Atrahasis builds a reed hut as a place to receive portentous dreams, Enki gets around the oath by telling the wall of the hut what he must do to survive:

> Flee house, build boat,
> Forsake possessions, and save life. . . .
> Roof her over like the depths,
> So that the sun will not see inside her,
> Let her be roofed over fore and aft,
> The gear should be very firm,
> The pitch should be firm, make her strong![36]

As the Flood overwhelms the land, Atrahasis, his wife, and selected animals are safe in the ark:

> Its destructive power came upon the people like a battle,
> One person did not see another,
> They could not recognize each other in the catastrophe.
> The deluge bellowed like a bull,
> The wind resounded like a screaming eagle.
> The darkness was dense, the sun was gone.[37]

In the version of the Flood story preserved in the *Epic of Gilgamesh* (see chapter 5 and the Epilogue), we read what happens next:

> Six days and seven nights
> The wind continued, the deluge and windstorm leveled the land.
> When the seventh day arrived,
> The windstorm and deluge left off their battle,
> Which had struggled, like a woman in labor.
> The sea grew calm, the tempest stilled, the deluge ceased.
> I looked at the weather, stillness reigned,
> And the whole human race had turned into clay.
> The landscape was flat as a rooftop.

I opened the hatch, sunlight fell upon my face.
Falling to my knees, I sat down weeping,
Tears running down my face.[38]

After the third bird he releases finds dry land, the survivor and his wife emerge from the ark and make offerings to the famished gods, who have been starving without people to provide for them. Enlil institutes mortality, celibacy, and childlessness as better ways to control human population.

4. KINGS OF THE FOUR QUARTERS OF THE WORLD

As Sargon made his invasion, . . .
The very forest might have been his enemy,
It cast darkness over heaven, the sun grew dark!
[But] many stars came out and were set toward the enemy.
The enemy strongholds, nine of them, were founded well,
But he captured every man, ox, and sheep.

Sargon, King of Battle

The First Empire

Some historians see in Lugalzagesi's conquests the culmination of several generations of efforts to unite Sumer by conquest from within. Unification would, however, come from without, through the new order initiated by Sargon, a near-legendary conqueror from Akkad. Sargon appears in the Sumerian King List as one of the eight most famous kings of the past. Already in the late third millennium, only a century or so after his death about 2279 B.C.E., he was deemed of special importance. Moreover, according to a Sumerian story about his youth, early in circulation, the goddess Inanna foiled a murder plot against him. When an Assyrian king of the late eighth century adopted the name Sargon, perhaps out of admiration for his achievements, a fable was composed about the first Sargon's infancy, childhood, and career, claiming that he was born in secret to a high priestess and set adrift on the Euphrates in a basket. Rescued by a man drawing water, he was brought up as his son and put to work in a date palm orchard. He rose rapidly to leadership, just as Moses, Cyrus, Ardashir, and other great men are reputed to have done, all overcoming unpropitious beginnings as foundlings or abandoned children. According to another tale, the young Sargon was cupbearer to the king of Kish. Some even said that the goddess Ishtar fell in love with him, giving him strength and protection.[1]

The significance of this accretion of stories is not their specific content so much as their unequivocal testimony that there was something quite remarkable about Sargon and what he accomplished. Later Mesopotamian thinkers saw his reign and empire as a new departure, glorious and worthy of particular study. His surviving inscriptions were carefully copied in later schools. Heroic poems told of Sargon's campaigns to parts of the world no Mesopotamian king had reached before, of his bravery and eloquence. This was the first period of history about which Mesopotamian scholars of later periods knew authentic details. The rise of Uruk may have been forgotten, but the career and conquests of Sargon remained vivid in historical and literary memory for more than two thousand years. Sargon harnessed the hitherto untapped forces of his native land and set forth to conquer the world.[2]

Akkad was the home of people who spoke a Semitic language we call Akkadian, after the native term for it, *akkadu*. What occasioned their rise to prominence is unknown. The history of Iraq, however, shows numerous such instances of northern states rapidly expanding northwest toward the Mediterranean, once their eastern and southern frontiers had been secured. The environmental cohesiveness of the steppes, the relative ease of communication across them, and the availability of supplies along the Euphrates and its tributaries certainly favored the formation of large, northern political entities. Whereas the rulers of Sumer based their power primarily on staple finance, that is, wealth from agriculture and animal husbandry, the Akkadian rulers derived theirs from wealth finance, that is, prestige goods, such as gold and silver, taking them by force from other peoples or exacting them as tribute, and using them to sustain substantial armed forces. At the same time, agrarian management remained a cornerstone of Akkadian imperial policy.[3]

Sargon created his empire through the prowess of a great standing army. In one of his inscriptions, Sargon claims he fed daily 5,400 able-bodied men in his service. Speed and mobility were certainly factors in Sargon's military success, his main force consisting of bowmen and lancers, lightly armed. The Sumerians, by contrast, seem to have favored heavily armed, dense formations, backed up by cumbersome battle wagons, as we see on the Stele of the Vultures (figure 7), no match for able archers. As city after city fell before him, Sargon, "victorious in thirty-four battles," pushed far into Iran, his army defeating even major coalitions raised against it. To the west, he surged up the Euphrates past Mari. To the north, he invaded Turkey, the "Silver Mountains," and, according to a later account, penetrated "woods hung about with tangles."[4]

Throughout the new empire, Sargon installed native Akkadians in governorships, implying a permanent presence, the establishment of an administrative apparatus, and the designation of provinces. He rebuilt Kish, perhaps intending it to be his capital, but he or one of his successors founded a new imperial capital, Agade, whose precise location is still undiscovered.[5] Into this place flowed all the wealth of the Akkadian conquests. A Sumerian poem waxes lyrical about its splendors, marveling that Inanna so endowed Agade that she had to store up its treasures like ordinary grain:

> She filled its very granaries with gold,
> She filled its gleaming granaries with silver,
> She apportioned copper, tin, and chunks of lapis among its
> granges,
> She even sealed them up in silos![6]

Sargon appointed his daughter Enheduanna as high priestess of the moon god Nanna-Sin at Ur. Her image survives on a limestone plaque from Ur showing her and her attendants making offerings at an altar.[7] To this talented, long-lived, and fascinating woman we owe the first literature of any civilization that can securely be associated with a specific author. She wrote a series of Sumerian hymns commemorating reconstruction of the principal sanctuaries of Sumer, as well as some ardent love lyrics.[8] She also composed a powerful autobiographical poem without parallel in Sumerian literature, in which she tells us that she was threatened when local rebels seized power at Ur. She prayed for help to the moon god, whom she had served all her life, but he did nothing. In her fear and distress, she even temporarily lost her power of speech, a motif often used later in Mesopotamian literature. Then she appealed to the warlike nature of the goddess Inanna, begging for help, which came with terrible swiftness. Once Ur was regained from the rebels, Enheduanna resumed her offices.[9] She then felt something stirring inside her, dark and intimate, which was her poem. She produced it in a private agony of creativity, and it stood apart from her as words for all to hear:

> This fills me, this overflows from me, Exalted Lady, as I
>   give birth for you!
> What I confided to you in the dark of night, a singer shall
>   perform for you in the bright of day![10]

Her work is so individual in stamp, though obscure and difficult to the highest degree, that she stands forth as a singular personality, even in the extraordinary times in which she lived.

No one knows how far Sargon's direct rule extended or how effective it was, but we can judge the heaviness of his hand from the fact that a widespread revolt broke out upon the succcession of his son Rimush. Determined to restore his father's empire, he moved first against the cities of Sumer, treating them with merciless cruelty, massacring their forces and deporting men, women, and children to forced labor camps, where many died. From the records of one of these camps, we see that free citizens and slaves alike were sent far from their homes, apparently to cut stone. After a short, harsh reign, Rimush was murdered in a palace conspiracy about 2270 B.C.E. and succeeded by his brother, Manishtusu.[11]

This king built on Rimush's reconquest of Sumer to invade Iran once again. He boasts in an inscription that he "quarried the black stone of the mountains across the Lower Sea, loaded it on ships, and moored them at the wharf of Agade." As we have seen (figure 8), diorite was considered the prime stone for royal statuary, esteemed for its exotic origins, as well as for the challenges it posed in quarrying, carving, and polishing. The numerous Akkadian royal monuments of diorite, fragmentary though they are today, embody the autocratic pride of these first rulers of an empire.[12]

By this time, the land of Sumer had been reorganized into an imperial province, a move designed to break down the boundaries of the old city-states by creating a new entity administered centrally by high royal officials, many of whom disdained titles, and by local professionals who were proud of theirs. The administrative capital of this new province was none other than Lagash, which now prospered afresh. Nearby, a gigantic domain was carved out, more than a hundred times the area of the manor at Jemdet Nasr (see chapter 3), and assigned to the support of crown officials, perhaps already by Rimush in retaliation for the revolt.

In Akkad, Manishtusu himself purchased extensive lands for distribution among his own retainers. These were a new class of people, who became directly dependent upon the king's patronage, withdrawing from the old ties of their native communities to serve at the king's pleasure. They fanned out, seeking opportunity and preferment throughout the realm, their wealth and income derived from estates awarded them in the conquered countryside.[13] A later legend portrays the plight of local residents displaced by these policies: "Where should we go?"[14] Like his brother before him, Manishtusu perished at the hands of conspirators.

Naram-Sin: When Kingship Went up to Heaven

The thirty-seven-year reign of Manishtusu's son, Naram-Sin, became a byword for imperial grandeur in Mesopotamian tradition for the next two thousand years. No other royal personality of the entire third millennium, save Sargon himself, left such an impression on history. In his inscriptions, he proclaims himself a peerless conqueror, before whom the massively walled cities of northern Syria fell for the first time. To the north, he explored the Tigris tunnel; to the south, he won a sea battle in the Gulf. There seemed no limit to his powers.[15]

Naram-Sin also carried out important administrative reforms. Standardized summary records were to be kept in each locality for the inspection of royal officers, documenting the harvest taken from their lands, the twenty percent set aside for the king, and the expenses of cultivation. In Akkad, many of these records were written in Akkadian, though Sumerian was still used in Sumer. A clear, elegant new script and a new rectangular tablet shape became hallmarks of the imperial administration, replacing local styles of writing and rounded tablets. Beginning at the turn of the third millennium, writing and sealing had developed as separate actions, not used in the same record. Akkadian practice recombined them, sometimes sealing written documents, sometimes writing on sealed surfaces.[16]

In the art of the reign of Naram-Sin, we see the finest pictorial expression of the Akkadian worldview.[17] Figure 9 shows the Victory Stele celebrating Naram-Sin's defeat of the Lullubi people of western Iran, an event commemorated in a now-fragmentary boxed text above the king's head. Gone are the registers and huge god of the Stele of the Vultures (figure 7). Instead, we are meant to admire Naram-Sin as he strides vigorously up the wooded slopes, supremely confident, with regal disregard for the dead and dying enemy in his path. This is the first landscape we have in Mesopotamian art, an innovation intended to impress the viewer with the geographical reality of Akkadian conquest in lands of exotic trees and foreign terrain.[18]

Alone and slightly larger than the rest, Naram-Sin ascends heavenward, where the gods are rendered as astral symbols, rather than anthropomorphized beings. Before him rises a rounded cone, the standard element in the iconography for mountains. The stele itself probably echoed this shape, as if it was a free-standing rock relief. In fact, similar depictions of Naram-Sin were carved high on the Zagros cliffs, homeland of the Lullubi, whose kings copied the Akkadian imagery in their own rock reliefs in the same mountains.[19]

Only Naram-Sin, though, wears a helmet with the horns of divinity, a sign that he had assumed the honors of the gods, which

Figure 9. Victory Stele of Naram-Sin from Susa, limestone, height 2 m, Louvre, Paris. (Moortgat 1967: pl. 155) *For over a century, with few interruptions, the French have excavated the site of Susa, sending most of the finds back to Paris in accordance with a treaty signed with the Shah in 1900. Many of the discoveries, including the Victory Stele, were unearthed in the first decades of fieldwork, when scant attention was paid to recording stratigraphy or tracing mud-brick walls. As a result, we cannot say with certainty where the Elamites set up the Victory Stele and other monuments they had seized from cities in Iraq.*

no other king before him had done. In an inscription on a massive copper statue, he tells us that the citizens of Agade begged leave of the great deities to worship their ruler as a god after he had saved their city in a time of crisis. The gods agreed, and the people built a temple in his honor in the capital. In administrative records thereafter, the king was sometimes referred to as "the god of Agade." Instead of kingship coming down from heaven, as Sumerian tradition had it, Naram-Sin's kingship had gone up to heaven, as we see vividly on the Victory Stele.[20]

In the mid-twelfth century B.C.E., the Elamites of Iran invaded Iraq (see chapter 6) and took the Victory Stele and other works back to their capital at Susa. Many of these pieces had been part of a treasury of heirloom sculptures kept in the temple of the sun god Shamash at Sippar. Though the Elamites are usually blamed for defacing them and chipping off their texts, the damage may have been done either before they got to Susa or during some subsequent destruction of the capital. As for the Victory Stele, the Elamite king left Naram-Sin's inscription, informing us in his own, carved across the pristine surface of the mountain top, "I took it, I transported it, I brought it to Elam."[21]

Other victory proclamations of Naram-Sin include narratives in Akkadian and Sumerian, replete with lists of vanquished kings, their officers, and the numbers of their defeated troops. In these the king speaks directly to his audience, sharing what he imagines were the reactions of his enemies, challenging the future, and giving for the uninitiated his own interpretation of the events he narrates: "The deed I performed is too great to describe."[22] Later ages envied the supreme self-assurance and highly wrought self-expression of the Akkadian kings.

Under Naram-Sin, the empire continued to prosper. Boatloads of grain, livestock, and tribute flowed into Agade, which became a center for international trade. Akkadian colonies were founded at Susa, as an administrative center and trading post, as well as far up the Khabur, perhaps for management of agriculture there.[23] As befit a great king, Naram-Sin also undertook construction projects throughout his realm. One of the most lavish was the rebuilding of the Ekur, the temple of Enlil at Nippur, under the auspices of the crown prince.[24] No expense or precious materials were spared in this project, but a later Sumerian poet looked with horror upon the king's demolition of the old temple:

> Like a boxer striding into the great courtyard,
> He clenched his fist at Ekur,
> Like a wrestler bent to start a match,
> He treated the precinct as if it were a lightweight.[25]

Indeed, empire came at a price. Many despised the serene arrogance of the Akkadian royalty and elite, whose domains had disrupted long-standing land-use patterns, and whose manors formed independent enclaves apart from the old cities. When the royal family passed through a region, they had to be entertained in extravagant style, wined and dined, seated on fine furniture in great pavilions, while the laborers struggled in the fields and the sharp-eyed scribes checked and sealed the contents of the barges passing in review, laden with choice goods to be taken to Agade. No doubt the people of Kish regarded with special distaste this upstart people who had usurped their city's ancient position as the heart of a great kingdom. While Sargon and his sons had kept the venerable, widely respected title of King of Kish, Naram-Sin called himself King of Akkad, dropping Kish from his titulary, because, according to him, the people of Kish were ungrateful for all the benefits Sargon and his dynasty had brought them.[26]

The gathering discontent culminated in a revolt that broke out first perhaps at Kish, then was joined by Uruk, Ur, and a coalition of other Mesopotamian cities, who sought support from abroad too. As Naram-Sin tells it, the foreign rulers were afraid to help; according to embroidered later tradition, a demonic horde of uncounted ghastly creatures was raised up against Naram-Sin from foreign lands.[27] Be that as it may, he utterly defeated the rebels, emerging as the savior of Agade and Akkadian rule:

> Naram-Sin the mighty, king of Akkad, when the four quarters of the earth attacked him together, through the love Ishtar bore him, was victorious in nine campaigns in one year and captured the kings they raised up against him.[28]

So far as we know, Naram-Sin died about 2218 B.C.E. in the fullness of years, the very type of the hero-king. What happened next is obscure. His son Sharkalisharri, whose grandiose name means "king of all kings," was eventually crowned at Nippur, where construction of the new Ekur temple resumed. We know little of his reign, save that the empire contracted drastically. In the northwest, a people called the Amorites moved steadily toward Akkad from their homeland up the Euphrates in Syria. As to why the Amorites would press at this time, one controversial explanation holds that this was a period of severe drought in Syria, meaning first that the Akkadian colonies there had to be abandoned, and second that the local population had to emigrate south to the irrigated lands, or starve. On the east, a people called the Gutians, stockbreeders in the Zagros, took advantage of the disorder to enter the lowlands and set up kingdoms in some of the Sumerian and Akkadian cities. Agade was rent by civil war, no doubt heavily damaged and looted, possibly destroyed.[29]

With savage glee, this traditionalist Sumerian poet crows over the downfall of Agade:

> Agade, may your strong man lose his strength,
> May he be unable to lift his sack of provisions to the saddle,
> May your riding donkey no longer rejoice in his strength
>   but lie motionless till nightfall.
> May that city die of hunger,
> May its citizens who dined on the finest foods lie down in
>   grass (like cattle),
> May the man who rose from a meal of first fruits
> Eat the binding from his roof,
> As for the grand door of his family home,
> May he gnaw its leather hinges![30]

According to later Sumerian and Akkadian literature about these events, it was Naram-Sin himself who had brought a curse on Agade by ignoring the diviners, who had told him that he must not tear down the old Ekur temple of Nippur. These texts also say that Inanna had forsaken Agade, turning against it because she was no longer happy there. In a literary work written fifteen hundred years after his death, a penitent, chastened Naram-Sin addresses future kings, ruing his pride, telling them of his ordeals, and enjoining them not to take the risks he did:

> Wrap up your weapons and lean them in a corner,
> Restrain your valor, take care of your person.[31]

To us, this sounds like the author's wishful thinking.

There seems to have followed a period of anarchy. The Sumerian King List asks, "Who was king, who was not king?" But within a few years, a prince at Lagash received a letter announcing, "There is a king in Agade."[32] We know, in fact, of a dynasty there that lasted another century, even campaigning in Iran. However this period ended, we can be sure that the ideal of the Akkadian kings was shattered forever, and we suspect that rulers of later ages looked back with nostalgia on the glory years of Sargon and Naram-Sin. They had created something new in world history, and the most any imperially minded king could do was to imitate their achievement.

A Golden Age of Sumerian Culture

Lagash, which appears to have been spared in the civil war, was favorably poised to take advantage of the decline of Akkadian power in Sumer. She had been the administrative seat of a prosperous province, and her rulers, accommodating to whatever dynasty or group was in command of the land at large, presided over a compact and flourishing little state. One of these rulers, Gudea, commissioned numerous diorite statues showing him seated or standing, his hands piously clasped in age-old Sumerian style.[33]

Under his aegis, Sumerian literature blossomed in eloquent inscriptions, epic poetry, and hymns to the gods. One of the most elaborate is a composition that recounts in prolix detail how Gudea, who took a personal interest in architecture, built a new temple to the local god, Ningirsu, and how craftsmen and precious materials came from near and far, all nations cooperating eagerly in this undertaking. One would never know from its labored lines that there was any other place or power of importance on the horizon:

> The Elamite came to him from Elam, the Susian from Susa,
> Magan and Meluhha, coming from their mountain lands,
>   bore timbers on their shoulders for him.
> They joined forces with Gudea on his way to Girsu to build
>   Ningirsu's temple.[34]

But Uruk was, at last, in a position to revive her fortunes. A vigorous new king by the name of Utu-hegal tells us that he drove the Gutians, those "serpents from the mountains," out of the land, so Sumer could finally come to life again.[35] How this claim squares with Gudea's rosy vision of the world at nearby Lagash we do not know. When the Sumerian King List was updated, Kish, Uruk, and Ur were cast in leading roles, but collaborationist Lagash was never mentioned. A scribe at Lagash responded with a heavy satire of the list, ridiculing its long antediluvian reigns and cosmic verbiage.[36] Akkad, perforce, had to be included, but not its grandeur. Utu-hegal may have had in mind a revival of the former imperial order of Akkad, this time based at Uruk, for he adopted Naram-Sin's royal title, "king of the four quarters of the world." His plans were cut short by his accidental death by drowning about 2013 B.C.E.. Ur-Nammu, a relative and the military governor of Ur, succeeded him, beginning the final chapter of Sumerian political history.

Of the five kings of the Third Dynasty of Ur, as it is known, two may command our attention here: Ur-Nammu and Shulgi.[37] At Ur, the capital city of the new dynasty, Ur-Nammu undertook numerous building projects, some of which were shown within traditional registers on a stele depicting busy construction scenes, with workers on ladders and the king himself carrying tools.[38] One of his most ambitious monuments was a temple precinct dedicated to the moon god Nanna-Sin. At its center, he built the first ziggurat, a massive three-stage structure of solid brick, both sun-dried and baked, its corners oriented to the cardinal points, with three steep staircases joining and leading to a sanctuary at the top (figure 10).

Figure 10. Ziggurat at Ur, base 64 × 46 m. (Author photograph) *The site of Ur was damaged during the Gulf War when shells landed very near the ziggurat, because Iraqi aircraft were parked in its shadow. In 2003, an American military installation was constructed in the vicinity, encroaching on the ruins.*

Beginning in the Ubaid period, temples had often been set on platforms, which gradually increased in height and complexity. The idea seems to have been to provide the gods with mountain-like settings, closer to the heavens, a concept furthered by calling ziggurats by such names as "Exalted Mountain," and possibly by planting trees on the terraces. As the divine bride of Nanna tells him in a Sumerian love song,

> I will come to dwell in your heavenly house, the house
> you love,
> O Nanna, I will come to dwell on high in your cedar-
> scented mountain,
> O my husband Nanna, I will come to dwell in your
> city, Ur.[39]

Ur-Nammu erected ziggurats of similar type at Eridu, Uruk, and Nippur. Later kings from the Old Babylonian to the Assyrian periods built some two dozen ziggurats throughout ancient Iraq and into Syria and Elam, whose architectural variations included as many as seven stages and internal staircases. In the Bible, the ziggurat of the temple of Marduk at Babylon was transmuted into the Tower of Babel, emblematic of the vain desire of the human race to rival God.[40]

Ur-Nammu's scribes turned out florid Sumerian hymns in his honor, the earliest examples we have of this genre of court literature. He was killed in battle in the prime of life, and a bitter outpouring of grief at his demise, in the name of Inanna herself, suggests that he had been a charismatic leader of great potential:

> Oh that my shepherd bring me back his charms, no longer
> can I be intimate with him!
> Oh that my strong man be vigorous once more for me, as
> the grass renews in the steppe!
> Oh that once more I, like a boat on a river, could find
> haven at his pier, now silent![41]

About 2094 B.C.E., Ur-Nammu's son Shulgi succeeded to the throne at a young age and reigned for forty-eight years, a longevity comparable to that of Louis XIV or Queen Victoria.[42] Like theirs, his era was marked by a distinctive style and was a golden age of literature. Under his approving patronage, Sumerian poets produced a whole series of hymns, glorifying his accomplishments in such grandiloquence as to suggest a personality cult. He was a ruler, warrior, athlete, strategist, musician, and linguist without rival in the world. In this excerpt, Shulgi boasts of a heroic long-distance run he made through a storm in order to celebrate festivals at Nippur and Ur on the same day:

> Then did the storm shriek, the west wind whirl,
> North wind, south wind roaring at each other!
> Lightning with seven blasts consumed the whole of
> heaven,
> The howling storm made the earth tremble,
> While thunder boomed and boomed again in the
> boundless sky.

The downpour flung its arms around the water on the
    ground,
Hailstones, large and small, were pounding on my back!
I, the king, felt no fear at all, nor was I dismayed,
I charged forward, like a savage lion for the kill,
I galloped onward, like an onager on the steppe,
On and on I ran, my heart rejoicing![43]

Shulgi and his court also listened to epics about the ancient Sumerian rulers of Uruk, whom they claimed as kin. They made scant
reference to the Akkadian kings, and they seldom used the Akkadian language in inscriptions, despite the fact that some of them
had Akkadian names, as did their wives. Scribes may have collected and suppressed the literature about Sargon and his dynasty,
even as they glorified the deeds of their more legendary ancestors.
Prime among them was Gilgamesh, whose exploits were celebrated
in narrative poems, forerunners of what would become the out-
standing masterpiece of Mesopotamian literature (see chapter 5).

Some of these epics are light-hearted, replete with barbed references to current politics, no doubt timely and amusing to a savvy
courtier, and daring jokes on the limitations of royal power and
the necessity of diplomatic bluffing. Two of them concern Enmerkar, another king of ancient Uruk, and his dealings with the
lord of Aratta, a mythical city across the mountains. In one, Uruk
desires exotic goods that Aratta is unwilling to provide, so the
kings engage in a series of riddle-challenges that end when a mysterious wise woman, more intelligent than either king, suggests
that the two cities trade instead of contend, thus initiating international commerce.[44] Perhaps later schoolboys especially liked
copying a passage where Enmerkar invents the first tablet, which
the lord of Aratta stares at in stupefaction.[45] Other of these epics
feature talking animals, magic contests, and a good witch who
triumphs over a wicked sorcerer.[46]

The court was entertained as well by masques or debates, pit-
ting characters representing seasons of the year, raw materials,
crops, or animals against each other in flowery self-praise and in-
vective, to show which was the more useful to the human race.[47]

In some cases, the king may have decided the winner, in others, the god of wisdom. In this example, the hoe ridicules the plow:

> When you finally arrive at the field after me,
> The one furrow you make is a delight to behold.
> When you finally buckle down to the task,
> Your blade gets snagged in brambles and thorns,
> Your point snaps off, then your point is repaired,
> You won't keep it for long.
> The plowman calls you "The Plow That's Always Broken
> Down."[48]

This rich and delightful literature suggests an elite sure of itself and of its values, ready for both fulsome praise and a light touch of mockery.

Some modern readers suggest there was a second agenda, that of creating a literate hierarchy of people who had read the same compositions in school, learning from them the importance of kingship and tradition, and who recognized in their peers the same education and values.[49] We see this at work most clearly in that old seat of Sumerian learning, Nippur, where students worked through a standard curriculum, from lists and literary excerpts to major compositions. Their own city and Ekur-temple they glorified in a ponderous, euphuistic hymn to the god Enlil, which, in its pompous verbosity, sums up the self-satisfied worldview of the educated Sumerian elite:

> You founded it in the center of the world, to link the earth
>   and sky,
> The very soil of its bricks is the vitality of this land, the
>   vitality of foreign lands,
> Its masonry is fiery gold, its foundations lapis blue.
> Like a wild bull, it tosses up its horns in the land of Sumer,
> While foreign lands droop their heads low in awe,
> And our people celebrate its great feast days in abundance![50]

Royal patronage of the decorative arts is attested by abundant references to the commissioning of statues, furniture for sanctuaries, ceremonial boats, and musical instruments in year names, for instance, "The Year of Lightning Bolts Made of Gold and Silver" and "The Year of an Image of Justice, Splendidly Made." A royal workshop at Ur employed jewelers, leather, reed, and textile workers, joiners, sculptors, smiths and metalworkers, seal-cutters and lapidaries.[51] The cylinder seals of the period mainly depict presentation scenes, in which the seal owner is led by one or more goddesses before a seated king or deity. The figures progress calmly across the space, empty save for a crescent moon or sun disc. As career administrators moved up through the ranks, they were issued a new seal with each promotion, on which they announced their titles, parentage, and subservience to authority in neatly boxed inscriptions.[52] Far from the vibrant, risk-taking work of the Akkadian empire (figures 5 and 9), the art of the Third Dynasty of Ur satisfied the aesthetics of an ordered, status-conscious society.

Management and Crisis

The foundations of this society rested upon tens of thousands of workers, those of menial status sustained by the distribution of a bare living ration of raw staples—barley, wool, and vegetable oil—and those of higher status, such as administrators and officials, receiving finished products, including bread and other baked goods, beer, textiles, and processed animal fats.[53] Laborers in fields, irrigation works, flour mills, breweries, bakeries, and boat yards toiled long days in large teams to meet fixed quotas of output. The king's bureaucrats could calculate exactly the expenses and work needs of a project, estimating to a nicety how much time it would take to clear weeds from a given set of fields, how many workers and how much seed would be required to cultivate it, and what the fields would yield. Backbreaking work was to be signed and sealed for, like any other commodity. Moreover, the administration had detailed schemes of tasks and output. For each major temple complex, for example, the scribes knew how much land was available and what condition it was in. They could compute the harvest in advance by comparing the previous records with the present state of the fields. Gathering the information from many such temple complexes and considering the land as a whole, they could even compute regional expectations on the basis of past performance.[54]

More than 35,000 administrative records document other areas of administration, as well as the foreign affairs of the period. The royal bureaucracy was subdivided and diversified, using, for greater efficiency, standard writing and tablet shapes to keep its myriad records. A complicated system of rotating obligations, nominally for the cult centers of the land, coupled with certain taxes and benefits, laid the burden of supporting the royal administration on local governors, rather than on the king's household.[55] Merchants spread out across the Middle East, under royal and private commissions, to secure metals, aromatics, stones, oils, woods, and other goods.[56] Shulgi's diplomats traveled abroad and reported on what they saw, while his treasurer dispensed silver rings and fine clothing to visiting dignitaries, who were expected to attend lengthy state festivals. Convinced of the benefits of diplomatic marriages, Shulgi sent off at least three of his ten known daughters to grace foreign courts.[57]

For the Third Dynasty of Ur, success was a function of careful planning and precise record-keeping. No detail was too small to escape attention; even when nothing was done, a record was made.[58] Prosperity and good order were the watchwords of the day. Ur-Nammu tells us, for example, in one of history's first collections of laws, that the roads were conveniently supplied with way stations, each with an agreeable garden.[59] Private initiative was stifled by restricting the sale of land.[60]

Yet all was not well. The agricultural accounts reveal an ominous trend. During the Akkadian period, the mode of agricultural exploitation was based on extensive community engagement in production on crown and temple lands. The Akkadian manor had few resident full-time workers, but many lessees and beneficiaries of grants, who provided their own labor and paid a portion of their harvest to the manor. The Akkadian king took his share from these manors, netting only a fraction of the yield from the land, but minimizing the cultivation costs for his administration.[61] The kings of Ur, by contrast, initiated a radical approach whereby government-supported teams of workers did as much cultivation as possible on government-owned lands. At first, this meant higher returns, because the royal administration was not sharing the harvest with lessees and beneficiaries. But it soon entailed greater expenses, for the workers had to be provided with food, drink, and lodging, and their teams of thousands had to be managed and disciplined. Although the real costs of such a system were known to administrators, official policy seems to have set these concerns aside in the quest for greater control of production. At the same time, yields were dropping. By the end of Shulgi's reign, the shortfall on agricultural projections in the Lagash region was twenty percent. Was this the result of overexploitation, in the bureaucratic drive to increase production without due regard to customary patterns of crop rotation? Was the land declining after millennia of agriculture? Or were the bureaucratic expectations unrealistic? We do not yet know the answer.[62]

Disturbing pressures, moreover, were mounting beyond the heartland. To the north, after a long period of peace and despite his diplomatic efforts, Shulgi was driven into a protracted, inconclusive war with the Hurrians, a people who lived in Assyria and northwestern Iran (see chapter 6). At home, in empty propaganda, his scribes dutifully proclaimed the same victories, year after year.[63] To the west, Amorites began moving onto the alluvial plains in large numbers. The Sumerians deemed them barbarous people from the grasslands of Syria, sneering that they neither lived in houses nor honored their dead.[64]

During the reign of Shulgi's grandson Shu-Sin, a wall named "Fortress to Keep Out the Tribespeople" was constructed between the Tigris and the Euphrates to hold these infiltrators at bay, but they came anyway. Sumerian poetry began to paint a grim, though cliché-ridden, picture of foreign invaders, pestilence, disorder, marauders in the ancient cities, and loss of respect for the old ways:

> Disorder befell this land, the like of which no one had ever known,
> Nothing of its ilk had ever been seen, no name could be put to it, it was beyond comprehension.
> The lands were bewildered in their fear,

The very gods of this city turned away from it in anger, its
    ruler disappeared,
The people could scarcely breathe for terror,
The tempest paralyzes them, the storm does not let them
    return,
There will be no return for them, the time of their captivity
    will never pass.[65]

By the reign of Shulgi's great-grandson, Ibbi-Sin, inflation was
out of control and productivity was way down. How were the
workers to be disciplined and fed? The capital began to starve.
Food was available in the countryside, but the price was high:
suppliers demanded that the king grant extortionate payments in
silver, as well as titles and authority.[66] The end came when the
great teams of workers rose up in a disorderly rabble. Country
people, wealthy from their flocks, moved to the impoverished cities, buying, lending, or forcing their way into becoming a new,
arriviste elite.

In 2004 B.C.E., the Elamites seized the moment, sweeping
down upon Ur, looting and wrecking the capital and carrying off
Ibbi-Sin to die in unhappy captivity in their land. Sumerian poets
lamented the destruction of Ur and her realm, even as they acknowledged that no human rule can last forever:

Ur was indeed given kingship, but no eternal reign was she
    given.
From time out of mind, from the foundation of this land
    and the multiplying of its people,
Who has ever seen a reign of kingship that endured
    uppermost for long?[67]

5. The Age of Hammurabi

> For all time in the future, may any king who
> shall arise in this land observe the words of
> justice that I inscribed on my stele. May he
> not change the law cases of this land I judged,
> nor the verdicts of this land I rendered. May
> he not repeal my ordinances.
>
> *Stele of Hammurabi*

The Amorites

After the fall of the Third Dynasty of Ur, Amorites were to be found everywhere in Iraq, from the uplands east of the Tigris to the major urban centers of the alluvial plains. Though the Sumerians had loftily dismissed them as barbarous tent dwellers, and though in their own language "Amorite" meant nomad, who really were these people? Some Amorites were indeed nomads and pastoralists living along the Middle Euphrates, but others were city people at home in northern Syria.[1] They all spoke a widely understood West Semitic language, though they wrote in Akkadian and their scholars tried their hands at Sumerian as well.[2] Once established in Iraq, the Amorites adapted to their new environment in three principal ways.

One was slavish imitation. In 2017 B.C.E. a new dynasty emerged at Isin, a center of traditional Sumerian learning, whose major sanctuary was dedicated to Gula, the goddess of healing.

The dynasty's founder, Ishbi-Erra, had served as a provincial official under Ibbi-Sin, and he came to power by demanding concessions from his beleaguered sovereign. Ishbi-Erra and the Isin kings who followed him portrayed themselves as the legitimate successors of the Third Dynasty of Ur. Thus, for example, they listened to Sumerian hymns cranked out in their honor; they solemnly proclaimed the old Sumerian titles of kingship; and they added the Isin dynasty to the ancient list of Sumerian and Akkadian kings.[3]

A second Amorite adaptation took the form of pragmatic assertion of their own customs and business behavior. At Larsa, seat of a rival dynasty, we see a largely Amorite community, where, for the most part, only academics and priests had Sumerian names. The notables of Larsa had money to spend and did so, buying and selling urban house lots and gardens until, within a few generations, they owned nearly all the available land in central Larsa, whose best quarter was filled with their spacious mansions. The newcomers also invested in labor and raw materials, speaking the language of business with only a faint Sumerian legal gloss, though the royal family cultivated a pedantic, baroque Sumerian literary style at court. This was a world of enterprising men of affairs who held responsible positions in the chamber of commerce, whose sons studied Sumerian literature in private academies, though their grandfathers may well have herded sheep. The Larsa kings relied on them to manage urban administration, just as they relied on the sheikhs of nomadic tribes in the countryside to collect taxes, to conscript military contingents and work details, and to administer justice. In return, the Larsa notables controlled local commerce, taxation, and agriculture, developed profitable opportunities and a network of patronage, and bought themselves a kind of urban social legitimacy.[4]

A third way was to vaunt one's Amorite background, to subscribe to a myth of origins that had nothing to do with the old Sumerian kings, but harked back to legendary nomadic ancestors, proudly called "kings who dwelt in tents."[5] For these Amorites, the official means of expression was the new Babylonian formal language, partly Akkadian, partly Amorite, with Sumerian influences too, which was understood from Syria to the Gulf. They shared as well a certain worldview, with numerous claimants to power, deeply and with good reason distrusting each other. A king of Babylon tells us he defeated twenty-six kings in less than six months, and the Mari archives know of 160 different kings within their horizon over a period of thirty years.[6] This was a political culture of constantly shifting alliances, both military and marital. One king wrote of another:

> He makes peace with one king and swears an oath, then he makes peace with another king and swears an oath, then he repudiates the previous king he made peace with, as well as the new king he made peace with. His peace-making and repudiation will change in a few months![7]

From among the many dynamic personalities of the era, we may single out three: Rim-Sin, Shamshi-Adad, and Hammurabi.

Rim-Sin, King of Larsa

In 1822 B.C.E., Rim-Sin succeeded to the throne of Larsa, which had been competing with Isin over the past century for control of Babylonia, as well as for recognition by Nippur of its dynasty as the true "kings of Sumer and Akkad." Midway through his reign of sixty years, after gradually solidifying his dominion over most of the old Sumerian cities, Rim-Sin finally destroyed Isin. His conquests followed the basic military strategy of the period: march upstream from the enemy city, cut off or diminish its supply of water, then attack. Isin was perhaps the culmination of his ambitions, for he dated the remaining years of his reign from "Year 1: Isin conquered" to "Year 30, Isin conquered."[8]

The abundant correspondence and commercial documents of the leading families of Rim-Sin's kingdom reveal a society busy lending money and buying and selling houses, fields, and orchards. International trade flourished as well, which we know best from the business records of a half-dozen prosperous families at Ur, some of whom imported metals from Dilmun (Bahrein) in the Gulf. This involved outfitting a ship, raising capital, and hoping to gain a significant return from the venture. Thankful for profitable voyages, they often dedicated silver ship models in the temple of Nanna-Sin at Ur.[9] From the merchants' letters to their agents and fellow traders, however, we learn more of their daily vexations than of their long-term successes:

> Now when you came [to Ur], you said this, "I'll give good ingots to Gimil-Sin [the writer's agent]." You came and you said that, but you didn't do it. You offered poor quality ingots to my agent, and you said, "If you're going to take them, take them, if you're not going to take them, go away." Would you indeed treat me in such a manner and be so contemptuous of me, we being gentlemen? . . . Who else among the Dilmun traders has ever treated me this way?[10]

Shamshi-Adad, King of Upper Mesopotamia

Shamshi-Adad was a dominating figure of the late nineteenth and early eighteenth centuries B.C.E. He grew up in a region subservient to the kings of Eshnunna, who saw themselves as continuing the grand tradition of the Akkadian rulers, just as the kings of Isin had seen themselves in the bright glow of the Ur dynasty. One king of Eshnunna even took the name Naram-Sin, conquered Assur, and pushed west into Syria. We know little of Shamshi-Adad's early life and family origins. From Ekallatum in Assyria, Shamshi-Adad went to Babylonia, all the while, it seems, biding his time and nursing his own ambitions to follow the example of the famous Akkadian warrior-kings, whom he honored as ancestors. When Naram-Sin of Eshnunna died, Shamshi-Adad's opportunity had come, nor was he slow to seize it. He returned to Ekallatum, raised an army, and swiftly conquered a vast territory, from the big bend of the Euphrates in Syria to northern Babylonia. He was destined to rule at least sixty years, calling himself "King of Akkad," among other titles. Toward the end of his life, he made a sentimental visit to the ruins of Sargon's capital, according to a letter in which he says, "I am now staying at Agade."[11]

At the city of Shehna (modern Tell Leilan) in eastern Syria, Shamshi-Adad established his own capital, renaming it Shubat-Enlil, "Abode of Enlil," perhaps an unsubtle equation between himself and the chief god of the Mesopotamian pantheon. He installed two of his sons as kings in geographically strategic cities: Yasmah-Adad at Mari in the southwest, and Ishme-Dagan at Assur in the northeast.[12] Shamshi-Adad's letters to them make lively reading for us, but in many cases must have been rather a trial for the confidential clerk to read aloud to the king. Here, for instance, is a typical tirade addressed to Yasmah-Adad:

> Are you a child? Haven't you grown up yet? Is there no beard on your chin yet? When are you going to take charge of your household? Don't you have the example of your brother, who commands huge armies? Now then, you too take charge of your palace and your household![13]

However much Shamshi-Adad fussed, it must have given this formidable man great satisfaction to see his sons as kings under his aegis. But the days of his kingdom were numbered. After Shamshi-Adad's death in 1781 B.C.E., his palace was overrun and looted, and his enemies, including young Hammurabi of Babylon, no doubt breathed a sigh of relief at his demise. An all-out scramble to divide his kingdom ensued.

At Mari, the ousted prince Zimri-Lim, who had languished in Aleppo during the tenure of Yasmah-Adad, returned to rule. He retained some prominent figures as members of his inner circle, including the chief diviner Asqudum (see chapter 6). Zimri-Lim also refurbished and enlarged the already impressive palace, which at its height had over five hundred rooms, with perhaps a thousand people in residence. There was even a building in which ice could be stored. Among the wall paintings recovered from the courtyards, throne room, and other official areas is an investiture scene depicting a ruler receiving a blue rod and a red ring, the insignia of kingship, from the goddess Ishtar. Below, on the same panel, other goddesses carry vases from which issue streams of water teeming with fish, symbolizing abundance and prosperity. In the antechamber to the throne room was found a statue of such a goddess, fitted with a channel so that water could actually flow from the vase she holds.[14]

About 1760 B.C.E., Mari fell to Hammurabi. Much was removed from the palace, including some royal correspondence and other documents, before it was burned. The fire preserved more than 20,000 of the tablets that had been left in the archives, giving us a vivid idea of the diplomatic, military, administrative, religious, and social and economic life of the palace and city. Here, for example, an official writes about materials for a statue:

> The woodworker from Aleppo who is supposed to make the statue of the protective deity has asked me for sixty pounds of ligament. The stock of ligament in the palace has been considerably diminished. May my lord command that I be provided with 120 pounds of caning rush to replace the ligament.[15]

Another official is anxious about the death of a lion in his care:

> A lion was captured at night in a loft at Bit-Akkakka. They came to inform me of it early the next morning. I was on the point of going away but I stayed on in Bit-Akkakka the entire day so the lion wouldn't be done in, saying to myself, "I have to get it to my lord alive." I threw it some piglets but, after it killed them, it left them and wouldn't eat them at all. I myself sent word to Bidaha to bring a cage. By the time they brought the cage the next day, the lion had died. I examined that lion: it was old and had something wrong with it. My lord shouldn't say, "They must have done that lion in." On my oath, no one touched it, in accordance with my lord's prohibition. Now that the lion is dead, I'll have its skin taken off and sent to the tannery. The lion was old and died of natural causes.[16]

Hammurabi, King of Babylon

Hammurabi, king of Babylon from 1792 to 1750 B.C.E., may be taken as the archetype of the successful Amorite ruler.[17] From his modest base in the city of Babylon, he craftily built an empire using brute force, alliance, and betrayal. During Shamshi-Adad's lifetime, which spanned the first seventeen or eighteen years of his reign, Hammurabi comported himself with respect toward his great northern neighbor. In the south, he initially maintained an alliance with Rim-Sin, but when he deemed the moment opportune, he turned on him and conquered Larsa. Moving north, he took Kish. In his campaign of 1757, he marched up the Euphrates as far as Mari, putting an end to the reign of another former ally, Zimri-Lim. Two years later, he defeated Eshnunna, his last serious rival, by diverting the Diyala River from the city.

In his inscriptions, Hammurabi boasts of his conquests and his ability to find his way out of crises. He was certainly a tactician of the first order. He was also proud of his lavish repairs to important cult centers, claiming that the gods of the cities he vanquished were pleased with him. We doubt, however, that his new subjects so cheerfully accepted his magnanimous offer of dwelling places elsewhere: "I brought happiness to the people, I made all the people of the realm lie down in green pastures, I allowed no one to alarm them."[18]

Under Hammurabi's policy of centralization, Babylon became for the first time the political, religious, and economic heart of the land. The business families of Larsa, for example, saw their livelihoods and patronage networks turned over to Babylonian agents; likewise, the merchant families of Ur saw their profitable commerce diverted to Babylon. The old city-state pattern was steadily absorbed into a Babylonian territorial state.

Hammurabi's extensive correspondence with his subalterns reveals his close attention to detail: no local dispute over a field was too slight a matter to engage his concern. He frequently seems to be curbing administrators' abuse of their powers and insisting that previous rights and practices be upheld:

> The arable land that has been given to the census takers and the fishermen, just as it has been given, so it is given! Not a single square cubit of that arable land shall be touched![19]

Some scholars read in this evidence of a hard-working king, who did not shirk the burdens of effective management; others consider it a sign of an insecure micromanager unable to delegate responsibility. In any case, he knew his realm well and had clear ideas and policies on how it should be administered.

Today, Hammurabi is most famous for his Law Code, best preserved on both sides of a massive basalt stele (figure 11).[20] The

Figure 11. Law Code of Hammurabi from Susa, basalt, height 2.25 m, Louvre, Paris. (Moortgat 1967: pl. 209) *In many ways, this stele is emblematic of how Mesopotamian artifacts have ever been enmeshed in the fortunes of war: taken to Susa as booty, broken into three pieces in a later sack of the city, evacuated from Paris in World War II. Susa yielded basalt fragments from the text portion of at least three additional Hammurabi Law Code monuments (Nougayrol 1957/8). There may originally have been a matched set of seven stelae, erected in the Babylonian cult centers mentioned prominently in the Law Code prologue, perhaps each depicting Hammurabi with that center's patron deity.*

scene at the top encapsulates Hammurabi's approach to statecraft, combining tradition with innovation. The king wears a Sumerian-style bordered cap of royalty and raises his right hand in the age-old gesture of reverence or prayer. Shamash, the sun god and supreme judge, holds out the rod and ring, emblems seen from the Third Dynasty of Ur onward, with which the king is to drive and lead his people like obedient livestock. The god's feet rest on a platform patterned in the convention for mountains, and sun rays shine from his shoulders, reviving a motif last used in Akkadian art. But the horns of divinity on his headdress are among the earliest shown in naturalistic profile, rather than frontally (compare figure 9). And here god and king meet in a direct personal encounter, without the interceding goddesses or intervening date palm altar previously present. As Hammurabi puts it in another inscription, "When Shamash, great lord of heaven and earth, king of the gods, looked joyfully with his radiant face upon me, noble Hammurabi, his favorite, he gave me everlasting kingship and a lengthy reign."[21]

Hammurabi's Code is one of the earliest and most comprehensive collections of legal material we have. Already in antiquity it was a classic text, copied and studied in Babylonian schools a thousand years later. For the most part, it lists hypothetical cases, from which we assume one could reason analogously to the circumstances of one's own case. They cover a vast range of subjects, including wrongs to individuals, such as assault or rape, false accusations, management of fields held in tenure from the palace, theft and robbery, adultery, witchcraft, ransom of prisoners, liability, and medical malpractice. Several articles treat the rights of married women:

> If a woman turns against her husband and says, "You shall no longer have marital relations with me," her circumstances will be investigated by the authorities of her city quarter. If she has been heedful and without fault, but her husband has been inconstant and treats her very badly, that woman shall bear no penalty, she may take her dowry and go off to her father's house. If she has not been heedful but has been

inconstant, is a spendthrift, or treats her husband badly, they shall throw that woman into water.[22]

Since some Babylonian legal documents mention a "royal decree," the interest of the palace in legal matters was palpable, despite lack of reference to the stele itself, which may be more of a commemoration of the king's legal thought and activity than a "code," as that term is presently understood. Local matters, such as disputes about property, were handled by neighborhood bodies. Lawsuits could be heard by professional judges, apparently for a fee. Capital cases may have been sent to the palace for final disposition, for we have royal letters ordering executions of convicted offenders.[23]

There is little evidence for the impact of the provisions of the Law Code on legal affairs in everyday life. Of far greater significance were periodic edicts issued by the king, apparently with a view to bringing the economy back into balance and to garnering local support. These edicts remitted certain types of debts and service obligations, and were clearly intended to relieve the burdens of the impoverished:

> With respect to arrears due from tenant farmers, shepherds, tanners, seasonal herdsmen, and those liable for support of the palace, to protect them and to treat them justly, it is decreed: the government collector shall take no action against the household of those liable for support of the palace.[24]

Hammurabi's Code is not the only corpus of laws from ancient Iraq. The fragmentary collections of earlier Sumerian laws, including the Code of Ur-Nammu (see chapter 4), show that the connection between kings and law-giving certainly antedated the coming of the Amorites to Mesopotamia. The discovery of another large group of laws at Eshnunna, however, dating just prior to the reign of Hammurabi, suggests that promulgation of law was an important prerogative of the Amorite kings. Furthermore, we see that the Hammurabi Code reflects fundamental principles of Amorite law: an eye for an eye, a tooth for a tooth; some offenses punishable by heavy fines, many others, including adultery, by death. Another principle was the method of arriving at the truth of a case. If investigation failed to establish the facts, one or both parties could take an oath. If even this procedure failed to establish fact, one could resort to an ordeal, such as plunging an accuser in the river to see if he or she surfaced (thus vindicated) or was about to drown (thus guilty of making a false accusation).[25]

Parallel to the law collections is a substantial body of legal documents, among them witnessed contracts of sale, hire, or rental, as well as an assortment of court cases that sometimes record the actual testimony of the participants. Numerous suits at law give evidence for a litigious age. These often involved property rights or social status, such as whether a certain person was free or a slave.[26]

There were two types of slavery, chattel and debt. The wealthy sometimes owned foreign-born chattel slaves in domestic service; debt slavery apparently stemmed from a shortage of reliable skilled and agricultural labor. Especially at critical times like the harvest, agents for hired men could exact very favorable terms for their clients. A way around this problem was to exploit a situation in which indigent families had been lent money or food at high rates (18 to 33⅓ percent), for which there could be little realistic expectation of repayment of the principal. The families pledged themselves or their children as collateral for these loans, and thus were obliged to work for the creditor solely to pay the interest, the principal becoming, in effect, the price of the debtor's freedom.[27]

From what we see in Babylonian business documents of this period, the early centuries of Amorite rule were times of considerable economic growth, with much buying and selling of land, activities apparently forbidden under the Third Dynasty of Ur. After Hammurabi, this pattern seems to taper off in favor of lease and rental, suggesting that much urban property and arable land was in the hands of notables. The south, moreover, may have become economically depressed in some areas, owing to the centralization of resources and opportunities in Babylon.

Arts of the Table and Bedroom

The twin pillars of the good life in Babylonia seem to have been fine cooking and the arts of love. Indeed, the world's oldest extant proposal of marriage, written a generation or two before Hammurabi, holds up proper meals as a reason to take a wife:

> Your father has written to me about you that I may marry you. For my part, I have sent my servants and my letter to your father about you so that he will release you. Please, as soon as you receive this letter, ask your father and get started with my servants. I am by myself, there is no one to look after me, and no one to set the table for me.[28]

A collection of recipes for elaborate cookery has come down to us, calling for a variety of ingredients and containing brief instructions for multiple stages of preparation, and for proper presentation at the moment of serving:

> When you have taken it from the fire, you set the cooked bird on the platter, then you loosen the joints, and you attach the legs to the sides with a string, and you tie the neck.[29]

Although such pains and expense may have been as rare in private life as they are today, the discovery of these recipes has opened an unexpected window into an otherwise unknown aspect of Babylonian life. Normal fare, even for people in comfortable circumstances, consisted of simple dishes of dairy products, bread, dates, vegetables, and legumes, served with wine, ale, or beer, and sweets made of honey and syrups, with a roast of meat or poultry only for holidays.[30]

Babylonian love literature illumines the tender passion with ardor, humor, and sometimes bitterness.[31] Here a woman arouses her lover:

> Your heartbeat is my reveille,
> Up then, I want to make love with you,
> In your smooth loins, as you come awake.
> How sweet your caress,
> How voluptuous your charms, . . .
> O my loose locks, my ear lobes,
> The contour of my shoulders and the opulence of my breast,

The spreading fingers of my hands,
The love-beads of my waist!
Bring your left hand close, touch my sweet spot,
Fondle my breasts!
[Oh come inside], I have opened my thighs![32]

Popular art of the time includes mass-produced clay plaques depicting erotic themes: nude or scantily clad women lying on beds or playing musical instruments, nude and clothed couples embracing, and nude men strumming lutes. Some of these plaques illustrate heterosexual and homosexual positions of intercourse.[33] A treatise preserved in an Assyrian manuscript of the seventh century B.C.E. offers prognoses of success based on different sexual practices:

If a man keeps saying to his wife, "Turn your rear towards me," that man will not have a good appetite.
If a man usually has intercourse during the afternoon siesta, that man will have good luck and will be happy. . . .
If a man talks with a woman in bed and after getting out of bed has an erection, that man will be happy and blissful.[34]

At Isin, a tablet of magical spells intended to enhance sexual performance was found broken in half and buried in a clay jar, for what reason is not known. Most such spells were used by women to arouse men or to keep other women away:

Look at me, be joyful as a harp,
May your heart glow as with liquor,
Keep bursting forth like the sun upon me,
Keep renewing yourself for me like the moon![35]

The Epic of Gilgamesh

In this period originated the most celebrated work of Mesopotamian literature, the *Epic of Gilgamesh* (see frontispiece and figure 22).[36] Although Sumerian narrative poems about Gilgamesh were composed or compiled at the courts of the Third Dynasty of Ur (see chapter 4), the material was transformed into an Akkadian epic about the time of Hammurabi. The story tells of a long-ago king of Uruk named Gilgamesh, who tyrannized his subjects until the gods created a wild man, Enkidu, to be first his rival, then his boon companion. The two set off to the distant cedar forests on a quest for eternal fame, despite the warnings of the elders of Uruk, and despite the portentous dreams of Gilgamesh. Undaunted, they reach the forest, kill its guardian monster, Huwawa, and return triumphant to Uruk with a magnificent beam for the Ekur at Nippur. When Gilgamesh rejects the marriage proposal of Ishtar, smitten by the dazzling hero-king, she wreaks vengeance by sending down the Bull of Heaven to ravage Uruk. In a coordinated attack, Gilgamesh and Enkidu kill the bull, a crime for which, along with the slaying of Huwawa, the gods decree that Enkidu must die.

Gilgamesh, inconsolable after the death of his friend, undertakes another quest, this time for eternal life. He decides the only hope is to find Uta-napishtim, the sole survivor of the Flood, to ask him why and how the gods granted him immortality. Along the perilous route, he meets a woman who keeps a tavern at the edge of the world. She advises him to abandon his hopeless quest:

> Gilgamesh, wherefore do you wander?
> The eternal life you are seeking you shall not find.
> When the gods created mankind,
> They established death for mankind,
> And withheld eternal life for themselves.
> As for you, Gilgamesh, let your stomach be full,
> Always be happy, night and day.
> Make every day a delight,
> Night and day, play and dance.
> Your clothes should be clean,
> Your head should be washed,
> You should bathe in water.
> Look proudly on the little one holding your hand,
> Let your mate always be blissful in your loins.
> This, then, is the work of mankind.[37]

But still he presses on, even crossing the waters of death. At last, on the far shore, he finds Uta-napishtim, who berates him for forsaking the honors and duties of kingship for such a selfish, futile purpose. He learns that the Flood, which Uta-napishtim describes, was a unique event that the gods will never bring about again (see chapter 3). Gilgamesh, crushed, must return to Uruk empty-handed.

As a parting gesture, though, Uta-napishtim tells him of a plant of rejuvenation growing on the ocean bottom. Gilgamesh dives deep and finds it, but on his homeward journey with Ur-shanabi, Uta-napishtim's boatman, a snake eats the plant and promptly sheds its skin:

> For whom, Ur-shanabi, have my hands been toiling?
> For whom has my heart's blood been poured out?
> For myself I have obtained no benefit,
> I have done a good deed for a reptile![38]

The epic ends with Gilgamesh once more by the great walls of Uruk, his most lasting achievement, finally accepting that he too must die, like everyone else. What is important is what one does with the life he or she is given:

> Go up, Ur-shanabi, pace out the walls of Uruk,
> Study the foundation terrace and examine the brickwork.
> Is not its masonry of kiln-fired brick?
> And did not seven masters lay its foundations?[39]

The End of Amorite Rule

After Hammurabi's death, his son Samsuiluna succeeded to the throne with high expectations of ruling an empire, but was doomed to go down in history as a king who lost a great inheritance. Partway through his reign, a savage rebellion broke out in the kingdom, led by a man who had taken the name Rim-Sin, and who was no doubt aided and abetted by the many enemies of Babylon. Although the Babylonians ultimately achieved victory, the cost was terrible. Many of the ancient cities of the land, such as Ur, Uruk, Nippur, and Larsa, lay in ruins, their once prosperous neighborhoods burned, looted, and silent, their public buildings in shambles, their fortifications dismantled. The main Euphrates channel seems to have abruptly shifted, possibly diverted by Samsuiluna to starve the rebels into submission. Whatever the cause, many cities in southern Babylonia now lacked the water they needed to survive. To the misery of the land was added the suffering of thousands of refugees, who made their way north to Babylon, Kish, and other centers. There they tried for a generation or two to maintain their customs and traditions in a new environment, but were gradually absorbed into the local population.[40]

The dynasty of Babylon lasted for another century, presiding over a shrunken kingdom and grandly claiming dominion over ruined cities. The countryside, especially to the south, was depopulated and abandoned. Local officials grew more independent of the palace and sufficiently well entrenched to pass on their offices and perquisites by inheritance, thus becoming notables.[41]

Larger events may also have had their impact on Iraq. People we call the Hittites were forming a powerful kingdom in central Turkey. At the same time, new people known as the Kassites were entering Iraq from the northeast. What pressures brought the Kassites into the alluvial plains we do not know, but their names begin to appear in Babylonian documents as workers and soldiers.[42] In 1595 B.C.E., the last king of Babylon was dethroned by a daring invasion of the Hittite king Mursilis and his army.[43] After sacking the city, Mursilis withdrew homeward, no doubt savoring this extraordinary triumph, but apparently not intending to occupy Babylonia. Into the resulting vacuum stepped the Kassites, inaugurating a new dynasty and kingdom.

6. Babylonia
in the Family of Nations

Down south, the marauders, the Kassite horde, were on the move,
But there, in the south, the ones who stood against them hit them hard.
Then, in the north, the robbers, starving, took to their heels,
Those who stood against them, in the north, triumphed over them.

    Sumerian poem about the Kassites

The Kassites

As the Amorites, especially under Hammurabi, had amply demonstrated, Babylonia could be the center of a powerful, prosperous regional state. The Kassites embraced this vision, reinvigorating it with a strong tradition of military service and organization, as well as developing a broader Babylonian sense of identity that effectively displaced the old Amorite ways and rendered them obsolete. Like the Turks who would enter Iraq in the Islamic period, the Kassites were culturally highly adaptive and receptive, but still maintained their linguistic identity and social values. The Kassites had their own language, but did not write it, so only scattered words are known today, too few for us to know its possible relationship to other ancient languages of Western Asia. Kassite social patterns involved what they called a "house," headed by a "lord of the house." This was a more inclusive concept than that of the

Babylonian family, because it could apply to numerous people and considerable land, so is probably best translated as tribe or clan. The Kassite domains were often referred to by the names of the family groups that owned them.[1]

At the same time, the Kassite ruling elite took their relationship to the indigenous Mesopotamian culture with the utmost seriousness. They adopted and supported the ancient cults, rebuilt and restored the gods' temples, and maintained their rites, even if they never forgot their own Kassite deities. Within a century or so, the Kassite court at Babylon was the proud patron of Akkadian literature in its most elegant and carefully wrought style. They also revived the long-dead Sumerian language as a scholastic idiom. Kassite dignitaries carried seals with elaborate Sumerian prayers inscribed on them; royal inscriptions were also worked up in that ancient tongue.[2]

Many works of Kassite art and architecture likewise continued in traditional Mesopotamian modes, while others reflected new approaches or veritable innovations. At the new capital at Dur-Kurigalzu, for example, a massive ziggurat was built, its three stairways similar in layout to those of Ur (figure 10) and elsewhere. Reed matting and plaited ropes were inserted as reinforcement every seven courses of brick, again a technique seen in earlier ziggurats. But the nearby palace has a new arrangement of rooms and courtyards, including one court with a square-pillared ambulatory, a type of colonnade not seen before in Iraq. Fragmentary wall paintings show stiff processions of officials or courtiers, apparently another new feature. The latest levels of the palace were built using an unusual technique in which bricks were laid alternately flat and on edge.[3]

At Uruk, the Kassite king Karaindash built a small temple to Ishtar, siting it near the ziggurat of Ur-Nammu and the Uruk-period Eanna complex. Although the temple retains the old Sumerian niching and tripartite plan, its entrance is on the main axis, rather than on the side. All four corners extend in stepped bastions, reminiscent of some Ubaid temples. The façade is of particular interest (figure 12). Male and female deities stand in niches, holding overflowing vases whose streams cascade down the buttresses onto pairs of round-topped stelae or summits. The

Figure 12. Molded brick façade from Uruk, height 1.8 m, Vorderasiatisches Museum, Berlin. (Matthiae 1997: 88) *During World War II, many of the museum objects in Berlin were packed in crates and moved to various locations for safekeeping. The works included material from the German excavations at Uruk, Babylon, Assur, and elsewhere in the Middle East. It was impossible, however, to move architectural monuments, such as the Ishtar Gate, the Pergamon Altar, the cone mosaics (figure 2), and this façade from Uruk. Protected by sandbags, they nevertheless suffered some damage in the bombing of Berlin at the end of the war. U.S. military units recovered most of the crates and their contents.*

gods and goddesses wear long robes patterned with mountains and ripples respectively, fitting fertility emblems for Ishtar.[4]

Much of this iconography we have encountered before: the deities with overflowing vases, the mountain and water patterns, the hands held in front, and so on. What is innovative is their rendering in molded baked brick, which creates a kind of three-dimensional mosaic, integrating the wall and its embellishment in a novel way. One wonders if the Kassite builders were inspired by remains of the low-relief designs achieved in cone mosaics (figure 2), possibly turned up during the construction of this or previous projects in the Eanna precinct. Molded baked brick appears elsewhere in

Kassite Mesopotamia, and, as we shall see, at Babylon a millennium later in the Ishtar Gate and Processional Way (chapter 8). We also find such brickwork in Elamite and Persian Susa, almost certainly made by Babylonian conscripts in both periods, and it may also lie behind certain aspects of Parthian ornamentation (see chapter 9).[5]

Other Kassite sculptures include stone monuments called *kudurru*s, most of which record royal grants of large landed estates. About a meter high, often made of black limestone or diorite and divided into registers, kudurrus depict kings, as well as a multitude of emblems and attributes of divine witnesses to the transactions.[6] On a much smaller scale, these images also occur on the cylinder seals of the period, engraved in hard, colorful stones, thanks to the development of new drills and cutting wheels. Earlier Kassite seals tend to be more formulaic and derivative than later ones.[7] Seal inscriptions are sometimes written horizontally rather than vertically, another innovation of the Kassites. This change in the orientation of cuneiform writing had already developed on tablets, perhaps just prior to the Akkadian period, but it was not reflected in glyptic until now.[8]

Kassite Statecraft and Society

The Kassite state was organized into provinces, within which certain important cities acted as regional centers. At one of these, Nippur, archaeologists discovered an archive of about 15,000 tablets, some of them administrative documents, others correspondence, dating to the fourteenth and thirteenth centuries B.C.E.. These give a picture of a strongly centralized state, with extensive work teams at its command. These teams could be moved from place to place, especially for irrigation projects, as reported in technical detail:

> I have dammed up ten spillways, I have dug out twenty-one irrigation terraces, I have moved up one of the weirs for the terrace inlets which was lying in the channel. Then when I pulled the workers from that, I got started on piercing

the weir for fifteen cubits in length, 7.5 cubits across, 2.25 cubits high. With only forty workers doing the piercing, there aren't enough workers, so send some orchard hands to do the piercing with me.[9]

The mobile teams may have been necessary because of the depopulation or impoverishment of local rural resources, an interpretation borne out by surveys of settlement patterns. The demands of the palace economies and the expensive armies of this period seem to have been major factors in the decline of the countryside.[10]

Society was divided between the king's retainers, who served him alone and had no particular ties to a town or village, unless it was granted to them by the king, and the citizenry, whose livelihoods were based on the land, who acknowledged extended family connections, and whose allegiance was primarily to their home city, clan, or lineage grouping, but whose produce was levied to support the king and his court. Members of the Babylonian ruling elite owned very large estates, which included villages and towns, bordering on crown lands and on the even greater domains of some of the Babylonian temples. According to one document, a Kassite king granted the temple of Ishtar at Uruk nearly 525 square kilometers of land; royal land grants to individuals and their families averaged 486 hectares. The revenues of the government depended upon the systematic taxation of agriculture and land, as well as on fees and tolls.[11]

Part of this income was invested in a professional military caste, also supported by land grants. The Amorite kingdoms had used seasonal levies as well as professional soldiers, but in the Kassite period the professional warrior class seems to have greatly expanded. Some of these soldiers were skilled in the new tactics, which involved the deployment of horse-drawn chariots in a single charge to break through and scatter the enemy lines.[12]

Horses had been in Iraq since the late third millennium, probably introduced from the Eurasian steppe, where they had been domesticated about 4000 B.C.E.. The Kassites may have initiated their large-scale military use in Mesopotamia. Within the Kassite army, the chariot warriors were the elite corps, whose expensive maintenance included equipment needs and equine care, as well as the lengthy, specialized training of men and horses. An Assyrian manual of the time explains how to feed, exercise, and prepare horses for the eventualities of warfare, including crossing rivers or canals:

> When they are supposed to go through water, you have them go through water in three stages. The first time you have them go, you just show them the water; the second time you have them go, you don't give them grass; the third time you have them go, you rub them with the water, you bring them out, you rub them with oil, you give them plenty of grass.[13]

By the Late Assyrian period, the image of the king hunting on horseback was a standard aspect of royal iconography; Assurbanipal boasted of his equestrian skills. Pleasure and war horses were fitted with elaborate bits, bridles, and reins, and elegantly or protectively caparisoned.[14]

Urban life in the Kassite period is illuminated by legal documents from Ur dealing with family and business matters. In one scandalous case, a woman lent a man money, then foreclosed and jailed his wife for his debt. She then proceeded to have an open love affair with him. At the complaint of the man's brother, perhaps concerned about the reputation of his family, the neighborhood authorities summoned the woman to court, where she swore off the relationship in picturesque language: "Since your honor has interrogated me, he'll not get over the edge of my bed again!" The judges thereupon ordered the straying husband not to go to her house, either for the afternoon siesta or at night.[15]

Rural life in Kassite Babylonia is best known from a family archive dealing with farm management. The documents detail the farmer's problems in finding reliable labor, vexation over missing implements, and other anxieties, culminating in a lawsuit. Perhaps in the hope that the suit would go his way, the farmer wrote out on a tablet a little prayer in both Sumerian and Akkadian, but we do not know if this worked, for the outcome of the case is not in the archive.[16]

The Club of Great Powers

The military prowess, extensive domains, and sophisticated culture of the Kassites entitled Babylonia to membership in the international club of great powers of the mid-second millennium, along with Egypt, Mitanni (Syria), Hatti and Arzawa (central and western Turkey), Alashiya (Cyprus), and Assyria (northern Iraq). This was a new concept, unknown to Hammurabi and his successors, linking much of the Middle East in a diplomatic and political network based on a fundamental acceptance of each other's frontiers. Relations were cultivated through treaties, correspondence, and the exchange of embassies and gifts, such as gold and gems, weaponry, art objects, and textiles, as well as physicians, princesses, and singing girls. The members of this kingly club addressed one another as brothers, sending constant reassurances of good will, but to the modern historian's regret they generally avoided comment on international issues or politics in favor of personal remarks and requests. The etiquette of the time precluded expressing enthusiasm for a gift received, so they usually complained of its skimpiness, while noting with satisfaction the magnificence of their own renderings.[17]

We know all this mainly through the discovery of the Amarna letters, as they are called, nearly four hundred cuneiform tablets found in the ruins of the Egyptian pharaoh Akhenaten's capital of Akhetaten (modern Amarna). Some Egyptian scribes were obliged to read and write Akkadian, the lingua franca of the day, in order to carry on international correspondence, not only with the other great powers, but also with Egypt's vassals in the Levant.[18] The Amarna letters include fourteen documents and letters sent between the pharaohs Amenhotep III and Akhenaten and the Kassite kings Kadashman-Enlil I and Burnaburiash II, between about 1375 and 1335 B.C.E.

In one letter, Burnaburiash, who had been miffed that the pharaoh did not send get-well wishes for his recent illness, grasps that Egypt is far from Babylonia:

[The pharaoh] for his part addressed me as follows, saying, "Ask your own messenger whether the country is far away and as a result your brother did not hear about you and did not send a messenger to greet you." Now, since I asked my own messenger and he said to me that the journey [to Egypt] is long, I was no longer offended.[19]

In another, Burnaburiash says that if he cannot have an Egyptian princess, he could pass a beautiful Egyptian woman off as one, for who would be the wiser:

You, my brother, when I wrote to you about marrying a daughter of yours, you wrote to me, consistent with your practice of not giving a daughter, "From time immemorial, no daughter of the king of Egypt is given to anyone." Why not? You are a king, you can do as you please. Were you to give me one, who would say anything? When I got this message, I wrote to say, "Some grown daughters, beautiful women, must be available. Send me a beautiful woman as if she were your daughter! Who is going to say, 'She's no daughter of the king'?"[20]

Yet we know little of the reigns of the Kassite kings, beyond occasional references to their achievements. So too, we know little of Babylonian relations with her eastern neighbor, Elam, save that at least one Babylonian princess was sent to Elam to cement a diplomatic marriage.[21] As for Assyria, the Kassite kings regarded it as a hinterland within their sphere of influence. But Assyria by the mid-fourteenth century was emerging as an independent kingdom (see chapter 7), and had been admitted to the club of great powers, to the indignation of the Babylonian court:

Now, as for my Assyrian vassals, it was not I who sent them to you. Why have they come to your country [Egypt] on their own? If you love me, they will accomplish nothing at all. Send them off to me, empty-handed![22]

Science and Literature

The Kassite period was a high point in the development of Babylonian science and literature. The branch of their science best known to us today is divination, that is, reading the portended future from systematically observed and analyzed phenomena of the past and present, seen on earth or in the heavens, both provoked and unprovoked. Royal patronage of divination may have begun during the Akkadian period, for Akkadian kings are the first historical figures mentioned in omens, and diviners are known to have accompanied their armies.[23]

Early detailed evidence for its practice, and for the high status of the diviner, comes to us from the Amorite kingdoms of the late nineteenth and eighteenth centuries B.C.E. (see chapter 5). Letters and other documents from Mari shed much light on the career of Asqudum, the chief diviner at court there. A native of Ekallatum, he was sent to Mari by Shamshi-Adad to assist his son Yasmah-Adad. He was kept on by Zimri-Lim as a trusted plenipotentiary, housed in a grand residence near the palace, and involved in all important affairs of state, often to his personal financial gain. His closeness to the royal family was such that he wed a Mari princess and negotiated Zimri-Lim's marriage to Shibtu, daughter of the king of Aleppo in Syria. Reports that a certain Asqudum drowned in a boating mishap may refer to the demise of the diviner.[24]

Among their other duties, diviners at Mari frequently had to check the reliability of what various people uttered when they went into prophetic trances. This letter and its accompanying packet from Queen Shibtu concern a slave girl's prophecy about Zimri-Lim:

> In the temple of Annunitum in town, Ahatum, the servant girl of Dagan-Malik, went into a trance and said this: "O Zimri-Lim! Even though you have no regard for me, I will smite on your behalf. I will deliver your enemies into your power. Then I will seize the men who steal from me and I will gather them into Camp Belet-ekallim." The next day, Ahum, the high priest, brought me this information, a lock of her hair, and a piece of her garment fringe, so I have written to my lord and sent the lock of hair and piece of garment fringe to my lord under seal.[25]

The most arcane and prestigious subfield of the discipline involved framing a question, posing it, often to the gods Shamash and Adad as lords of divination, and then sacrificing a sheep to examine its liver, intestines, and gall bladder for certain tissue formations or marks. In this observation from the Kassite period, a diviner found the following:

> The gall bladder was firm at the right; the left side of the gall bladder was split. There was a pattern on the *processus papillaris*. The lung was suspended at the right. Twelve convolutions of the colon.[26]

The features were tabulated and then evaluated in the aggregate as favorable or unfavorable. This expensive form of divination, called extispicy, was often used prior to state decisions, as well as for private concerns, such as the health and welfare of one's family or the cause of illness or misfortune.[27]

To interpret omens, diviners consulted large reference works in which omens and their outcomes were listed in detail. Some omens were historically based: when a liver, for example, had a certain mark on its lobe, a certain king had died. Others were worked out by analogy: if a mark on the right side was potentially favorable, a similar mark on the left side was potentially unfavorable. There were also drawings and clay models of viscera for study, some with explanatory labels such as "This was the omen for the destruction of Agade" or "This was the omen for Shulgi, who dropped his crown."[28]

Beginning in the Kassite period, older collections of omens were systematically gathered, evaluated, and standardized into comprehensive works called "series," some running to hundreds of large tablets, with such titles as "When the Physician is on the Way to the Patient's Bedside," "Painful Muscles," and "When a City is Situated on a Height." These four omens are excerpts from the last:

> If there are green and red fungi in a man's house, the owner of that house will die.
> If half-green, half-red fungi fill a man's house, the man's son will enrich the father's house.
> If green fungi fill a man's house, the owner of that house will become poor.
> If a fungus keeps putting out protuberances, the government will have a claim on that house.[29]

Another important Babylonian science of the period was philology, the study of words and language. Kassite philologists collected rare words, mastered long lists of words and signs, then learned the techniques of manipulating words, parts of words, and cuneiform signs as a way of explaining both their meanings and what the words signified. The practice of writing commentaries on important works of literature and scholarship may have originated at this time.[30] Babylonia was still formally a bilingual culture, and the ability to translate to or from Sumerian and Babylonian was the sign of an educated person. As a Sumerian proverb put it, "The scribe who does not know Sumerian, what kind of scribe is he?"[31] At some point in the Kassite period, perhaps at Nippur, a translation school tackled the problem of producing Akkadian renditions of major works of Sumerian literature. These translations tended to be explanatory or dynamic, rather than exact or literal. Their purpose seems not so much to aid someone who could not read the Sumerian original (though they have been a great help indeed in the decipherment of Sumerian in modern times) as it was to recast the text into Akkadian as another version of the same composition. In some instances scholars even altered the original to correspond better to the translation. For the benefit of those writing legal documents, scholars also compiled handbooks of Sumerian legal phraseology with Akkadian translations.[32]

With respect to medicine, the Kassite archives from Nippur preserve various letters from physicians referring to treatments based on herbal medicines, poultices, and other remedies. Here, the patient is improving:

> Since Ayaru's daughter had trouble breathing early in the evening and since, after midnight, after I sent my message to my lord, she fell asleep until daybreak, no one put on the mask that they usually put on her at night. At daybreak, when she woke up and asked for a mask, they put one on her, and, although previously she was having a lot of trouble breathing, now she has no trouble breathing at all. . . . [33]

Since none of the letters of Kassite physicians mention surgical procedures, known already in the Law Code of Hammurabi, perhaps surgical specialists were considered distinct from general practicioners.[34] Later medical texts often incorporate the techniques used by magicians and exorcists to deal with physical and psychological illness.

One of the finest literary works of the Kassite period is known as the *Poem of the Righteous Sufferer*, an eloquent self-narrative and lament by a certain Shubshi-meshre-Shakkan. As a person of importance at the royal court, he assures us that he was meritorious in every way. Suddenly, for no discernible reason, Marduk, the chief god of Babylon, struck him from his high position:

> I, who walked proudly, learned slinking,
> I, so grand, became servile. . . .
> As I went through the streets, I was pointed at,
> I would enter the palace, eyes would squint at me. . . .
> My slave cursed me openly in the assembly of gentlefolk,
> My slave girl defamed me before the rabble.
> An acquaintance would see me and make himself scarce,
> My family set me down as an outsider.[35]

As his life went from bad to worse, he paid lavishly for divination to determine what was amiss, but this served only to exhaust his resources. Then he was assaulted by a battalion of fell diseases, and, like Enheduanna (chapter 4), his powers of speech and concentration deserted him:

> My robust figure they flattened like a bulrush,
> I was dropped like a dried fig, I was tossed on my face.[36]

Soon he was bedridden, losing control of his bodily functions and lapsing into a moribund coma. His family assembled at his bedside, his grave was dug, and his grave goods were set out. His enemies glowed with pleasure at his imminent demise.

In his last conscious moments, Shubshi-meshre-Shakkan sees a resplendent woman who promises him relief, followed by a mysterious exorcist with a scholarly Sumerian name, who recites the magic spells needed to banish his afflictions. Rising from his death bed, he parades through the streets of Babylon, redeemed from misery. He gives a feast at his grave site, turning the funerary repast into a celebratory banquet of his healing. Just as Marduk was powerful enough to bring him low, so the god's wonderful majesty snatched him from the very jaws of destruction.

Various Mesopotamian compositions of different periods likewise confront the question of undeserved suffering. The Kassite poem stands out for its exquisite poetic refinement, immense learning, and passionate expression, bespeaking deep reflection on the nature of human woes and the fragility and strength of human achievement. The biblical Book of Job, written in the same vein, is sometimes said to be Mesopotamian in origin.[37]

The Hurrians

North of Babylonia was the Hurrian kingdom of Mitanni, which at its height stretched from the Mediterranean to the Zagros. The Hurrians, originally from somewhere in Turkey, had settled in northern Syria in the late third millennium and adopted cuneiform to write their language. In the early second millennium, they spread into northern Iraq. About 1500 B.C.E., the kingdom of Mitanni emerged by uniting the Hurrian city-states. Mitanni and Egypt battled for control and influence over the Levant during the mid-fifteenth century; Thutmosis III won decisive Egyptian victories at Megiddo and elsewhere. Subsequent treaties with Egypt and with the Hittites, who had been pressing from the north, cemented by diplomatic marriages, brought a measure of peace to the region, which is reflected in the Amarna letters.[38]

Excavations in northern Iraq at the site of Nuzi, the center of a small Mitanni vassal kingdom called Arrapha, have yielded the remains of a palace and private homes from the late fifteenth and early fourteenth centuries B.C.E. Thousands of court administrative records and large family archives, written in Akkadian but often strongly influenced by Hurrian, illuminate life on the fringes of the Mitanni realm. The Nuzi finds are particularly important, since the location of the Mitannian capital, Washukanni, is unknown. The palace archives include such documents as accounts, rosters of rations, muster lists for military service, and receipts for oils, textiles, wool, and other commodities.[39]

The private records reveal the activities of a thriving local economy, based on arable land, as well as details of the business dealings of several generations of prominent Arraphan families. Scattered across the landscape were small manors, whose family members, by tradition at least, held their land in common and worked undivided shares. In practice, however, typically one family or one aggressive individual, often an eldest son taking advantage of a preferential inheritance, gradually built up their own private land holdings through purchase, loans, and foreclosure. To circumvent the custom that land shares could only be sold or exchanged within families, the buyer and seller needed only to go through a fictive adoption procedure, the seller in some cases continuing to work the land he had sold for the benefit of his creditor.[40]

In this general region of northern Iraq, the world's first glass industry developed in the sixteenth and fifteenth centuries B.C.E. Although some earlier glass may have resulted from experimentation with faience (see chapter 3), large-scale production of this artificial material for vessels, cylinder seals, and jewelry began with the invention of core-forming techniques. To make the goblet shown in figure 13, whose top-heavy shape is typical of pottery of the period, hot glass was poured over a clay core. For the festoon pattern, threads of colored molten glass were wrapped around the outside, then reheated so the viscous surface could be combed up or down with a fine tool. The foot was attached, the vessel cooled, and the core broken and removed. In another method, glassmakers achieved similar designs by arranging thousands of tiny colored glass rods in chevrons, fusing them by firing, then grinding and polishing the surface to create shimmering mosaics. They also produced figurative work, such as the inlays from Dur-Kurigalzu with inset stars and raptors, all of glass. Related pyrotechnical essays led to the invention of glazed ceramics, small vases at first, then architectural elements such as tiles and decorative knobs.[41]

The End of Kassite Rule

The beginning of the twelfth century saw unrest and widespread population movements throughout the Middle East. In Babylonia, Kassite rule collapsed after more than five centuries. In 1165 B.C.E., the Elamite king Shutruk-nahhunte invaded Iraq, capturing seven hundred towns, according to his account, and taking

Figure 13. Glass goblet from Tell al-Rimah, height 13.4 cm, Iraq Museum, Baghdad. (Roaf 1990: 127) *The British excavated Tell al-Rimah in the 1960s, when the antiquities law in Iraq still permitted foreign archaeologists to take a share of their finds out of the country. The rest were divided between local muse- ums and the Iraq Museum. After nine of the thirteen provincial museums were looted during the Gulf War, many of their holdings were shipped to Baghdad, only to be caught up in the events of April 2003. The fate of the fragile glass from Rimah, some of it previously in Mosul, is unknown.*

dozens of monuments back to Susa, among them the Victory Stele of Naram-Sin (figure 9): "All the cult centers of Akkad and their sanctuaries he burned with fire."[42]

His son, Kudur-nahhunte, murdered him, then demanded to be king of Babylon, as well as of Elam, on the basis of his descent from a Kassite princess who had married into the Elamite royal family. He threatened reprisals if thwarted:

> If you go up to heaven, I will seize your coattail, if you go down to hell, I will grab you by the hair! I will destroy your cities, I will wreck your towns, I will carry off your wives, I will cut down your orchards, I will throw open the locks of your waterworks![43]

The Babylonians rejected his ultimatum with scorn: "Shall livestock and ravening wolf come to terms? Shall firm-rooted thorn and soaring raven love each other?"[44] Elamite troops thereupon invaded again, looting some of the most sacred sanctuaries, including those at Babylon, Uruk, and Nippur.

Onto this scene a new dynasty arose at Isin, whose most important ruler, Nebuchadnezzar I (1126–1105 B.C.E.), figures prominently in later Babylonian tradition as the savior of his city and land, an inspiration to his namesakes, especially Nebuchadnezzar II, of biblical renown (chapter 8). His first task was to establish a convincing claim to the Babylonian throne, countering that of the Elamite royal house. Like the Isin rulers of eight hundred years earlier (see chapter 5), Nebuchadnezzar chose to graft himself onto Sumerian tradition, in his case claiming descent from a Sumerian sage who had lived long before the Kassites, or even the Amorites, had ruled the land.[45]

His next task was to secure the safe return of the statue of Marduk, held in seemingly hopeless captivity in Elam. In a maneuver intended to catch the Elamites off guard, Nebuchadnezzar set forth at the height of summer. His army nearly perished from the heat, according to an eyewitness account:

> The heat glare scorched like fire, the paths of march were burning like open flames. There was no water in the bottoms,

and drinking places were cut off. The finest of the great horses gave out, the legs of the strongest man faltered.[46]

Nebuchadnezzar's tactics worked, for he surprised and routed the Elamite army at the Karun River. The precious statue was escorted back to Babylon, amidst rejoicing, restoring national morale and the well-being of the land.

A Babylonian poem in seven tablets, known today as the *Epic of Creation*, tells how Marduk became king of all the gods and reorganized the universe after his victory, in a cosmic battle, over the monstrous forces of Tiamat, the sea. This nationalistic composition, which places Babylon at the center of the world and considers it the gods' preferred dwelling place, was likely commissioned in honor of Marduk's triumphal homecoming from Elam:

> Then the great gods convened,
> They made Marduk's destiny highest, they prostrated themselves.
> They laid upon themselves a curse (if they broke the oath),
> With water and oil they swore, they touched their throats.
> They granted him exercise of kingship forever,
> for lordship of heaven and netherworld.[47]

To the north, Nebuchadnezzar and his successors faced Assyria across a frontier guaranteed by treaty, but which witnessed violations, skirmishes, and raids by both sides, enumerated in a detailed Babylonian chronicle. Nebuchadnezzar himself captured Ekallatum in Assyria, but not long after, an Assyrian king, Tiglath-Pileser I, invaded Babylonia and took both Babylon and Dur-Kurigalzu. Increasingly, however, the Assyrians and the Babylonians recognized their need for peace between them, to defend themselves against the Aramean tribesmen who were pushing into Iraq from Syria, very much as the Amorites had, and settling in the open countryside. These tribesmen acknowledged only their own leaders, and were regarded by city dwellers as uncivilized bandits. The period from about 1050 to 900 B.C.E. is a dark age in Babylonian history, with few written sources.[48]

As the Assyrians renewed their imperial ambitions during the ninth to eighth centuries, relations between Babylonia and Assyria vacillated between alliance and hostility, with mutual defense pacts made and broken. Babylonia was sometimes independent, under dynamic kings of her own, including several from the Chaldean tribes in the far south, but just as often Babylonia found herself under the direct or indirect rule of Assyria.

7. THE ASSYRIAN ACHIEVEMENT

> They say "Man is the shadow of God" . . .
> but Your Majesty is the mirror image of God.
>
> *Letter from a scholar to Esarhaddon*

The Rise of Assur

The city of Assur sits on the northernmost spur of a range of hills along the Tigris, whose ancient channel passed below its principal monuments. Although Assur lacked the extensive agricultural hinterland of other cities in the region, such as Arbela and Nineveh, the site did have two strategic advantages. First, important caravan routes crossed the Tigris there, following the natural corridors through the terrain. Second, its position on a promontory, just at the edge of the rainfall-agriculture zone, meant that Assur could serve the south or the north equally well as a fortress.[1] Because the name of the city and the name of its god were identical, the rocky outcrop itself may have been an object of worship in remote prehistory.[2] Assur remained a god without mythology or distinctive imagery in historical times, even though he stood higher in the Assyrian pantheon than the other gods.

As we recall, northern Mesopotamia is a broad steppe, where rainfall- and well-agriculture are possible, stretching from the

Zagros to the Euphrates Valley, bordered on the far west by the mountain ridges of Syria and Lebanon, on the north by the foothills of the Anatolian plateau, and on the south by the alluvial plains. The Akkadian empire and Shamshi-Adad's kingdom, as well as the state of Mitanni, had shown the potential of this region for the rapid creation of a broad political entity, but little in the early history of Assur presaged the future destiny of this city.[3]

Rather, during the last few centuries of the third millennium, Assur had been a provincial outpost, the residence of a governor under first the Akkadian kings, then the Third Dynasty of Ur. At the time of the Amorite kingdoms, Assur became a compact city-state whose ruler served also as chief priest to the god Assur. The city grew to be the center of a bustling international trade, from which it greatly prospered.

By the early nineteenth century B.C.E., Assur was founding colonies and trading posts throughout Turkey. Assyrian commerce was based on long-term contracts and partnerships, especially with relatives or trusted associates. Caravans carried woolen textiles and tin from Assur to Turkey, where the goods, as well as the donkeys, were sold for cash in the form of silver or sometimes gold. Tin was the most expensive commodity, since this essential ingredient for bronze had to be brought from a distant source, perhaps Iran or Afghanistan.[4]

A major colony was established outside the city of Kanesh, where excavations have uncovered the remains of the private houses of the Assyrian merchants, as well as the palace of the local Anatolian ruler. The colony at Kanesh was largely self-governing, through a chamber of commerce run by leading merchants, and maintained its own court for the frequent lawsuits that arose. The local ruler levied tolls on the caravans, but otherwise left the Assyrians to themselves.[5]

Kanesh has also yielded more than 22,000 tablets detailing the merchants' activities over several generations. Figure 14 illustrates a typical tablet, a letter still in its clay envelope bearing the name of the addressee and the seal of the sender. The texts were written in a simplified cuneiform, with dividers between words, suggesting that the merchants were sufficiently literate that they did not have to rely on scribes. Study of the seal impressions indicates that

Figure 14. Tablet and envelope from Kanesh, height 8.4 cm, Yale Babylonian Collection, New Haven. (Yale Photographic Services) *At the end of the nineteenth century, tablets of this type began appearing on the antiquities market and were acquired by numerous museums and collectors around the world. Their provenance, the site of Kanesh in Turkey, was concealed for decades to protect a lucrative source of income for the sellers, from the farmers unearthing them in their fields to the international dealers. Today, study and publication of the tablets and associated material found during the scientific excavations of the site have made it possible to fit many of the illicitly dug tablets back into their archival context.*

many of the seals were made in Assyria, frequently with staid, conventional presentation scenes, whereas others (as here) were cut locally, their fields crowded with lively motifs and creative adaptations of Mesopotamian iconography. A few envelopes were sealed by Syrian and Babylonian merchants, or by traders using seals from these regions.[6]

The letters deal with both business and family affairs. The merchants' wives usually stayed home at Assur, while their husbands might live abroad for years, rarely seeing them. Some of the women wove textiles that they dispatched to the colony on the regular donkey caravans; their husbands were to sell the weavings and send them the proceeds. The wives' letters are the earliest large corpus of women's writings known from the ancient world.[7] In this one, a woman indignantly defends the quality of her work against her husband's unfair complaints:

> Why do you keep writing me, "The textiles you're sending me each time are no good"? Who is this person living in your house who criticizes the textiles when they get to you? For my part, I'm the one who makes every effort to produce and send you textiles so that, with each caravan, your house takes in at least ten shekels of silver.[8]

Little is known of the Old Assyrian period, as it is called, at Assur itself, beyond a few documents and brief inscriptions left by its rulers, because these remains underlie the later monuments and have not been excavated. According to the Assyrian King List, a record probably begun in the Old Assyrian period but now known from manuscripts of the first millennium, the only true kings were those who ruled at Assur, although the title of king was not actually used there until the time of Shamshi-Adad. All other dynasties in the Sumerian King List were ignored.[9] This self-aggrandizing aside, for most of the second millennium Assur was no more than a small, if prosperous, city-state on the outer fringes of greater Mesopotamia, sometimes a vassal of larger kingdoms, controlling an area hardly more than 150 kilometers across. But beginning in the mid-fourteenth century B.C.E., a series of successful warrior-kings of Assur laid the foundations for an empire that soon became a member of the club of great powers.

The Middle Assyrian Empire

Middle Assyrian inscriptions and works of literature attest to a determined imperialism. In fact, the very coronation oath of the Assyrian kings had them vow to extend the land's dominions, and they were expected to lead their armies, in person, on annual campaigns.[10] The basic strategy was to secure the southern boundary with Babylonia and to conduct preventive and punitive raids against the mountain peoples to the northeast and north. Once this was accomplished, expansion by conquest targeted the rich lands to the northwest and west, including the valleys of the Euphrates, Balikh, and Khabur, and, ultimately, the lands beyond the big bend of the Euphrates, the crossing of which was a major military, economic, and psychological advance. The going was not easy, and there were natural limits to seasonal campaigns without forward bases. During the late second millennium, therefore, the Assyrians established military and agricultural colonies in areas such as the Khabur Valley, where small garrisons remained year-round to cultivate fields and stock supplies for the army.[11] This enabled the Assyrian military machine to penetrate as far west as Carchemish by the twelfth century, and the colonies anticipated the later provinces, created beginning in the eighth century and ruled by Assyrian governors, which ultimately extended as far as Egypt. In these and other ways, the Middle Assyrian empire set the pattern for later Assyrian history.

Of the energetic Middle Assyrian rulers, several stand out. Assur-uballit I (1368–1328 B.C.E.) solidified control of the Assyrian heartland and, according to the Amarna letters, sent Akhenaten a chariot with a matched pair of white horses, asking the pharaoh in return for gold, which "in your country is dirt; one simply gathers it up."[12]

One of the most vigorous warrior-kings was Tukulti-Ninurta I (1243–1207 B.C.E.), who boasted of his far-reaching conquests, which brought home to Assur enormous quantities of booty and tribute. He dug a moat around the capital, rebuilt the Ishtar Temple in traditional mode, and began construction of a palace beside the double temple of Anu and Adad, overlooking the Tigris. For some reason, he stopped work on that palace and began a new city across the river, called Kar (port)-Tukulti-Ninurta.[13]

The palace there was lavishly adorned with polychrome glazed bricks and wall paintings depicting panels of heraldically arranged trees, palmettes, and deer. These subjects also appear in Middle Assyrian seals, which are noteworthy for their naturalistic modeling of plants and animals, and for their innovative use of pictorial space (figure 5). Some of these images perhaps have significance beyond the purely pastoral or decorative, given the symbolic representation that often characterizes Assyrian art. The gods, for instance, are seldom fully anthropomorphic, but take shape instead in such forms as emblems, winged disks, or hands reaching down from clouds.[14]

A stone cult plinth of Tukulti-Ninurta I, found in the Ishtar Temple at Assur, encapsulates the period's artistic developments. On its side, the king is shown praying before a divine emblem that rests on a plinth of the very same type (compare the self-reference in figure 4). The inscription below says that Nusku, the messenger god, repeats the king's prayers every day before the gods Assur and Enlil. The representation is among the earliest instances of narrative conveyed through separating the action into component parts, a device we see again in the Late Assyrian palace reliefs, especially at Nineveh. Here, the king appears twice: he approaches the plinth holding the divine symbol, then kneels before it, maintaining his grip on his mace and keeping his right arm upraised in the time-honored gesture of reverence (see figure 11).[15]

Unlike his predecessors, Tukulti-Ninurta turned against Babylonia, on the pretext that the Kassite king, Kashtiliash, had repeatedly violated a long-standing treaty between their two countries. Attacking Babylonia, crossing its recognized border with Assyria, was a serious measure requiring justification, whereas attacking any other land was a divinely sanctioned, inherent right of the Assyrian kings. The Assyrians were proud of their cultural and political traditions, but they were well aware that their literature and scholarship were largely Babylonian in origin. They even used

Babylonian, rather than their own Assyrian dialect, in their official inscriptions and other formal expression. Nevertheless, Tukulti-Ninurta invaded the land, occupied the city of Babylon, and declared himself king there. Kashtiliash was taken in battle, supposedly by Tukulti-Ninurta himself, who claims, "I trod with my feet upon his lordly neck as though it were a footstool. I brought him, bound as a captive, into the presence of Assur my lord."[16] He also carried off to Assyria the statues of the gods, the royal archives, and the scholarly libraries, among other booty.

Assyrian rhetoric cast all this in a positive light. An erudite psalm, written in Sumerian in the king's name, lamented that the world did not appreciate the new order and glory of his dominion.[17] A royal epic commemorated in turgid detail his war with Babylonia, portraying Tukulti-Ninurta as a righteous, wronged monarch, the Kassite ruler as a scoundrel and coward, and the war as a trial-at-arms before Shamash, god of justice, who ruled in favor of the Assyrian "mighty king":

> Tukulti-Ninurta, having put his trust in his observance of
>   the oath, was planning for battle,
> While Kashtiliash, insofar as he had trespassed the
>   command of the gods, was altered within himself.
> He was appalled on account of the appeal to Shamash and
>   became fearful and anxious about what was laid before
>   the gods,
> The mighty king's utterance constricted his body like a
>   demonic presence.[18]

Later Babylonian historians, however, saw Tukulti-Ninurta's murder, by one of his own sons in his new palace, as divine punishment for his sacrilegious attack on their city.[19]

The campaigns of Tiglath-Pileser I (1114–1076 B.C.E.) took the Assyrian army from Lake Van to the Mediterranean, where the people of Arwad, an island off the Syrian coast, escorted the intrepid king on a whaling expedition.[20] According to his own account, he harpooned a whale himself and had a basalt statue of it made for the gate of his palace, along with a statue of a yak he had received as a royal gift from a distant land.[21]

Court life of the period is illuminated by a set of edicts regulating the behavior of palace staff toward the sequestered palace women. If a courtier caught sight of or even heard the voice of a palace woman, he was liable to severe corporal punishment:

> If a woman of the palace sings or quarrels with another of her rank, and one of the royal eunuchs, courtiers, or servants stands listening, he will be beaten one hundred times and one of his ears will be cut off.[22]

The same impression of harshness is conveyed by the Middle Assyrian laws and by contracts in which parents sell their children to a creditor, an act whose legal term was, ironically, "revival." The creditor could put the child to work at some task like weaving, keep the goods' proceeds toward the interest of the debt, and, if the child was a girl, marry her off at his discretion, retaining the traditional bride price paid by the groom.[23]

Middle Assyrian rural life was centered in the small fortified manors that dotted the steppe, each presided over by a male head of an extended family, which often included several closely related families, since brothers might choose not to divide the fields at their father's death, but to keep the manor intact and farm the land in common. A portion of the land, referred to as "the king's share," may have been worked by the families as a form of service or taxation.[24]

The twelfth century, which saw the collapse of Babylonia, was followed by a retrenchment of the Assyrian state in the eleventh. Many consider these events part of the convulsions besetting the whole region at the end of the Bronze Age: the Mediterranean incursions by the groups the Egyptians called the Sea Peoples; the destruction of many urban centers and palaces throughout the area; the collapse of the Hittite Empire in Turkey.[25] Among other troubles, Assyria was invaded by Aramean tribesmen from northern Syria, who, like the Amorites before them, were largely village and nomadic folk.[26] There are scattered reports of famine, disorder, political instability, and military weakness. Two centuries would pass before Assyria reasserted herself as an imperial power.

The Neo-Assyrian Empire

At the turn of the first millennium, the kings of Assur controlled the same core area with which they had started, five hundred years before. Beyond, to the north and west, they faced powerful, fortified urban centers with rich agricultural hinterlands and extensive stock-breeding, united by wide-ranging trade networks, various alliances and coalitions, and a sense of common culture. Some were Aramean, others Neo-Hittite kingdoms. Along the Mediterranean coast, there were wealthy Phoenician cities, such as Tyre and Sidon, which were founding colonies far across the Mediterranean. Inland, Arameans had established independent city-states, such as Damascus and Hamath. To the south lay the kingdoms of Israel and Judah, Moab and Edom. In Arabia, there were prosperous urban cultures in the south and east, and nomadic tribes in the north and center. In due course, the empire of Assyria would reach all these lands and more.

As in previous periods, the basic Assyrian military strategy was first to secure the boundary with Babylonia, pacify the mountain peoples on the eastern fringes of Assyria, and then thrust northwest and west, up the Tigris and Euphrates and their tributaries. The next phase, especially in the eighth century, was to cross the big bend of the Euphrates and invade northwest Syria, then to turn south into Lebanon, and eventually Palestine. This typically entailed conquering the cities of northern Syria, such as Aleppo and Qatna, the lands of Israel and Judah, with their capitals at Samaria and Jerusalem, and the Phoenician cities of the Levantine coast. At its greatest extent, under Esarhaddon and Assurbanipal in the seventh century, the empire stretched from Elam to Cilicia, from the Gulf to Urartu, and far up the Nile Valley.

Neo-Assyrian rulers dealt with the perennial dilemma of Babylonia in different ways. Some, like Sargon II and Esarhaddon, presented themselves as Babylonian kings in Babylon, whereas Sennacherib, furious at the death of his son and crown prince as a result of Babylonian resistance to his rule, tried to obliterate the city in 689 B.C.E. and ordered that Babylonian mythology be rewritten to replace their national god Marduk with the Assyrian national god Assur.[27] The Assyrians' problems were compounded by the increasingly complex political situation in the south. Certain cities deemed loyalty to the Assyrian kings a safe expedient, but others resisted Assyrian control. The Aramean tribes, who had settled in Babylonia in great numbers and lived largely in rural areas, were difficult to subdue, and made no common cause with the cities in whose hinterlands they camped. In the marshlands of the far south, the people called the Chaldeans not only effectively fought Assyrian domination, they put forward claimants to the throne of Babylon itself.[28]

Intervention in Babylonia drew Assyria into confrontation with Elam, which tended to back opponents of Assyria and to give them haven. In 647 B.C.E., Assurbanipal put an end to this by annihilating Elam for its support of a rebellion led by his own brother, Shamash-shum-ukin (remembered in later tradition as Sardanapalus). The Assyrian king leveled the capital, cut down its trees, even desecrated its cemeteries and sowed thorn bushes in its fields:

> The ziggurat of Susa, which was built of glazed bricks, I destroyed, I tore down its horns of shining bronze. . . . I carried off to Assyria their gods and goddesses, together with their adornment, their belongings, their vessels, as well as their priests and attendants. I carried off thirty-two statues of kings, made of gold, silver, bronze, and alabaster. . . .[29]

In this brief essay, we would make two points about Iraq in the Neo-Assyrian period. First is the internationalization of Mesopotamia: the horizons of the land had widened to encompass all of Western Asia, including significant areas of Iran, Turkey, the Levant, Arabia, and Egypt. The insular city-state of the third millennium was long extinct. The empires of Naram-Sin and Hammurabi were dwarfed into insignificance by the conquests of the Assyrians, which brought them into contact with peoples "whose names none of the kings my ancestors had ever heard spoken."[30] Even the great powers of the Amarna letters had no realistic expectations of conquering each other, but now an Assyrian king was sacking Thebes in Upper Egypt.

An important aspect of the internationalization of the period stemmed from the Assyrian policy of deporting people from one area of the realm to another, apparently as a way of Assyrianizing the empire and populating both rural areas and the grandiose new cities and palace complexes.[31] Mountain people were marched to the plains; villagers and townsmen were forced to forsake their homes and begin a long, sad journey to some land they had never seen. Once the former leaders were gone, Assyrian governors took over local rule. In the last century of Assyria's power, as many as a million human beings from all strata of society were displaced, according to Assyrian inscriptions, though this number may have been exaggerated.[32] The result was the creation of a polyglot population in Mesopotamia comprising peoples of many lands, among whom Aramaic was the most widely spoken and understood idiom. This gave rise to its role as the great world language of the Persian Empire and as the primary language of Judaism and Christianity.[33]

Despite this internationalization—and this is our second point—Assyria and Babylonia maintained parallel identities. Babylonia was never completely Assyrianized, even in the presence of Assyrian garrisons, administrators, puppet rulers, and informers. If Assyria had the greater military glory, Babylonia enjoyed the ultimate triumph, not only keeping her individuality, but inheriting the Assyrian conquests in the late seventh century. Moreover, the city of Babylon was destined to be one of the largest, most prosperous, and most cosmopolitan cities on earth, thanks to her central position in the Persian and Hellenistic worlds. So it was, then, that in 612 B.C.E., when Assyria fell to the Medes and the last Assyrian king fled the flames of Nineveh, native Mesopotamian tradition had centuries more to live in Babylonia.

We may choose two rulers, Assurnasirpal II and Sennacherib, as archetypes of the Neo-Assyrian king.

Assurnasirpal II and Nimrud

Assurnasirpal II (883–859 B.C.E.) consolidated the territorial gains of his father and grandfather, extended Assyrian control to new areas, and moved the capital from Assur to Nimrud (ancient Kalhu, biblical Calah). As a warrior, he was both effective and successful, leading a powerful Assyrian military machine and laying the foundations for a system of provincial government in certain annexed regions. Some of his annual campaigns were pursued simply to seize booty; others were evidently undertaken to add to Assyrian dominions. His primary psychological weapon was to instill terror, or "calculated frightfulness,"[34] committing mass executions, incinerating defeated civilian populations in bonfires, skinning defeated rulers alive and impaling their heads on stakes, leaving heaps of skulls as an admonishment to survivors. We need hardly be surprised that people in the Assyrian path hastened to buy their lives with gifts and tribute. Assurnasirpal describes his gruesome tactics with relish, in long detailed accounts; unlike the clandestine atrocities of other societies in world history, his were proudly proclaimed.

Early in his reign, Assurnasirpal decided to transform a small town near the confluence of the Tigris and the Upper Zab into a grand capital. Over the course of fifteen years, the king dug an irrigation canal from the Upper Zab, enclosed the city with massive walls, 8 kilometers long, and built a citadel with temples and a magnificent complex now known as the Northwest Palace.[35] A stele set in an alcove near the throne room describes the construction of Nimrud and the opening ceremonies, including a feast lasting ten days attended by 69,574 men and women "invited from all the districts of the land," who dined on 14,000 sheep, 20,000 pigeons, and 10,000 jars of beer, not to mention 10,000 jerboas.[36] It is striking that among all this slaughtered livestock there was not a single pig, though pork had been esteemed as a delicacy since the third millennium in Iraq.[37] The Nimrud banquet stele provides the earliest evidence we have for this dietary proscription, perhaps reflecting Aramean custom.

In plan, the Northwest Palace followed the usual Assyrian arrangement of outer and inner courtyards surrounded by administrative offices and royal apartments. Colossal human-headed winged bulls and lions flanked many of the entrances, protecting the palace and king. The walls were dazzling: polychrome glazed bricks and plaques, colorful murals, and carved stone panels painted in black, red, white, and blue. For the reliefs, Assurnasirpal seems to have been inspired by the orthostats (stone slabs) decorating some of the Neo-Hittite and Aramean palaces he had conquered. Using

Figure 15. Relief from the throne room of Assurnasirpal at Nimrud, gypseous alabaster, height 1.93 cm, British Museum, London. (Moortgat 1967: pl. 257) *In 1845, Austen Henry Layard began digging at Nimrud, the first of seven Assyrian palaces he eventually investigated. With the science of archaeology then in its infancy, Layard tunneled through walls, could not keep freshly excavated ivories from crumbling, and had little awareness of stratigraphy. The British Museum, his financial backers, for their part insisted that he ship back the largest possible number of art objects "at the least possible outlay of time and money" (Collon 1995: 26). Nationalism was at stake too, for the rival French were sending boatloads of Assyrian art to Paris from their own palace site at Dur-Sharrukin. Accordingly, Layard worked rapidly to extract the reliefs, cutting them up and sawing the backs off to reduce their size and weight for shipment.*

soft local gypseous alabaster, the sculptors working on the Northwest Palace produced hundreds of monumental panels, most of which glorify the king as he performs religious duties, wins battles, receives tribute, and slays wild beasts.[38]

The relief illustrated in figure 15 was originally behind the throne dais. Assurnasirpal appears on either side of a new design often called a "Sacred Tree" or "Tree of Life," though it may represent a garden viewed from above or a cult object with arboreal elements attached.[39] The king wears a fringed ceremonial robe finely embroidered or appliquéd with bands of typical Assyrian motifs, such as winged beings with human and eagle heads (see also fig-ure 5). On the throne room reliefs and elsewhere, these creatures often carry in one hand a small bucket and in the other an object usually identified as a date palm cone. Although the precise mean-ing of the iconography is not clear, it is thought to signify a purifi-cation or protective ceremony to ensure the well-being of Assyria.

Here, as on the other palace reliefs, a text known as the Standard Inscription was engraved across the images, relentlessly setting forth the royal titles and accomplishments, bombarding the viewer with Assurnasirpal's self-predication to the ages:

> Assurnasirpal, attentive prince, worshipper of the great gods, ferocious dragon, conqueror of cities and the entire high-lands, king of lords, encircler of the obstinate, crowned with splendor, fearless in battle, merciless hero, he who stirs up strife, praiseworthy king, shepherd, protection of the four quarters, the king whose command disintegrates mountains and seas, the one who by his lordly conflict has brought under one authority ferocious and merciless kings from east to west. . . .[40]

The visual message of Assyrian power is likewise omnipresent, from the horrific scene of soldiers playing ball with decapitated heads to the poignant vignette, in a tribute procession, of a leashed monkey turning to look homeward. The royal forearms bulge with rippling muscles, even when at rest. The king's expression conveys implacable resolve and complete confidence in the suc-cessful outcome of a campaign or hunt. Compositionally, he and the other figures move within an ordered realm, hinting at time and space through spare, controlled overlapping (see, for example, the tree and royal toes in figure 15), or through a careful depiction of foreign features in the conquest reliefs.[41]

We glimpse the material wealth of the empire in the intact tombs of several queens and members of their entourage, recently discovered beneath the domestic quarter of the Northwest Palace. Because ancient robbers emptied the burials of the Assyrian kings at Assur, the finds here offer a unique opportunity to study a com-plete corpus of Assyrian grave goods. Among the 57 kilograms of gold ornaments are many items of royal accouterment familiar from the palace reliefs, such as armlets (see figure 15), as well as adornments new to us, such as a jeweled version of the traditional bordered cap, found on a child's head.[42]

Sennacherib and Nineveh

Sennacherib (704–681 B.C.E.) was born into the court of the Assyrian empire at one of the moments of its greatest glory. His father had dared to take the name of Sargon of Akkad, the first monarch to do so in more than a thousand years. Sargon II (721–705 B.C.E.) seemed destined to live up to his namesake, for he was the ideal type of the warrior-king, marching to the farthest reaches of his vast empire, even vanquishing the powerful kingdom of Urartu, a state that had emerged in the rugged intermontaine valleys of Armenia—a remote and difficult objective for an Assyrian force.[43] His master scribe produced a lavish, fervid tribute to this exploit, implicitly comparing it to those of the legendary Gilgamesh and the near-legendary Sargon of Akkad, whose reign was understandably of intense interest.[44] In this passage, the army comes to

> . . . a great mountain covered with clouds, the peak of which reaches to the sky, which no living creature had traversed since time immemorial, nor any wayfarer seen its fastnesses, nor even a bird of heaven passed over, nor built a nest to teach her little ones to spread their wings, a peak sharp-tipped as a dagger point, where chasm and mountain ravines yawn. . . .[45]

In 717 B.C.E., following the example of Assurnasirpal and others, Sargon II founded a new capital city, called Dur-Sharrukin (Fort Sargon), north of Nineveh. On this virgin site (modern Khorsabad) sprang up walls and monumental gates, temples, a palace complex, and residential quarters.[46] The king's correspondence shows how eagerly, despite the pressure of the many campaigns and administrative tasks that confronted him, he followed the progress of the work, as reports arrived of construction quotas met: "Day and night I planned the building of that city."[47]

Despite his successes on the fringes of his empire, Sargon had considerable difficulty controlling Babylonia. Although it seems that he himself admired Babylonian culture and saw himself as fulfilling a very ancient Babylonian imperial tradition, there were many opponents to Assyrian rule, both in the cities and the countryside, men like the swamp-fox Chaldean king Merodach-Baladan, who, from the marshes, pressed his own claim to the throne of Babylon, which Sargon held proudly in his grip.[48]

In this heady atmosphere of empire- and city-building, young Sennacherib grew up. Then, at the height of Sargon's power and achievement, just two years after his new city was inaugurated, the king was killed in battle, far from Assyria. So total was the rout that his body could not be recovered for proper burial with his ancestors, a terrible calamity. Sennacherib succeeded to the throne amidst gloom and foreboding: what had his father done wrong to receive such a fate from the gods? Teams of diviners sought the answer to this question. One scholar made a special copy of the *Epic of Gilgamesh*, perhaps for reading at the king's funeral the grim description of the netherworld, which Enkidu relates to Gilgamesh:

> If I tell you, my friend, if I tell you,
> If I tell you the way things are in the netherworld,
> You would sit down and weep, I would sit down and
>   weep too.
> My body you once touched, in which you rejoiced,
> It will never come back.
> It is infested with lice, like an old garment,
> It is filled with dust, like a crack in parched ground.[49]

Sennacherib proved himself more than capable of meeting the enormous challenges presented to him. The demoralized Assyrian army was regrouped and readied for a series of campaigns abroad, the best known of which today are the sieges of Lachish and Jerusalem in 701 B.C.E. (see Epilogue). At home, Sennacherib abandoned his father's new city, perhaps believing it a place of ill omen. He moved to Nineveh (modern Kuyunjuk), a site occupied since the seventh millennium. An engineer by inclination, Sennacherib directed a series of sophisticated projects that would transform the ancient city into a capital of astounding features, from its fortification walls and moat, 12 kilometers in circuit, to its impressive system of aqueducts, canals, dams, and other waterworks, some of which are still in use. He seems to have invented the water-raising machine we call the Archimedes screw, after its third-century B.C.E. Greek inventor.[50]

The crowning marvel was what he named the "Palace Without Rival," built overlooking the Khosr River.[51] Sennacherib envisioned the palace as a microcosm of the world he ruled. While on campaign, he prospected for unusual building stone for the winged bulls, hauling them rough-hewn back to Nineveh on specially constructed sledges and rafts. In the wall relief shown in figure 16, the king himself supervises a phase of the operation, shaded by a parasol. The largest blocks were put in place at the gates, using ingenious mechanical devices. The king was also keenly interested in metallurgy and wrote in technical language of his experiments in casting. He tells us he designed a portico for the palace, its columns supported by solid cast bronze lions.[52]

The king took particular pride in his botanical and zoological gardens and hunting park. At least since the third millennium, the royal acquisition of exotic flora and fauna had been an important element in demonstrating dominion over distant lands and peoples.[53] Many rulers of ancient Iraq and elsewhere had kept foreign plants and animals, but Sennacherib may have been the first to construct authentic habitats for them. The innovation was a great success, as he tells us: "The high-flying heron, whose range is remote, built his nest there, and the wild boars and buffaloes multiplied in abundance."[54] Among the new exotic plants that thrived at Nineveh were "trees bearing wool," probably cotton from India.[55]

It is very likely that the greatest glory of the "Palace Without Rival" was its Hanging Gardens. Centuries later, when Nineveh had long been in ruins, Classical writers thought that this wonder of the ancient world must have been at Babylon, a city still flourishing. They spun a tale of a queen homesick for her native Median hills, for whom Nebuchadnezzar II had built gardens, each description of how they hung more fantastic than the last. Though

Figure 16. Relief from Court VI of Sennacherib at Nineveh, gypseous alabaster, original height ca. 2 m, British Museum, London. (Layard 1853: 93) *On the positive side, Layard and his French counterparts made accurate drawings of the palace reliefs at the time of their discovery. These records, such as the one seen here, are invaluable, since some slabs were lost or damaged in transit, whereas on others the details are no longer so visible. Many of the colossal winged guardians of the Assyrian palaces, one of which makes its way to Nineveh in this relief, were also removed and shipped to London, Paris, and other destinations. Those that remained in situ have suffered at the hands of looters. In 1999, Iraqi television showed the decapitation of ten people for having cut off the head of a winged bull from Dur-Sharrukin in order to sell it. The head was recovered and sent to the Iraq Museum.*

there is no Mesopotamian evidence for any aspect of this story, the legend persists.[56]

Two recent studies have suggested what the Hanging Gardens of Nineveh may have looked like. The first, based in large part on an intriguing garden relief from the Nineveh palace of Assurbanipal (668–627 B.C.E.), sees the gardens as cascading from elaborate colonnades and terraces along the Khosr.[57] The other proposes that these were the world's first carpet gardens, intended to be admired from above, so that the flowers and shrubs appear wondrously suspended, a living, dazzling display of color and pattern.

Subsequent carpet gardens are found within palaces from Iran to Muslim Spain and in the textile-inspired parterres of Europe.[58]

Several of Sennacherib's reliefs, including the one in figure 16, attest to a complementary concern with new perspectives in art. For millennia, scenes had been rendered in side or aerial view, often using both in the same image to convey maximum information. But here we watch the scene obliquely, with all the complicated transport mechanisms naturalistically spread before us as the colossal block moves through the undulating landscape.[59]

Sennacherib no doubt planned his government and succession with the same flair and attention to detail. His eldest son, Assurnadin-shumi, was given the sensitive position of king of Babylon, replacing various unsatisfactory and unreliable puppets that Sennacherib had tried before. If the young man could meet this test, he would be ready for kingship of the realm at his father's death. Fate decreed otherwise. The crown prince was deposed in a rebellion, with the connivance of the Elamites, and was carried off to die in miserable captivity in Elam, beyond Sennacherib's reach. The bereaved monarch turned his fury upon the city of Babylon: "I completely destroyed it by flooding and left it like an open field."[60] He tells us that he obliterated the place so utterly that its site could scarcely be identified; that he spared no one, man, woman, or child; that he carried off its dirt to Assur, trampling it underfoot in the temples he built there to replace the cult centers of Babylon; that the debris he dumped in the Euphrates flowed far out into the Gulf, to the awe of people in Dilmun.[61] This was his solution to the problem of Babylonia.

The death of the crown prince raised the inevitable question of which of his other sons was to succeed him to the throne of Assyria. Conspiracy and competition were in the air. Sennacherib himself fell victim to it, murdered by one of his sons. To a Babylonian historian, this was a divine judgment, the same that had been visited upon Tukulti-Ninurta I more than five centuries before.[62]

The Library of Assurbanipal

Assurbanipal (668–627 B.C.E.), the grandson of Sennacherib, was proud of his education, informing us that he had become expert in all he was taught, from chariot-driving to kingly deportment.[63] His academic attainments, he boasted, were superior to those of any Assyrian king before him:

> I have worked intricate mathematical problems that had no solution. I have read artful text in which the Sumerian was obscure and the Akkadian was difficult to interpret. I have studied inscriptions from before the Flood, a mishmash of cryptic enigmas.[64]

Tablets evidently written in the king's own hand, including a childhood letter to his father, Esarhaddon (680–669 b.c.e.), suggest that his claim to learning had some basis in fact. Assurbanipal was probably the author of several uninspired, plodding hymns in his name to Marduk and other gods, full of clichés, but no doubt applauded by his courtiers.[65]

Under his direction, thousands of tablets and writing boards were assembled at Nineveh and housed in at least two locations, his palace and the nearby temple of Nabu, god of wisdom and patron of writing. We do not know precisely how many documents the library originally contained, mainly because of the fragmentary nature of the material and the conditions under which it was excavated in the mid-nineteenth century. Estimates range from fifteen hundred to more than twenty-five thousand tablets and from several hundred to ten thousand boards, depending on how the individual pieces are counted and on the number of tablets thought to be needed for a given work in its entirety.[66] Even with a conservative figure of five thousand holdings, the library is the largest to survive from the ancient world.

Mesopotamian libraries had existed as early as the mid-third millennium. Temples, palaces, and scribal schools kept collections of literary works, practical handbooks, such as lists of dates and manuals for drawing up contracts, and scholarly works, such as magical procedures. Storage and retrieval systems included wooden shelving, built-in niches, clay and wooden boxes, baskets, and leather bags, as well as labeling in the form of perforated dockets, inscribed tablet edges, small clay knobs (see frontispiece and figure 22), and red-ocher stripes.[67] Catalogues usually listed works by their opening words, but occasionally by genre, such as "School-Days Compositions," by title, such as "The Series Gilgamesh," or by group, such as "Four Series and Twenty-One Songs." A few give shelving information: "In the container in the center, below."[68] The Middle Assyrian kings Tukulti-Ninurta I and Tiglath-Pileser I are sometimes credited with putting together a library at Assur. If so, this would be the first collection we can associate with a specific royal founder. The largest library surviving from that period was in private possession at Assur.[69]

Assurbanipal gathered the texts for his library from institutional and private collections throughout the land. Scribes recopied most of them in carefully prepared editions, adding colophons in the name of the king, stating that the work was done "for my life and for the well-being of my soul, to avoid disease, and to sustain the foundations of my throne," as well as "for my royal perusal." In letters concerning the formation of the library, evidently recopied as a historical dossier, Babylonian scholars assure the king that they are diligently procuring more material to send to Nineveh.[70]

The recovered contents of this great library have yet to be fully reconstructed, but it was no doubt as complete as the king's agents could make it. There were scholarly and reference works of magic, ritual, and divination, medical and lexical texts, technical prescriptions for making glass and aromatics, as well as literary, mythological, and historical compositions, oracles, and copies of letters written by famous rulers of the past. There were treatises on dream interpretation, series of omens from chance sounds heard in the street, rituals for the royal bath, and procedures for the consecration of a cult statue. There were hymns and prayers to the gods, and rituals to appease and appeal to them. There were fables and humorous sketches, love songs, laments, anthems performed in honor of current events, and dictionaries, encyclopedias, commentaries, and lists of rare words. There were historical chronicles about former kings as ancient as Sargon of Akkad, and copies of heroic epics about them.[71]

Of particular interest to many modern readers are the editions of the works considered both then and now to be the masterpieces of cuneiform literature. Most, such as the *Epic of Gilgamesh*, *Atrahasis*, the *Creation Epic*, the *Erra Epic*, and the *Poem of the Righteous Sufferer* (see chapters 5, 6, and 8), are known from other collections, but the Assurbanipal library manuscripts are often the most complete, and of the highest quality.[72]

The Fall of Assyria

The same harsh fate that she had dealt to so many other lands befell Assyria. During the eighth and seventh centuries, an Iranian people called the Medes had formed a state or confederation over the western half of the Iranian plateau.[73] Their power seemed invincible, for their archery and cavalry were more than a match for the less mobile Assyrian infantry and chariotry. Nor were the massive walls of the Assyrian cities proof against Median siege craft, which they had perfected in attacking the stone-built fastnesses of Urartu and Iran. The great prizes that lay before them were the Assyrian capitals and cities. By 612 B.C.E., these had succumbed, one by one, not without desperate resistance, as shown by recent excavations of the fortifications at Nineveh, whose defenders fought to the death on Sennacherib's "Wall That Awes the Enemy."[74] A letter from one of the last Assyrian kings to the Babylonian king pleads for his help on any terms, but the Babylonians allied with the Medes and joined them in the battle of Nineveh.[75] The Medes carried out such thorough slaughter, destruction, and plundering that nothing of Assyrian might and culture remained visible, including the library of Assurbanipal, which was smashed into thousands of fragments. It is likely that the Medes even mutilated a life-size, cast copper head of an Akkadian ruler, for archaeologists found the heirloom sculpture in the ruins, deliberately disfigured in just the way the Medes treated enemy notables.[76]

Yet the fires that swept through the palaces spared, indeed preserved, certain things, among them the stone wall reliefs, the broken clay tablets of Assurbanipal's library, a ground crystal lens, the oldest of its kind known, intended to correct astigmatism, and ivories.[77] From Nimrud comes the largest corpus we have of ancient carvings in this delicate medium, some hardened by the heat, others tossed down wells. The pieces include openwork plaques,

Figure 17. Ivory furniture panel from Nimrud, width 55 cm, Iraq Museum, Baghdad. (Matthiae 1997: 181) *Many of the Nimrud ivories had been kept in a basement storage room in the museum, where prior to the Iraq War they were damaged by flooding. The conservation laboratory, seriously affected by shortages owing to the sanctions of the 1990s, was unable to treat them beyond putting them in wooden trays to dry. When the looters came upon them in April 2003, they overturned the trays, pulverizing a large number of ivories in the process. Important pieces, some of which had been on display, are still missing as of this writing, and are posted on international registers of stolen art.*

decorative finials, inlays, panels, and cosmetic containers, dating from the ninth and eighth centuries B.C.E. Stylistically, they fall into three main groups, dubbed Assyrian, Phoenician, and Syrian, reflecting the internationalism characteristic of the period.[78] Figure 17 illustrates one of a group of similar chair backs or bedsteads executed in typical Syrian style, with sinuous plants and pudgy versions of Assyrian winged beings carrying buckets and cones (see figure 15). When the Medes broke into Nimrud, they stripped the gold sheets from these and other pieces of palace furniture. Someone then placed the ivory panels in orderly rows in a small storage room. Twenty-five hundred years later, archaeologists found them, still neatly stacked.

Assyria was gone forever. Even her hereditary enemies, the Babylonians, were shocked by what the Medes had done, and a contemporaneous historian commented, "They inflicted a crushing defeat on a great people."[79]

8. The Glory of Babylon

O Nabu and Marduk, as you go joyfully
in procession through these streets,
may words favorable of me be upon your lips.

Prayer of Nebuchadnezzar II

The Last Babylonian Empire

Although Sennacherib boasted that he had left Babylon ruined
forever, his son and successor Esarhaddon (680–669 B.C.E.) began
to rebuild the damaged areas of the city with treasure seized from
his invasion of Egypt.[1] His solutions to the perennial problem of
governing Babylonia were to reign himself as king of Babylon and
to name one son, Shamash-shum-ukin, to succeed him there and
the crown prince, Assurbanipal, to succeed him as king of Assyria
and the rest of the empire. Mindful of the civil war that had broken out at his father's assassination, Esarhaddon required all vassal
rulers in the empire to swear a loyalty oath to Assurbanipal,
drafted in over 650 lines of closely written script:

> [You have sworn] that if an Assyrian or a vassal of Assyria or
> an officer or a courtier or a citizen of Assyria or a citizen of
> any other country, or any living being whatsoever opposes
> Assurbanipal, the crown prince, in city or countryside, or
> brings about rebellion and insurrection, you will stand by

and guard Assurbanipal, the crown prince, you will whole-heartedly defeat the troops who revolt. . . .[2]

When Esarhaddon died, the queen mother Zakutu demanded that Shamash-shum-ukin also swear a loyalty oath to his brother, but he eventually rebelled, abetted by the Elamites, Arabs, and Chaldeans. Assurbanipal crushed the uprising; Shamash-shum-ukin's death in the burning city gave rise to the later legend of the pleasure-loving king Sardanapalus, who committed suicide by setting fire to his own palace.[3]

In the destruction of Assyria some forty years later, Babylonia was spared because her king, Nabopolassar (625–605 B.C.E.), had allied with Cyaxares, king of the invading Medes. After the last remnants of Assyrian resistance were quelled and an Egyptian force that came to their aid was annihilated, to Nabopolassar and his energetic son, Nebuchadnezzar II (604–562 B.C.E.), fell the task of forming a Neo-Babylonian empire on the ruins of the Neo-Assyrian, and this they set to with a will. One of the reasons for their success was that the new empire oversaw an amalgamation of what had once been rival groups in the land—Babylonians, Arameans, and Chaldeans—and thus avoided the local conflicts that had plagued Babylonia for centuries. At Nabopolassar's death, Nebuchadnezzar could look out over a dominion stretching from the Gulf to the borders of Egypt, secure in his alliance with the Medes. No significant power opposed him.[4]

His best-known campaigns were to Palestine, where he put down successive rebellions of Judah. When Jerusalem fell about 586 B.C.E., the defeated king Zedekiah was forced to witness the execution of his sons, then was blinded so that he could retain this last image before being led off into captivity in Babylon, along with many leading citizens of Judah.[5] With these and other deportations began the long history of Jewish culture in Iraq, which continued well into the twentieth century (see chapter 10).

Nebuchadnezzar transformed Babylon into the greatest city of the age, enjoying a peace and prosperity she had not known for centuries. The palace, inner fortress, temples, Processional Way, walls, and gates were lavishly refurbished, using, according to one estimate, 15 million baked bricks. Indeed, many Classical writers listed the walls of Babylon among the Seven Wonders of the World.[6] Special attention was given the ziggurat and other monuments associated with the god Marduk. Each spring equinox, the Babylonian New Year, Marduk left the city for a festival house outside the walls. Upon his return, amidst the rejoicing of the citizens, the god was borne in triumph down the Processional Way, a boulevard paved with great slabs of colored stone and faced with glazed, molded bricks depicting over 120 roaring lions. Where this avenue passed through the city walls, the king constructed the successive monumental portals of the Ishtar Gate, decorated by molded brick figures of bulls and dragons and guarded by bronze colossi of the same animals.[7]

The most famous description of Nebuchadnezzar's capital was written more than a century later by the Greek historian Herodotus (484?–425? B.C.E.), who was interested in Assyria and Babylonia as forerunners of the Persian Empire. He claims to have visited Babylon: in Book I of his *Histories*, we read, for example, that the walls were wide enough for a four-horse chariot to drive atop, and that every Babylonian woman had to prostitute herself once in her lifetime. Whether or not he ever in fact stood upon the walls, we can be sure that Herodotus grasped next to nothing of Babylonian history and civilization, and that his celebrated story of prostitution is rubbish. If he had known traveler's Aramaic, he could have spoken to people in public places, though Babylonian wisdom literature insists that speaking to strangers in the street is ill advised. How could he have met priests or scholars or the educated elite? We may freely doubt that he did so, for he makes no mention of cuneiform writing or clay tablets. His book was widely popular in antiquity and remained, for better or worse, one of the principal sources for Babylonian history, manners, and customs until the decipherment of cuneiform in the nineteenth century.[8]

At Nebuchadnezzar's death, the succession did not follow in an orderly manner. According to a Babylonian poem, the king had begun to act irrationally: "He paid no heed to son and daughter, family and clan were not in his heart."[9] Perhaps this is the basis for the later story that Nebuchadnezzar went mad.[10] Like many powerful monarchs, he seems at various times to have entertained deep suspicions of his sons. One of them, Nabu-shuma-ukin, supposedly a favorite, was jailed by his father because of untrue rumors fanned by his enemies. From prison, he appealed to the god of Babylon: "O Marduk! . . . Single out for harm the one who stirred up harmful talk of me! O Marduk, the artful devices of humankind, who can thwart them but you?"[11] Released through Marduk's intervention, so he tells us, he changed his name to Amil-Marduk (biblical Evil-Merodach) and did succeed to the throne, but ruled only two years. His brother-in-law followed, then his young nephew, who was murdered after two months as king. Intrigue, confiscations of property, and corruption cast long shadows over the times.[12]

Nabonidus, King of Babylon

In 555 B.C.E., under unclear circumstances, the throne passed to Nabonidus, son of an official and a priestess of the moon god. His redoubtable mother attained the age of 104, living through the reigns of seven Assyrian and Babylonian monarchs and informing us in her funerary inscription of her vigor:

> My eyesight is clear and my mind is excellent. My hands and feet are sound. My words are well chosen. Food and drink agree with me. My flesh is healthy, my temperament is cheerful. I have seen my descendants for four generations, I have reached a ripe old age.[13]

Nabonidus (555–539 B.C.E.) has left a vivid impression on Mesopotamian history because of his idiosyncratic religious ideas and the strong passions he inspired among his subjects.[14] He was eager to promote the cult of the moon god, a lesser Mesopotamian deity, over those of other Mesopotamian gods, and he took an increasingly hard line as resistance grew. In a series of rambling, formal compositions, he set forth his views, as in this prayer to the moon god: "The land you have resolved to make your dwelling, you will establish therein reverence for your great divinity for all time to come. The land you have resolved to shatter, you will remove reverence for you from it and you will overthrow it for all time to come."[15]

Even more extraordinary, Nabonidus moved his court to inner Arabia for a decade, to an oasis town called Teima, which was an important caravan station and had a sanctuary to the moon god. No one knows why he did this. Some consider it the act of a religious fanatic rusticating himself. Others see a prescient grasp of the precarious situation of the Babylonian empire. To survive with the great powers, such as the Medes, looking down, as it were, from the uplands, Babylonia would need a secure, alternative line of communication with the West. Traveling across the desert was not easy, but with camels it could be done. Further, this would gain Babylonia access to the surprising wealth that preceding rulers had found when they invaded Arab territory. Whatever the reasons, Nabonidus built a palace and enclosure at Teima, leaving his son, Belshazzer, to rule at Babylon as his viceroy. Belshazzer was not so interested in the cult of the moon god as his father, and seems to have acted with rather too free a hand during Nabonidus's prolonged absence. Belshazzer figures in the biblical book of Daniel in the story of his feast, during which the mysterious writing appears on the wall. As suddenly as he had left, Nabonidus returned, and carried out a thorough shake-up of the Babylonian court.[16]

According to a later satirical Babylonian poem, Nabonidus embarrassed the learned with his scholarly pretensions:

> He would stand forth in the collegium, boasting about himself, "I am wise, I am an expert, I have seen hidden things. I don't know how to read cuneiform writing but I have seen esoteric lore."[17]

He also recorded his dreams in commemorative inscriptions:

> In the same dream appeared Nebuchadnezzar, the former king of time gone by, and an attendant, in a chariot. The attendant said to Nebuchadnezzar, "Speak to Nabonidus and let him tell you the dream he had." Nebuchadnezzar assented and said to me, "Tell me what propitious thing you saw." I thereupon answered him, saying, "In my dream I saw a great star, Sin and Marduk had risen high in heaven. . . ."[18]

Nabonidus may also have seen himself as a lawgiver like Hammurabi, whose laws were still studied in Babylonian schools. In an account of royal justice that may date to Nabonidus's reign, the king tells us that he drew up, after careful deliberation, numerous cases of national significance. In one instance, when a man made a false appeal after a verdict had been issued in a case, the king had him beheaded, then commissioned an image of the cut-off head to be set up at the entrance of the law court, with an inscription reminding people not to make false appeals. In another case, in which a man brought a charge of murder against another man but could not prove it, accuser and accused were both put to the water ordeal (as provided for in the laws of Hammurabi), in which the false accuser drowned. When his corpse was finally recovered, "the top of his head was burned, as with fire, his body was covered with blisters."[19]

Learning and Memory in Babylonia

Educated Babylonians of the time were well aware of the great antiquity of their civilization. The study of ancient history flourished in professional circles, producing a new style of chronographic literature. Babylonian and Assyrian chronicles had long listed current events such as battles, deaths and accessions of kings, and happenings of cultic interest, but now similar information was collected for the distant past, beginning with the Akkadian kings.[20] In the Babylonian chronicle of Sargon of Akkad, for example, we read:

> Sargon, king of Akkad, arose during the reign of Ishtar. He had neither rival nor opponent, his fame spread over all lands, he crossed the sea in the East. In the eleventh year, he conquered the country of the West up to its farthest boundary and placed it under his sole authority, had his statues erected there and booty ferried across on barges. He made his courtiers dwell at a distance of every five double hours and governed the community of his countries as one.[21]

Scholars also studied, copied, and displayed their decipherments of very old writing, even as the official language of prayers and royal inscriptions became steeped in what were deemed old-fashioned expressions, written in archaizing spelling.

Figure 18 illustrates one of the antique objects allegedly discovered by Nabopolassar during his restoration of the temple of the sun god Shamash at Sippar, and preserved in his foundation deposit in the renovated building.[22] The piece, if not a clever forgery of Nabopolassar's own time, would then have been about 250 years old, dating to the reign of Nabu-apla-iddina, a Babylonian king of the ninth century B.C.E. On it, Nabu-apla-iddina records his own restoration of this temple, including his replacement of its long-gone statue of Shamash with an exact copy made from the very model used for the original, which he claims was fortuitously unearthed by a priest on the west bank of the Euphrates. The scene at the top shows the king approaching the refurbished shrine, the god enthroned within and his solar symbol being lowered to an outside stand by two minor gods. Much of the style and iconography is familiar from Babylonian works we have already seen—the interceding figures leading the worshipper, the reverential gestures, the proffered rod and ring, the bull-men on the throne. New elements, perhaps reflecting Assyrian and other, more northern influences, include the only partially anthropomorphic gods and the volutes on the column, which prefigure the Ionic capitals of Greek architecture. The deckled edges have few parallels.

Nabonidus was a keen antiquarian and one of the world's first archaeologists and collectors. In his inscriptions, he says he made great efforts to restore ancient rites and sanctuaries "as of old," and in his correspondence with his officials he urges them to pay close attention to such matters. He went so far as to revive the practice, first known under Sargon of Akkad, of appointing a daughter to serve as high priestess of the moon god, an office that had lapsed for centuries. He carried out excavations at the Akkadian capital of Agade, the temples of which had long been abandoned, their cults moved to other cities. Nabonidus tells us that he could not find the remains of the temple of Ishtar at Agade, which kings had been looking for since the Kassite period, until a storm opened a gully around the foundation laid by Naram-Sin. This "made the king's heart glad and brightened his countenance."[23] When a statue of Sargon was discovered during excavations at Sippar, he

Figure 18. Limestone tablet from Sippar, height 29.5 cm, British Museum, London. (Matthiae 1996: 164) *In 1881, Rassam's workers smashed a bitumen-covered chamber at Sippar, finding inside a clay box containing this tablet and two clay impressions of its relief scene. There was also a third impression, apparently made from a nearly identical, now-missing tablet that the Arabs were said to have stolen from the site. Rassam's inadequate records and methods make further reconstruction of context impossible.*

ordered its restoration. He kept a kind of museum at Ur, which housed a statue of Shulgi and a Kassite land grant, among other antiquities. A broken monument of Hammurabi was displayed at Sippar. For a collection at Nippur, a scribe made a clay impression of an inscription of Sharkalisharri, "found in the palace of Naram-Sin."[24]

Since the literate person was supposed to have some knowledge of the ancient Sumerian language, high literary expression was sometimes salted with Sumerian loanwords. Educated people wrote in Babylonian, had read major works of Babylonian literature, and honored the scholarly achievements of the past. In daily life, however, Babylonian was increasingly influenced by Aramaic, which was probably much more widely spoken in the land. Over time, Babylonian may have become the formal language learned in school, analogous to Modern Standard Arabic today in Iraq, whereas Aramaic was the language of everyday discourse, like Iraqi colloquial dialect. In its written form, usually on papyrus, parchment, or waxed writing boards, Aramaic used a simple alphabet that was much easier to master than the complex cuneiform system. Aramaic linked Babylonia with a much wider world than that of the few people who still spoke Babylonian. Some works of Aramaic literature have survived, among them the tale of a wise man called Ahiqar who served at the court of Esarhaddon and eventually triumphed over a perfidious nephew.[25]

Education in Babylonia was often a family affair. Certain families were repositories of scholarly, religious, and literary tradition and trained their descendants in what they knew. They had specialties, such as divination or singing the long laments in Sumerian dialect in the major sanctuaries to appease the hearts of the gods. The sons, having achieved a certain competence, demonstrated their proficiency by making new copies of the family collection of tablets, thus mastering and carrying forward the family's learned tradition. Some of these men, however, preferred to make their living drawing up legal documents for a fee, or by surveying, or working as administrators.[26]

Scholars naturally gravitated toward centers of wealth and power, where patronage and employment could be found. At

Babylon, perhaps elsewhere too, a small, highly trained guild was adept at mathematical and observational astronomy, compiling over the course of 800 years neatly written astronomical diaries that yield a wealth of information when analyzed in their entirety, the longest sustained research project in world history. Babylonian astronomers and astrologers were particularly concerned with predicting, observing, and interpreting solar and lunar eclipses and calculating the motions of the moon and the planet Venus.[27] Because eclipses were deemed portents for the stability of society and the government, astrologers enjoyed royal patronage:

> On the 14th of this month, an eclipse of the moon will take place. This is bad news for our neighbors, in the southeast or the northwest, but it is a good omen for His Majesty. His Majesty may therefore rest assured. In any case, I had already foreseen and predicted this eclipse as soon as the planet Venus appeared.[28]

In addition to practical and scientific uses for astronomy, such as deciding when to insert extra months in the lunar calendar to keep it consistently correlated with the seasons, evidently there was also interest in using astronomy for such subsidiary purposes as predicting the market price of selected commodities.[29] By the late fifth century, the motions of the stars and planets were thought significant for anyone, not just kings, so the world's first horoscopes were cast for private clients.[30] At the same time, mathematical models for the motions of the stars and planets had made possible purely rational explanations of celestial phenomena.

Babylonian literature consisted of important works inherited from the past, such as the *Epic of Gilgamesh* (chapter 5) and the *Epic of Creation* (chapter 6), as well as newly composed prose and poetry, often written in a vivid, original style, showing a strong sense of personality, time, and place, and using neologisms and words not found elsewhere.[31] In this passage from a penitential prayer, for instance, the author describes his deep discouragement and suicidal thoughts:

Death has tantalized me like a precious stone,
I keep going up to the roof to jump off,
    But my life is too precious, it turns me back.
I try to encourage myself, but what is there to encourage?
I try to keep control of my thoughts, but what is there for
    me to control?[32]

Here is the lament of a woman dying in childbirth:

The day I carried the fruit, how happy I was,
Happy was I, happy my husband.
The day I went into labor, my face grew overcast,
The day I gave birth, my eyes grew cloudy. . . .
My husband, who loved me, uttered a cry,
"Do not forsake me, the wife I adore!". . .
All those days I was with my husband,
While I lived with him who was my lover,
Death was creeping stealthily into my bedroom.
It forced me from my house,
It cut me off from my lover,
It set my feet toward the land from which I shall not
    return.[33]

One of the last major compositions in Akkadian is the *Erra Epic*.[34] The poet, Kabti-ilani-Marduk, asks how, in a world controlled by self-interested and all-powerful gods, could violence overtake the very cities that sustained them and their earthly homes, the great temples of the land? How could the city of Babylon, center of the universe, the chosen dwelling of the god Marduk, built with the very labor of the gods, ever be given over to plunder and destruction? Kabti-ilani-Marduk responds with a passionate portrayal and a complex theological explanation: Erra, the god of violent behavior, grows bored and discontented if he has no outlet for his horrible energies; on some pretext, however flimsy, fighting begins, growing quickly out of control. Drunk on blood, Erra boasts of his powers:

I will tear out the mooring pole so the ship drifts away,
I will smash the rudder so she cannot reach the shore,
I will pluck out the mast, I will rip out the rigging.
I will make breasts go dry so babies cannot thrive,
I will block up springs so the tiniest channels can
    bring no life-sustaining water.
I will make hell shake and heaven tremble,
I will make the planets shed their splendor,
I will wrench out the stars from the sky![35]

These are but three samples of the rich and varied Babylonian literature of the period, which includes narrative, devotional, and scholarly compositions, humor and satire, laments, and love songs—in short, every form and style that tradition, imagination, and creativity could command.

Works and Days

The great temples in Babylonia were centers of religious, economic, and intellectual life. The temple of Ishtar at Uruk, for example, had a staff of hundreds, including scores of craftsmen, and controlled at least 17,000 hectares of agricultural land and extensive date orchards, many of which it leased out to citizens for a share of the crop.[36] All the major temples had their own administration and courts, as well as an elaborate system of prebends, in which citizens purchased the rights to certain offices, gaining thereby both the income from them and social prestige.[37] The king appointed the leading temple administrators, who normally belonged to prominent local families.

A tendency to allow close associates to take advantage of what would now be called government contracts expanded under Nabonidus's reign. A group of businessmen contracted to manage all the arable land of the temple of Ishtar at Uruk, and even when it became clear that they were far from meeting the terms of their contract, the king insisted that they be left unmolested. Perhaps the king thought that privatization would increase production, since the temple lacked the personnel to manage so much land itself. Or perhaps the temple officialdom had unrealistic expectations of what the temple should receive from its resources. In any case, it is clear that the results were not satisfactory, and that some contractors and temple staff resorted to embezzlement, theft, bribery, default, even murder for hire, as can be seen in the temple records.[38]

We also have documentation for many aspects of Babylonian private life in this period, especially those governed by written contracts among the wealthier classes. In dowries and inventories, for instance, we read of fine furniture, woven and knotted textiles, jewelry, cosmetics, and sets of metal cooking utensils. The well-to-do kept domestic slaves, a half-dozen or more. Only in this period of Mesopotamian history does chattel slavery achieve some prominence, and then only in domestic contexts, where slaves were servants, business agents, and confidential clerks. Slaves were permitted to marry, have children, and accumulate property of their own.[39]

Most families with capital accumulated wealth through partnerships and investments in real estate, especially houses, fields, and date palm orchards.[40] These last were particularly profitable, because once the trees were mature they gave a high, reliable yield, and vegetable gardens could be cultivated in the open spaces among the trees. The plots were typically leased out to orchardists in return for a percentage of the harvest. Date palm trunks were sold as timber, and the fronds used for baskets and matting.[41] Less is known about international trade. Iron, for example, was in common use in Mesopotamia for tools, chains, weapons, and the like, but we have no records telling how iron was obtained or in what form.[42]

Although the Babylonians drew up maps of their world and speculated about its shape and distances, no Babylonian ever described a foreign land or people as Herodotus did.[43] Were they so preoccupied with their own culture and affairs that they deemed it sufficient to master the demands of their milieu and pointless to inquire into those of another? Perhaps on a philosophical level they saw the world as unitary, with Babylonia at the center and all other peoples languishing on the periphery, though surely soldiers, merchants, and businessmen knew otherwise. Or perhaps we err by seeing them principally through the dark glass of their elitist cuneiform written tradition and luxury artifacts. Had more Aramaic sources of this period survived, we might have a broader and clearer perspective of what this dynamic and prosperous era was really like.

The Persian Empire

Within a few years of Nabonidus's return from Arabia, word no doubt reached the Babylonian court of unexpected developments in the land of the Medes.[44] A certain Kurash, better known today as Cyrus the Great, had rebelled against the Medes and defeated them. From his base in Parsua (modern Fars), Cyrus conquered in all directions and became sovereign of a realm stretching from the Indus to the Anatolian plateau. It was only a matter of time before the Persian armies appeared in Mesopotamia. Marching down the Tigris in 539 B.C.E., they routed the Babylonian army, and an advance Persian force entered Babylon. Shortly thereafter, Cyrus himself arrived; according to his own account, the god Marduk

> . . . delivered Nabonidus, the king who did not revere him, into his [Cyrus's] hands. All the people of Babylon, all the land of Sumer and Akkad . . . rejoiced at his kingship and their faces shone. . . . They greeted him with gladness and praised his name.[45]

As it proved, Cyrus was a humane and enlightened ruler by the standards of ancient conquerors, and Babylonia entered a new and vital phase of her existence.

At its height about 500 B.C.E., the Persian Empire stretched from Libya to Central Asia, linked by excellent roads and a postal service, by far the most successful political experiment of its kind in antiquity.[46] The empire was bound together by a rule of law and loyalty to the king, within which local laws were applied by local authorities. There was no interference with native religious or other institutions, no attempt to impose the Persian language. Rather, it was the destiny of Aramaic to become the common spoken tongue of this vast dominion, the language even the Persian nobility used to communicate with the stewards of their far-flung estates.[47]

Administratively, the empire was divided into satrapies, or provinces. Of these, Babylonia was among the wealthiest because, if we may believe Herodotus, it paid the highest tribute.[48] As for Assyria, it remained one of the poorest provinces of the Persian Empire, sparsely populated, with few important cities. So thorough had been the devastation by the Medes that nothing resembling the former Assyrian economy and agricultural regime seems to have reasserted itself. A few proud families at Assur kept alive some memory of their traditions by giving their children Assyrian names.[49]

The provinces were ruled by Persian noblemen drawn from several families often related to the royal house. The extensive Babylonian royal and temple domains passed into the control of the Persian crown and nobility. A file copy survives of a well-turned letter addressed to Darius I (521–486 B.C.E.) by the officials of the temple of Ishtar at Uruk:

> To the king of the world, our master, thus say your servants Amurru-dan, Kudurru, and Marduk-shakin-shumi: May Uruk and the Eanna-temple bless the king of the world! Every day, at opening the doors and closing the doors, we pray to Our Lady of Uruk and to the goddess Nanaya for a life long of days, health, happiness, stability of reign, and the downfall of the foes of the king of the world, our master. All is well with the administration of the Eanna-temple, the abode of your gods. We have begun the shearing in the abode of your gods. We have been praying constantly before Our Lady of Uruk and the goddess Nanaya for the king of the world, saying, "May this be the first of a thousand shearings at the pleasure of the king of the world, our lord!"[50]

We have the sense that under the early Persian kings Babylonia continued to develop economically, as she had under the last Babylonian kings, but with a much broader scope and an even more brilliant prosperity. Important irrigation projects were begun for the further reclamation of arable land, so as to increase production and revenues; the population increased and many foreigners settled in Babylonia.[51] The Persian authorities distributed agricultural land as military fiefs, whose holders were obliged to provide soldiers at the king's command. Although this practice, widespread in the empire, meant that troops were readily available, it also meant that local Persian administrators had significant numbers of soldiers at their disposal, and could use them in pursuit of power, extending even to claims on the throne itself. So numerous did these fiefs become that they were organized into districts that gradually replaced the old Babylonian provinces.[52]

Some enterprising Babylonians saw opportunity in the new organization of the countryside. They offered the Persian landlords or holders of military fiefs cash in advance for the harvest on their holdings, which they collected and marketed for their own profit, using their own transport agents.[53] No doubt this left the producing peasant just as much at the mercy of these local speculators as he had been under distant Persian noblemen. We may surmise that a large class of peasantry may gradually have begun to sink into debt and a kind of economic servitude from which there was no escape but to flee in secret, as interest rates soared.

The landed Babylonian urban class prospered during the first half-century of Persian rule, just as they had under the Neo-Babylonian dynasty. A prominent Babylonian who died during the reign of Darius I, for example, left an estate of sixteen houses in Babylon and Borsippa, other urban real estate, over a hundred slaves, and much cash, livestock, and personal belongings, even after he had handsomely dowered three daughters.[54] He and others like him presided over extended families that included several households and made it their task to manage and build up the family holdings, and to negotiate advantageous marriages for their sons and daughters.[55]

Many, however, chafed under the Persian occupiers, the first foreign people to rule Babylonia who did not embrace Babylonian culture. The Persian idea of nobility was especially galling to Babylonians, who had always recognized the intellectual or social prestige of certain families, but had no notion that by the accident of birth a small percentage of the population was entitled to a way of life inaccessible to others, whatever their achievements.

In Babylonia and elsewhere in the empire, rebellions sought to remove the Persian overlords from their land. Two Babylonian patriots took the name of Nebuchadnezzar, perhaps to evoke the glorious empire of Nebuchadnezzar II, some generations before, or even to recall Nebuchadnezzar I's summer triumph over Elam in the twelfth century (see chapter 6). Scholars recopied poetry about the latter event, perhaps in the hope that history would repeat.[56] It did not; Persian armies suppressed the rebellions with severe reprisals and looting. The great temples were naturally tempting targets, and some of them probably sustained heavy damage. Their archives end abruptly at this time, as do those of many leading families. We are not sure if they experienced disaster or were suddenly obliged to maintain their records in some other form.[57]

Yet is difficult to see what impact, if any, the new world of the Persian Empire had on Babylonian culture. Persian rule presented a situation Mesopotamia had never enjoyed before: unhindered access as far east as the foothills of the Hindu Kush and as far west as the Nile Valley. We see almost nothing of this in the Babylonian art and literature of the time. A few Persian words and technical terms crept into official parlance, and Babylonian historians duly noted the deaths and accessions of the Persian kings, but the age and durability of Babylonian culture seems to have kept it isolated from foreign influence.[58]

The Persians, for their part, borrowed certain Mesopotamian cultural features freely. In the construction and decoration of their palaces at Pasargadae, Persepolis, and Susa, for example, we see courtyard plans, carpet gardens, four-winged beings, composite creatures, façades of glazed molded bricks, and other venerable aspects of Mesopotamian iconography. To make his new palace at Susa a showcase of empire, Darius I summoned materials and craftsmen from every corner of his realm. Babylonians were set to making brick, Assyrians to bringing cedar from Lebanon.[59] At Susa as at Babylon, inscriptions of the Persian kings were composed in

Babylonian. When Darius commemorated his rise to power in a long narrative carved on a sheer cliff face at Behistun, Iran, he used three languages, Elamite, Persian, and Babylonian, all written using cuneiform characters. This trilingual inscription helped make possible the decipherment of cuneiform writing in the nineteenth century (see Epilogue).

9. Mesopotamia between Two Worlds

> The Chaldeans and the Indian wizards are the
> first people to my knowledge who ever said
> the soul of man is immortal, and one of the
> most important Greeks they convinced was
> Plato.
>
> *Pausanias, Guide to Greece*

Alexander the Great and the Seleucids

When Alexander crossed from Europe to Asia in the spring of 334 B.C.E., he may not have imagined that he, a young king from Macedon, might topple Darius III, King of All Lands. Nevertheless, in victory after victory, culminating in the battle of Gaugamela, near Nineveh, in 331 B.C.E., Alexander and his army indeed vanquished the Persians and inherited Darius's empire.[1] Shortly thereafter, he arranged at Susa a mass marriage ceremony between his soldiers and Persian women, an event meant to meld Macedonian and Persian cultures. Yet wintering at Persepolis in 331, he burned its magnificent palace built by Xerxes. We do not know why he did this. Some ancient writers said it was the outcome of a drunken orgy, or in revenge for Xerxes' attack on Athens; others claimed it was at the urging of the beautiful courtesan Thaïs. Modern historians have suggested that he resented the

Persians' not accepting him as the successor to Darius, or wanted to remove Persepolis as a rival to Babylon.[2]

Whatever the reason, laden with treasure, Alexander returned to Babylon, where he gave orders that the ruins of the temple of Marduk be cleared and restored, apparently for resumption of the ancient rites.[3] If Alexander intended to base his new universal kingdom at Babylon, it was a good strategic choice. Situated roughly in the center of his domains, and with a long imperial tradition that was not so closely identified with Persian kingship as Persepolis, Babylon might once again have ruled the world.

Over the next seven years, Alexander the Great marched and conquered from Samarkand to the Indus Valley, a personal triumph, but it is well to remember that he went almost nowhere the Persian kings had not been before him. Finally, he headed back to Babylon, where he fell ill, dying in the palace between 4 and 5 o'clock in the afternoon of 11 June 323, so the Babylonian astronomers tell us.[4] His empire was left in the hands of several Macedonian generals and followers. Whereas at first they maintained a pretense of waiting for Alexander's son, called Alexander IV, to come of age and take hegemony, when strife and betrayal broke out among them they abandoned that course, warring among themselves to succeed the brilliant fallen leader.

In 312 B.C.E., the general Seleucus seized power at Babylon, and as Seleucus I Nikator eventually ruled over the Iranian plateau, where Macedonian colonies were flourishing, as well as over Iraq, Syria, and parts of Turkey. Of all the successor states, his most closely resembled the shape of the old Persian Empire. But his rise to power did not go unopposed. Antigonus, another of Alexander's generals, invaded Babylonia in 310–307. Both sides fought hard, recognizing that Babylonia was crucial to their plans, and supported themselves by looting and terrorizing the local population. There were emergency taxes; holy places were pillaged. As a Babylonian historian wrote, "There was weeping and mourning in the country."[5]

Seleucus I Nikator prevailed, and his dynasty, called the Seleucids, continued to rule the Great Kingdom of Asia, as it was known, for two and a half centuries, down to the Roman and Parthian conquests, for the most part maintaining Persian administrative practices, respecting local customs, and supporting local religions. Their tenure was, however, not without serious challenges and setbacks. For one, they faced the difficulties of controlling such an enormous territory with a relatively small Macedonian army to rely on.[6]

To complicate matters, they never gave up on the idea of enlarging their kingdom to the west, for they considered themselves the sole legitimate successors of Alexander. As a result, Seleucid Iraq looked politically and strategically westward, and Babylonia was drawn directly and indirectly into the vicious politics of the Mediterranean. There, Alexander's successors in Egypt, Turkey, Greece, and Macedon were vying for their own supremacy, always hoping to outflank and protect themselves from Seleucid expansionism. In 281 B.C.E., Seleucus I Nikator sailed for Macedon to claim its kingship, probably not having set foot there since embarking with Alexander, more than fifty years before. Just as Seleucus's ship landed, Ptolemy Ceraunus, son of his former comrade Ptolemy I Soter, rushed forward and stabbed the aged warrior to death.[7]

There were also troubles to the east, in the former provinces of the Persian Empire in Iran, which the Seleucids could ill afford to ignore. The eastern dominions became an urgent problem in the first half of the third century, when nomadic peoples from Central Asia, whom the Greeks called Scyths, invaded Iran in large numbers, overrunning some of the former Macedonian colonies there and posing a threat for Seleucus's son, Antiochus I Soter (281–261 B.C.E.).[8] The immediate consequence of the disorder in Iran was that various local chieftains abrogated their allegiance to the Seleucid royal house and founded lineages of their own, prime among them Arsaces of Parthia.

Antiochus I Soter, King of Asia

Antiochus I epitomized the new royalty of the Hellenistic age (figure 19). Son of the Macedonian king in Babylonia and his Bactrian queen, he grew up bilingual in Greek and his mother's native tongue. From this dual heritage, he must have absorbed both Hellenistic concepts of kingship, whose principles held that the "best

Figure 19. Silver tetradrachm of Antiochus I Soter, minted at Seleucia, diameter 2.75 cm, private collection. (Kraay 1966: pl. 204, 743) *Most ancient coins, with the exception of the occasional small denominations, come from hoards hidden by their owners for safekeeping, usually in remote locations, and never recovered. For today's illicit finders and sellers of hoards, the rewards are great, since gold and silver coins in fine condition, singly or in groups, fetch enormous prices and pass fluidly through international channels. As a result, we rarely know anything of a hoard's findspot, overall contents, and associated material, vital information that would greatly contribute to our understanding of ancient monetary systems. The coins themselves are scattered about the world, often, as here, in private collections.*

man" ruled as mentor to his society and valiant leader of his army, and nomadic views of leadership, which involved a chieftain's pride in his lineage and canniness in dealing with the fiercely independent tribes of the steppes east of the Caspian and throughout the Iranian plateau.[9]

As king of Babylonia, Antiochus deemed it prudent to support the Babylonian cults. Certain deities, such as Nabu (Greek Nebo), god of learning and writing, and Nanaya, goddess of love, gained a wider following in his realm. A Babylonian hymn to Nabu, in a stilted though competent style, honored Antiochus and his family: "O Nabu, foremost son, when you enter Ezida, the eternal house, may there be on your lips a favorable word for Antiochus, king of the world, and favorable words for Seleucus the king, his son, and for Stratonike, his wife, the queen."[10]

During the reign of Antiochus, a Babylonian scholar named Berossus wrote a book in Greek called *Babyloniaca*, dedicated to the king, in which he explained Babylonian history and religion and listed ancient rulers. This, like the prayer to Nabu, suggests that Antiochus had some historical and cultural interest in his Babylonian domains. The book is poorly known today, as only fragments, quotations, and summaries remain, their authenticity open to dispute.[11] One of the best-known passages treats the origins of Babylonian civilization:

> There appeared from the Red Sea in an area bordering on Babylonia a frightening monster, named Oannes. . . . It had the whole body of a fish, but underneath and attached to the head of the fish there was another head, human, and joined to the tail of the fish, feet, like those of a man, and it had a human voice. Its form has been preserved in sculpture to this day. . . . This monster spent its days with men, never eating anything, but teaching men the skills necessary for writing and for doing mathematics and for all sorts of knowledge: how to build cities, found temples, and make laws. It taught men how to determine borders and divide land, also how to plant seeds and then to harvest their fruits and vegetables. . . . At the end of the day, this monster Oannes went back to the sea and spent the night.[12]

Though this story per se is not found in extant Babylonian tradition, there is an episode in the *Erra Epic* (chapter 8) in which the cult statue of Marduk at Babylon was purified by seven sages, "sacred fish, . . . perfect in sublime wisdom," so Berossus may have known of an association between fish and knowledge.[13] Fish-men or fish-garbed figures appear in Mesopotamian art from the Kassite to the Seleucid periods, but their meaning is obscure.[14]

As leaders of a cosmopolitan urban elite, Antiochus and his successors were prepared to be Hellenes in the Mediterranean world, Great Kings of their domains in Asia, and local kings in Babylonia. Nor were they unique in this. Their counterparts in Egypt, descendants of Alexander's general Ptolemy, were pleased to be pharaohs as well as Hellenistic kings.[15] There, too, cross-cultural books were written. An Egyptian priest named Manetho compiled his *Aegyptiaca* in the early third century B.C.E., including a list of pharaohs since earliest times, and Ptolemy II Philadelphus (283–246 B.C.E.) was said to have commissioned a translation of the Hebrew Bible into Greek for his famous library at Alexandria.[16]

But rather than projecting for Seleucid Iraq a grand synthesis of the Greek and the Mesopotamian, some historians are inclined to see parallel patterns of colonial rule and Babylonian culture. Perhaps this view is too much influenced by such recent situations as British rule in India, but the great complexity and extent of the Seleucid realm, its polyglot society, and the necessity that rulers come to terms in some way with the ruled invite the comparison, if it is not carried too far.

The Realm and Its Economy

The Seleucids administered their programs from Antioch and its military base at Apamea in Syria; from Ecbatana (modern Hamadan), the ancient Median capital in Iran; and from Seleucia-on-the-Tigris, a new city built about 60 kilometers northwest of Babylon at the confluence of a royal canal and the Tigris. As the capital of Mesopotamia and seat of the royal court, Seleucia must have attracted the ambitious and the colonist. In many ways, it was a model Hellenistic city, with gymnasia, a theater, a palace, and government buildings, but they were built of native mud-brick rather than stone.[17] In his *Natural History*, the Roman writer Pliny the Elder (23–79 C.E.) claims that Seleucia drew population away from Babylon, turning it into a backwater, nearly uninhabited.[18] Though the construction of a new capital nearby may have dismayed the

Babylonians, who had hoped that once again their city would rule Asia, Babylon was in fact still one of the most populous and important centers of the realm. Even at the height of the war with Antigonus, the restoration of the temple of Marduk continued apace. The Seleucids also adorned portions of the city with Hellenistic monuments, such as a theater and gymnasium.[19]

Although some leading Babylonians had both Greek and Babylonian names and occupied positions of responsibility in the local administration, beyond the ruling elite we do not know how much the Greek and Babylonian populations interacted.[20] Like the Ptolemies in Egypt, the Seleucids may have been wary of recruiting too many native soldiers, relying instead on Greek troops and foreign mercenaries to uphold their power. The Greek tax collector was of course everywhere, charging fees, tolls, and duties to maintain the Seleucid war machine, scarcely ever idle.[21] In an archive building at Seleucia were found some 36,000 bullae, the clay nodules used to seal documents, their sides stamped using signet rings engraved with fine portraits of the elite and with Greek dockets, such as "Tax on salt. Seleucia. Tax due."[22]

The economy of Hellenistic Mesopotamia was enhanced by the introduction of standardized coinage, spurred initially by the ready availabililty of tons of silver and gold from the Persian treasuries looted by Alexander. Previously, Mesopotamia had used mainly silver and grain as media of exchange and valuation. Coins first appeared in the seventh or sixth century B.C.E. in Lydia, a wealthy kingdom in western Turkey. Other regions soon developed their own coinage. After Cyrus the Great defeated the Lydian ruler Croesus in 547 B.C.E., the Persians began to mint gold and silver coins, including some types that were still being struck during the period of Alexander and his successors. Greek coinage, however, became the preferred currency throughout Western Asia and the Mediterranean world. The Babylonians, for example, specified "good quality *staters*" when selling temple prebends in Hellenistic Uruk.[23]

A considerable proportion of the best arable land in Babylonia was held by the crown and royal family, who had confiscated it from the Persian nobles they had displaced.[24] The producing population of peasants, many perhaps permanently tied to the land they worked, possessed limited civil rights. The irrigation projects of the early Persian kings may have suffered damage in the revolts and wars of the later Persian and Hellenistic periods, possibly leading to an aggregate decline in agricultural output.[25] But the Mediterranean world had an insatiable thirst for luxury goods from the East, such as fine textiles, aromatics, oils, and spices, not to mention precious and semiprecious stones. We thus have reason to believe that many sectors of the commercial activity of the major Mesopotamian cities continued to be bustling and profitable.[26] To take one index, market prices of basic commodities generally were stable or dropped in Hellenistic Babylonia, perhaps because the government intervened against inflation.[27]

The Culture of Hellenistic Babylonia

However robust other sectors may have been, the Hellenistic period witnessed the steady loss of Babylonian cultural vitality, save in the careful work of a few learned people. A priest at Uruk wrote out in detail various temple rituals, as if anxious lest they be forgotten or fall into disuse. The clerks of the great temples of Ishtar and Anu at Uruk still kept their records in neat Babylonian script. And the proud old Babylonian scholarly families still read the *Epic of Gilgamesh*, recited Babylonian spells and hymns, copied commentaries on works of divination and medicine, and sang ancient Sumerian laments in the time-honored way.[28]

There seems to have been scant mutual intellectual curiosity. A handful of magic spells in both cuneiform and Greek characters implies that some Greeks and Babylonians were intrigued by each other's writing systems, but this can hardly be seen as meaningful cultural exchange. As for Berossus's laborious Greek book on Babylonian culture, it was probably a failure. Copies were extremely rare, even in antiquity.[29] Native apologetics under colonial rule seldom make interesting reading for the ruling clique who tend, instead, to cling the more strongly to their own traditions when transplanted to a different clime. Few Greeks wanted to tackle a volume full of the strange, barbarous names of long-ago kings with fantastic life spans. Those who delved into its mythological sections must have been disappointed not to find revealed therein the secret, alien wisdom they imagined lay hidden in the ancient books of the East.[30]

Instead, Greek-speaking scholars in Seleucid and Parthian Babylonia taught at a Stoic academy in Babylon and pursued their own concerns. A certain Zachalias, for instance, wrote a book about how precious stones influence human behavior, which was known to Pliny the Elder, but has not survived.[31] Another author, the philosopher and poet Herodicus, wrote a satirical poem on fussy Greek grammarians, "buzzing in dark corners, mumbling monosyllables, whose sole business is the difference between . . . 'min' and 'nin.'"[32] This too survives only in a quotation cited by another writer.

The international nature of the sciences, however, transcended any insularities of the period. Scientific work, like military technology, has its own laws of circulation, which often reach far beyond the range of other kinds of cultural transmission. Greek scientists were well aware of the sophistication of Babylonian astronomy and began to translate astronomical tables into Greek, perhaps through some intermediary language. Babylonian astronomy, as well as astrology, thus made their way to the scientific treatises of the Hellenistic world and thereby enriched them considerably, many would say decisively.[33] Babylonian geometry and metric algebra were also of major importance in the development of mathematics in the Hellenistic world.[34] As for divination, the queen of the Babylonian sciences, some forms, such as examining the entrails and livers of sheep, were practiced by Mediterranean peoples using Babylonian techniques; a Roman historian recognized that Babylonia was "where the true art of divination first made its appearance."[35]

In the late third or early second century B.C.E., a Babylonian prince called Adad-nadin-ahe built a palace atop the ruins of Girsu (modern Tello). He was evidently interested in restoration and preservation, as well as in reviving ancient customs, often with a Hellenistic twist. He inscribed his name on bricks in venerable Mesopotamian tradition, but in Aramaic and Greek instead of cuneiform. In the course of his projects, he came across decapitated diorite monuments of Gudea seated and standing (see chapter 4). These he arranged by pose in his palace courtyard, apparently readying several for new, presumably Hellenized heads.[36]

As we might expect, much Seleucid art in Iraq reflects a similar admixture of styles, which is one of the hallmarks of Hellenistic work throughout the Mediterranean and Middle East. Small alabaster and terracotta statues of women from Babylonian cities and graves, for example, wear garments that drape over their bodies in the fluid folds characteristic of Greek sculpture, but they usually have the overlarge eyes typical of Mesopotamian votive figures across the millennia, awestruck as they come face-to-face with the deity in his or her temple.[37]

The same may be seen in Seleucid coins, especially earlier in the period. Figure 19, a silver tetradrachm minted at Seleucia about 255–246 B.C.E., represents Antiochus I Soter with a Greek fillet-diadem and windswept streamers and hair, but an enlarged Mesopotamian eye. On the reverse, this coin and many others of the dynasty depict the Greek god Apollo, from whom the dynasty claimed descent; some show an elephant, the new weapon in the Seleucid arsenal. Seleucus I Nikator had seen war elephants in action in India and, according to Strabo, surrendered his interests there for five hundred of them, some of which were later used to clear the ruins of the temple of Marduk at Babylon.[38]

We know little of the Seleucid kingdom's cultural relations with the East, mainly because there are no native Iranian sources, and because the Hellenistic historians focused on the Mediterranean and Syrian activities of the Seleucid rulers. Some have suggested that Babylonian astronomy spread to India, perhaps as far as China, conceivably through the medium of Aramaic or Greek translation, or directly from Babylonian to Sanskrit.[39]

The Rise of Parthia

The Seleucids and Alexander's other successors were not the only claimants to the territories of the old Persian Empire. In the steppes east of the Caspian Sea, where there is abundant seasonal pasturage for nomads, a new royal house arose in the third century B.C.E. This dynasty traced its origins to Arsaces, a charismatic Iranian leader, who in 238 B.C.E. seized control of the former Persian satrapy called Parthia. The nomadic peoples of Central Asia had no well-defined tradition of kingship. Instead, they recognized heads of families and a leader (*khan*) in time of war. The Parthians chose now to follow a Hellenistic model for kingship, later venerating Arsaces as a deified ruler somewhat akin to the way the deified Alexander was honored. And just as the Seleucid rulers numbered their regnal years from the beginning of the reign of Seleucus I Nikator, so the Parthian era reckoned continuously from the fixed date of the apotheosis of Arsaces.[40]

Even as they imitated the Seleucids, the early Parthian rulers expanded their realm at their expense, establishing a compact, powerful kingdom that essentially lay beyond the reach of Seleucid arms, despite temporary incursions. But the Parthians, in common with most rulers of the region from ancient to modern times, found greater Iran a challenging land to conquer and govern, in part because of the distinctive geography of the plateau, whose central area is largely desert. As a result, settled life tends to cluster in towns and cities rimming the edge, while nomads freely crisscross the rest of the country. The other nomadic peoples of the region proved difficult to subdue, unless surprised in their summer hillside pastures, where they had less mobility than in the winter, when they could move rapidly across flatter terrain to evade direct assault. We also see, time and again, that the steppes east of the Caspian and the pasturelands between the Syr Darya and Amu Darya rivers were the pressure points for peoples, such as the Scyths, forced west by developments as far east as China.

The Parthians eventually learned to manage their territory by seeking the allegiance of local chieftains and by building fortress cities at key locations. These cities were often circular for optimal defense, surrounded by massive walls that nomads lacking heavy siege equipment could scarcely hope to penetrate. Parthian military strategy was based on using elite units of archers on horseback, trained from boyhood in the equestrian arts and marksmanship. The Parthian bow, accurate to a distance of about 200 meters, with a drawing pressure of 30 kilograms, could readily pierce shields and armor. The archers were famous for the so-called Parthian shot, discharged at a gallop while pivoting backwards in the saddle, a feat requiring exceptional prowess, seen first in Assyrian hunting reliefs.[41] The mounted troops were supported by tactical units of heavily armed infantry. Their combined attacks could only be met in kind, but neither the Seleucid phalanx nor the Roman legion could do so.

The strength of Parthia was also its weakness, a situation similar to what had plagued the Persian Empire. The leading families, such as the Suren, commanded large forces of loyal troops, were proud of their lineage, and often asserted their own claims to kingship or served as king-makers. Even if they held the subordinate title of provincial governor, they reigned and acted nearly as sovereigns. The Roman historian Plutarch described the entourage of one scion of the Suren family as follows:

> Whenever he traveled privately, he had one thousand camels to carry his baggage, two hundred chariots for his concubines, one thousand completely armed men for his lifeguards, and a great many more light-armed; and he had at least ten thousand horsemen altogether, of his servants and retinue.[42]

Many of these men, like the knights of medieval Europe, may have thought of little beyond the arts of riding and war and the intense joys of life between battles. The Parthian kings could control them only by force and guile, playing them off against each other with an elaborate network of land grants, patronage, and intermarriage, as well as affording them sufficient outlets for their warlike energies. Thus the Parthians often ruled more as a confederation than as a monolithic state.[43]

Mithridates I and the Reunification of Iraq

Mithridates I (171–138 B.C.E.) transformed the Parthian kingdom into an empire. Making peace with the Greek king of Bactria, who ceded him the fortress of Merv in exchange for his support against the Scyths, Mithridates was ready to face his enemy in the west, Antiochus IV Epiphanes (175–164 B.C.E).

This Seleucid king had invaded Ptolemaic Egypt in 169–168 B.C.E., but was met by a Roman senatorial delegation that demanded his immediate withdrawal, primarily because Rome was becoming dependent upon Egypt for grain. According to the Greek historian Polybius, a fascinated eyewitness to the creation of the Roman Empire, the head of the Roman group

> drew a circle around Antiochus and told him to give his reply to the message before he stepped out of that circle. The king was astounded by the arrogance of this action and hesitated for a short time and said he would do everything the Romans asked.[44]

On the brink of at last fulfilling the Seleucid hope of regaining Alexander's kingdom in Egypt, Antiochus found his triumph snatched away. This was the moment the small Jewish state at Jerusalem chose to rebel against him; it paid heavily for its temerity and timing, for Antiochus vented his fury and frustration on the Jews and sought to obliterate their kingdom and religion. Some of his subjects thought him a madman, calling him Epimanes (insane) instead of Epiphanes (illustrious). Antiochus next turned on Elam, seeking wealth from its rich temples. On his return to Seleucia, he died mysteriously, said to have fallen from his chariot in a fit.[45]

Seeing his unexpected chance, Mithridates invaded Media, seized Ecbatana, then pushed across Assyria to Arbela, where Alexander had once defeated Darius. From there it was an easy march south on the same route Cyrus had taken to Babylon, to lay siege to Seleucia. He entered the city in triumph in 141, receiving delegations from Babylon, Uruk, and Assur, all hailing him as a liberator. Like Cyrus, he was a benevolent conqueror, taking pains to spare Seleucia and the other cities of Babylonia from looting.[46]

Across the Tigris from Seleucia, the Parthian court and army set up a large circular encampment that was to become Ctesiphon, the winter capital of the new Parthian Empire.[47] Its days of nomadic, tribal federation behind it, the Parthian state now included important urban centers, such as Seleucia, which had a population of perhaps half a million. Mithridates encouraged the adoption of stone in preference to mud-brick, as well as the development of Parthian as a written language, using the Aramaic alphabet.[48]

He also created a professional standing army on the Persian model to replace the tribal levies on which his predecessors had depended, dividing it into platoons, companies, and brigades, based on multiples of ten men. Their impressive ensigns were windsocks that looked like writhing dragons as they were borne aloft into battle, and their troops charged to the heavy beat of drums, calculated to unnerve the enemy.[49] Elite soldiers, especially the archers, were given plots of land by the king in return for their service, and were obliged to swear an oath of fealty to him.[50]

From Iraq, Mithridates invaded Armenia, but his plans for further expansion were interrupted by another incursion of Scyths into Bactria and Afghanistan. The Seleucid king Demetrius II Nikator took advantage of the situation to invade Iraq from Syria. He managed to retake Seleucia, and continued into Media. There he was defeated and captured by a Parthian general in 139 B.C.E. Paraded through Seleucia in chains, Demetrius, the first of the successors of Alexander to be captured in battle, was then sent off to Mithridates, who treated him well and gave him one of his own daughters in marriage. In exchange, Demetrius was expected to oppose any rival claimants to the Seleucid throne. Meanwhile, Mithridates reasserted his authority in Iraq, expanding it to include the region of Charax (modern Shatt al-Arab and Basra).[51] With the head of the Gulf under their control, the Parthians were ensured a route to the East, even if, as for the moment was the case, the Scythians were blocking the overland connections to India through Afghanistan. Iraq was once again a unified state, from Assyria to the Gulf. But in 138, as he mobilized for an invasion of Syria, Mithridates died, leaving a kingdom a hundred times larger than the one he had inherited.

Parthian Iraq

Under Parthian rule, many of the old Mesopotamian cities, among them Uruk, Nippur, Assur, and Nineveh, retained some importance, transformed into fortresses, trading centers, and provincial capitals. Parthian Babylon was a town of about 20,000 inhabitants, perhaps a third of its population a few centuries earlier, but still a substantial urban agglomeration, with an active religious center and a renovated theater, at the heart of an empire stretching from the Euphrates to Afghanistan.[52]

The Parthian kingdom lay astride the international land and sea networks that brought to the Roman and other western markets some of their most prized and expensive commodities, above all silk. It was much in the Parthian interest to promote this lucrative trade by providing security and way stations, particularly in northern Iran on the caravan route known as the Silk Road, exacting tolls and fees in the process. In the late first century B.C.E., the geographer Isidore of Charax wrote *Journey Around Parthia*, an account of the overland itinerary from Antioch to India via Afghanistan, summarized in his *Parthian Stations*, an annotated list of the caravanserais along the way and the distances between them. In his Mesopotamian sections, he notes such curiosities as the canal of Semiramis and a rock dam on the Euphrates, and he describes pearl diving at Bahrein in the Gulf, alluded to in Babylonian tradition where Gilgamesh brings up the plant of rejuvenation from the ocean floor (chapter 5).[53]

The secret of silk, the Chinese miracle fiber, was unknown in the Mediterranean and would remain so until the mid-sixth century C.E., thus giving the Parthians a monopoly on its trade. The Chinese for their part were curious about this market that brought such a flood of specie into China. In the early first century B.C.E., a Chinese delegation made the long journey westward, only to be discouraged by the Parthians on the pretext that continuing from Babylonia to Roman territory was accomplished only with great difficulty. To maintain cordial relations, the Parthians sent embassies of their own to China with exotic gifts, among them ostrich eggs and jugglers of astounding skill.[54] These niceties aside, the Parthians had deliberately misled the Chinese: in fact they had free access to the extensive transportation network across the Syrian desert, for which experienced guides and armed escorts were available in such caravan cities as Palmyra and Hatra.

Built originally as a fortress and religious center, Hatra's 6 kilometers of walls, studded with over 160 square towers, would enable it to withstand sieges by the Roman emperors Trajan and Septimius Severus.[55] In figure 20, we see the remains of the central temple complex, which included a pedimental temple of classical

Figure 20. Temple complex, Hatra. (Dominique Collon photograph.) *The first systematic excavations at Hatra were carried out beginning in the 1950s by Iraqi archaeologists, who also undertook considerable architectural restoration work. Important sculptures were removed to the museums in Mosul and Baghdad, while others remained at the site. In April 2003, many of the statues were decapitated so that the heads might be sold on the antiquities market. Explosive ordnance disposal in the area by American occupation forces has caused additional damage to the ruins.*

design, reflecting the Parthians' idiosyncratic embrace of Greek and Roman cultural elements. They also minted coins in Hellenistic style, on which they sometimes called themselves philhellenes, or "lovers of all things Greek."[56]

Parthian art also developed in more independent directions. To the right in figure 20 is the temple dedicated to the sun god Shamash, with large and small examples of the Parthian architectural feature called the *iwan*, a vaulted hall open at one end. The world's first use of the arch, dating to about 6000 B.C.E., is attested at the Mesopotamian site of Umm Dabaghiyah, which was probably a center for hunting onagers.[57] The first known vault comes from the fourth-millennium site of Tepe Gawra, with notable subsequent examples found in the early third-millennium round building at Tell Razuk, and in various late third- and early second-millennium structures at Tell al-Rimah (Qattara), with a certain continuity of tradition over the next two thousand years.[58] It was the Parthians' vaulted enclosure of interior space on a dramatic, monumental scale that was new. In later Islamic architecture, the iwan survives in a wide range of contexts, particularly in the mosques of Iran, Afghanistan, and Central Asia.

In addition to the iwan and the liberal use of creative polychrome stucco work, a third major innovation was the rendering of the human form in full frontal mode. Previously, Mesopotamian relief, glyptic, and painting nearly always presented profile or frontal heads, frontal torsos, and profile legs. Now the whole figure faced the viewer, with the feet splayed to either side. The pictorial effect is twofold. On the one hand, the viewer communicates directly with the image, setting up a potentially powerful exchange on a personal level. On the other hand, narrative is diminished, since the figures can no longer interact as readily with each other or their environment. Full frontality spread westward through Syria and Armenia and was adopted in Roman, early Christian, and Byzantine art, for it perfectly served the iconographic needs of both empire and Christianity.[59]

The equestrian and nomadic traditions of the Parthians influenced many aspects of their material culture. Male dress, a V-necked tunic worn over chap-like trousers and leggings, had its origin in riding apparel. One Roman historian quipped that the Parthians were so fond of riding that they even took their meals on horseback, by preference.[60] Long after the Parthians were settled, much attention was still lavished on portable items typical of nomadic culture, such as pins, buckles, belts, and hair ornaments, which were often inlaid with semiprecious stones in striking color combinations. At Hatra, votive statues, most of them representing wealthy merchants, their wives, and priests, stood in the temples, bedecked in a manner evocative of the Parthians' nomadic origins.[61]

We have almost no direct knowledge of Parthian literature, largely because it was transmitted orally by minstrels and survives only in much later retellings and translations. The romance of *Vis and Ramin,* for example, originated in the Parthian period, but has come down to us in a mid-eleventh-century Persian poem and a Georgian translation. Vis, the heroine, was promised before birth to Mobad the king, who had been smitten by her married mother. Sent to the king's court to be raised, she falls in love with Ramin, Mobad's brother. Their passion brings sorrow to all around them, but the two remain steadfast to each other through numerous tribulations, outwitting and outliving their enemies.[62]

The Babylonian Tree, another work of Parthian literature, is a debate between a date palm and a goat, reminiscent of similar Sumerian and Akkadian compositions (see chapter 4). The date palm tells the goat:

> I am superior to you in many kinds of things, . . .
> They make pegs of me which hang you upside down,
> I am fuel for fires which roast you terribly. . . .

In rebuttal, "like one who scatters pearls before sows and boars," the goat sings its own praises:

> The Mazdeans perform ablutions on my skin, . . .
> Harp and vina and lyre and flute and zither,
> Everything they play they sound upon me. . . .

With such "golden speech," the goat wins the contest.[63]

Roman Armies in Iraq

With Pompey's march into Palestine in 62 B.C.E., Rome definitively entered the Middle East. Over the preceding two centuries, Rome had gradually expanded eastward, from Italy into Macedon and Greece. During the Punic wars against Carthage in the western Mediterranean, the Romans had viewed the Seleucid kingdom as distant and invulnerable. Then the Carthaginian leader Hannibal journeyed to the Seleucid court to warn Antiochus III the Great (222–187 B.C.E.) of the serious danger posed by Rome. The Seleucids were thereupon added to the Romans' enemy list, a situation aggravated when they allied with Macedon against Rome. The decisive Roman defeat of Antiochus the Great at Magnesia in Turkey in 196 B.C.E. shattered the Seleucids' aura of invincibility, which had been fostered by their vast army and their terror weapon of trained elephants. A prodigious indemnity laid on the Seleucid kingdom went far toward destroying its economy, and cost Antiochus his life when he tried to loot an Iranian temple to pay it.[64]

By the end of the second century, the weakness of the Seleucid dynasty left Rome and Parthia in direct confrontation across the Euphrates, each with a strategic and economic interest in greater Syria, but each lacking the means to eliminate the other, their centers of power lying too far apart. To Roman authors, admirers of the heavy-handed, centralized, professional Roman provincial administration, the Parthian state seemed loose and disorganized, and the Parthian royal house appeared inconsistent of purpose, treacherous, and liable to conspiracies and revolutions:

> They are rather crafty than courageous, and to be feared only at long range. They are given to empty words, and talk madly and extravagantly. They are boastful, harsh and offensive, threatening in adversity and prosperity alike, crafty, haughty, cruel. . . .[65]

The Romans were to gain a healthy respect for Parthian military prowess, but little for their staying power, which lacked the tenacity of Rome's. Rapid Parthian conquests in Syria, for example, were followed by baffling withdrawals nearly as swift. But because we owe most of our knowledge of this period to biased Roman historians and military men, it is difficult to gain a true understanding of the Parthians' tactical and political thinking.

Some Romans imagined themselves latter-day Alexanders and dreamed of defeating the Parthians, as Alexander had defeated the Persians. The most tragic of these was a rich man, Crassus, who raised a Roman army and rashly invaded Parthian domains in 53 B.C.E., with visions of becoming a military hero. The Parthians were at first incredulous at his venture and hoped terms could be reached, but when his determination became clear, he was lured into a trap that allowed the Parthian archers to decimate the hapless Roman troops with showers of arrows. Crassus and his son were among the casualties, and Crassus's severed head was used as a prop in a performance of *The Bacchae* staged in Greek before the

Parthian king, Orodes II, and the king of Armenia. As for the victorious Parthian general, he was executed by Orodes, lest his stunning victory make him a rival for the throne.[66]

A small band of survivors was led back to Rome by Cassius, later renowned as one of the assassins of Julius Caesar. The disaster weighed heavily on the Romans, who thereafter deemed the Parthians their archenemies, though Crassus had been the aggressor. The Roman poet Horace exhorted his countrymen to "become the scourge of the wild Parthians," fanning an ideology of revenge.[67] Decades of diplomatic efforts finally succeeded during the reign of Augustus in freeing the captured Roman standards from Parthian hands. Their recovery was hailed in Rome as a triumph, and appears as the central image of the decorated cuirass Augustus wears in his Prima Porta statue.[68]

In the centuries that followed, the Syrian frontier seesawed back and forth, with successive Parthian and Roman victories and defeats. The once populous and productive Euphrates Valley became a grim wasteland of battlefields, military installations, and devastation. The Romans obstinately persisted, though their sieges of Hatra were failures. The high points of their efforts were Trajan's brief occupation of Ctesiphon from 114 to 117 C.E. and Marcus Aurelius's destruction of Seleucia in 165 C.E. Hailed by some as liberators, resisted by others as new tyrants, the Romans for their part saw Babylonia as an outpost of empire, deeming Armenia, not Mesopotamia, the key to controlling the Middle East.[69]

The End of Mesopotamian Civilization

Sometime during these first centuries of the Christian era, perhaps in the brutal campaign of Marcus Aurelius, a Roman soldier may have killed the last person who could read and write cuneiform.[70] The latest datable cuneiform tablets are astronomical diaries:

> Month 10 [75 C.E.], the 1st of which will follow the 29th of the previous month. Jupiter, Venus, and Saturn in Sagittarius, Mars in Libra. On the 14th, Mercury will be visible for the first time in the east of Capricorn. On the 14th,

moonset after sunrise. On the 19th, Jupiter will reach Capricorn. On the 26th, Mars will reach Scorpion. On the 28th, last lunar visibility before sunrise.[71]

We may take these texts as the effective terminus of Mesopotamian civilization, after well over three thousand years. The ancient cities were mostly in ruins, with the occasional Parthian fortification atop the debris. This is not to say that Mesopotamian civilization left no legacy. We see its survival in many contexts down to the present day—from literature and metaphor to geometry and astronomy, from cultic and magical practices to art and iconography.[72]

In the third century of the Christian era, a civil war between rival Parthian claimants to the throne weakened the central government so gravely that history could repeat itself in the old heartland of the Persian Empire. Near Persepolis, a Parthian governor named Ardashir deposed the king and in 224 founded a new dynasty that would rule the region for the next four hundred years.

10. Sassanian Iraq

There are five appointed temples of idol-worship.
They are the Temple of Bel in Babylon,
    the Temple of Nebo in Borsippa, . . .
What is meant by saying that these temples
    are appointed? . . . Regularly, all the year round,
    worship is taking place in them.

Babylonian Talmud

The Sassanian Empire and Religious Pluralism

The Sassanian dynasty faced many of the challenges the Parthians had, especially how to defend the eastern frontier from nomadic incursions and how to maintain the western frontier against an implacable Rome. And as with the Parthians, we have a dearth of surviving native records, chronicles, significant historical inscriptions, and works of literature. So again, our views are colored by Roman and other contemporaneous authors, as well as by later Iranian tradition, notably the *Shah-namah*, or *Book of Kings*, a Persian narrative poem in 60,000 rhymed couplets completed by Firdawsi in 1010. In his final section, after dismissing the Parthians in twenty couplets, the poet treats the Sassanians. Though he drew his material from authentic sources, now lost, the historicity of the *Shah-namah* is secondary to its literary qualities.[1]

The Sassanians rose to power in the ancient Persian heartland, but knew almost nothing of the Persian Empire, instead ascribing their origins to mythical Iranian kings of the distant past and claiming descent from a certain Sassan, who may have lived during the the mid-third century B.C.E., and who may in fact have been related to the Persian royal family.[2] They professed to disdain their Parthian predecessors as mere factional rulers or worse, as in this passage from a Sassanian treatise on government called the *Letter of Tansar*:

> Four hundred years had passed in which the world was filled with wild and savage beasts and devils in human form, without religion or decency, learning or wisdom or shame. They were a people who brought nothing but desolation and corruption to the world; cities became deserts, and buildings were razed.[3]

Notwithstanding their rhetoric, the Sassanians built upon the Parthians' achievements, established their capital at Ctesiphon, and likewise placed Iraq at the center of a strategy to found a single state throughout Western Asia. The first Sassanian ruler, Ardashir (224–241), was crowned at Ctesiphon (though the *Shahnamah* puts the coronation at Babylon). The great iwan that probably served as audience hall and throne room of the Sassanian kings still stands today, its vault soaring more than 30 meters, poignant remains with little trace of the gardens, palaces, and bustling walled city that once surrounded it.[4] Later Arabic verse often drew inspiration from the ruins of Ctesiphon; here is a modern Iraqi poet's apostrophe to the iwan:

> Despite the nights, the envious nights,
> Your immortality indeed transcends death,
> Defying through the ages any slap of obliteration's hand,
> Though time itself had raised the threatening arm.
> Time you withstood, firm as a towering peak,
> With stalwart strength a valiant warrior would wish were at
> his side![5]

Through forceful campaigning and building key fortress cities, the ablest of the Sassanian monarchs effectively controlled the

Iranian plateau, the steppe as far as the Syr Darya River, and Afghanistan as far as Herat. Constant pressures on the periphery of the region, however, meant that few Sassanian rulers had a free hand to achieve any lasting advances against Rome. Tensions escalated after the emperor Constantine moved his capital to Constantinople in 312, for the Roman Empire's increasingly tenuous hold over Italy, North Africa, and southwestern Spain strengthened its determination in Syria and Egypt, the most important of its remaining provinces.[6]

Moreover, the Christianization of the Roman state, starting in earnest with the conversion of Constantine and the establishment of Constantinople as a purely Christian city, elevated the status of cities such as Jerusalem and Antioch, which had historical associations with the origins and spread of Christianity. There, as elsewhere in the Empire, splendid basilicas were constructed, whose plans derived from the Roman tripartite halls of justice, with their apse and columned aisles. Lavish royal patronage of the Christian church not only showed off the emperor's wealth and power, but also served to identify Christianity more closely with Roman government. In its settings and iconography, Christianity became ever more imperial. Indeed, from the fourth century on, the Roman Empire presented itself as the temporal kingdom of God on earth, the emperor the image or shadow of God to his subjects. All Christians, even those not under his direct rule, owed him fealty.[7]

These developments and their implications were not lost on the Sassanian sovereigns, but the religious situation in their own domains was more complex. The best candidate for an official religion, if the Sassanian Empire was to have one, was Zoroastrianism, which had long enjoyed state patronage and was based on the teachings of a prophet and religious reformer named Zoroaster (Persian Zarathustra).[8] He gave strong moral content to Iranian religion, which had previously been focused on forces of nature, for he taught that people should think, speak, and do good, as well as perform certain rites of purification. In Zoroastrian belief, fire and water were sacred. The universe was a battleground between gods of goodness, whose leader was Ahura-Mazda (Ormazd), who would ultimately prevail, and forces of evil, led by Ahriman.

Zoroastrian theology shows influences of Babylonian tradition in its elaborate chronological schemes of cosmic history.[9]

According to Zoroastrian doctrine, the prophet lived during the seventh century B.C.E., and his teachings and poetry were collected after his death in a scripture called the Avesta. He may in fact have lived up to a thousand years earlier, since parts of the Avesta are written in an ancient Iranian language known as Zend Avestan, which by Sassanian times was difficult to understand.[10] Zoroastrians therefore relied on a class of priests, referred to as magi, to convey and interpret belief and ritual. The magi were virtually a separate class in society, though Sassanian statecraft officially saw the religious establishment and the state as mutually dependent: "Church and State were born of the one womb, joined together and never to be sundered."[11]

At the same time, many Sassanian subjects were not Zoroastrians, but Jews and Christians (see below, this chapter). Some Arab tribes in the Euphrates Valley were Christians, others revered Venus as the morning and evening star, a male deity they called Allah (God), and his consort Allat (Goddess).[12] Still other people of the realm worshipped traditional Mesopotamian deities, such as Hadad and Dagan, the thunder and storm gods; Sin, the moon god; and Shamash, the sun god.[13] There were practitioners of Iranian cults that had not been drawn into Zoroastrianism, as well as adherents to various Gnostic faiths and mystery religions, to Manichaeism, to the cult of Mithra, and to assorted pagan deities of the Mediterranean world, such as the Greek hero-god Herakles (Roman Hercules).

The Gnostics, such as the Mandaeans of southern Iraq, taught that a person could achieve salvation through esoteric knowledge of divine things, rather than through specific deeds or faith alone. This knowledge, they believed, had been vouchsafed to the human race through a hierarchy of divine beings emanating from a supreme, unknowable deity, and was set down in writings the uninitiated could not understand. Using teachers or adepts, people might work their way through various stages toward ever higher, more esoteric knowledge of the divinity. The Mandaeans, whose doctrines include late Babylonian elements, particularly venerated John the Baptist and recognized Jesus and other divine figures as emanations from the unknowable deity. Their rites centered on baptism in flowing water.[14]

The teachings of the prophet Mani, born in 216 in Babylonia, drew on Christianity by revering Jesus; on Zoroastrianism by portraying the universe as dominated by a struggle between good and evil; and on Gnosticism by establishing a hierarchy of believers, of whom the elect were assured of a happy afterlife. The elect lived a life of austerity, forgoing marriage and sensual pleasures, whereas laymen could marry and hope to be reborn after death, as elect. Manichaeism was preached by missionaries throughout the Roman and Sassanian Empires, but was persecuted by both the Zoroastrian and Christian churches. Protected by Shapur I, Mani died in prison in the reign of his successor, Bahram I. The faith persisted into the early sixth century and was incorporated into the beliefs of certain sects of the Middle Ages, such as the Bogomils, the Paulicians, and the Albigensians.[15]

The cult of Mithra had spread widely from Mesopotamia to Europe in the ranks of the Roman army, because its teachings emphasized such soldierly values as courage, perseverance, and valor. Its impressive ceremonies were held, with music and incense, in chapels called Mithraeums, often richly decorated with wall paintings showing the god Mithra slaying a bull or performing some other heroic deed. The initiation rites were frightening tests of bravery. To some adherents of this faith, Mithra appeared a kind of savior god who could bring believers safely through the trials and ordeals of their lives.[16]

A consequence of the Christian Roman Empire's increasing religious intolerance was the widespread purge of paganism, from the banning of rites to the closing and despoiling of temples. Paganism lingered on, however, especially in rural areas, among families who were determined to keep up the worship of the old Greek and Roman gods, and among philosophers who believed that no single book, such as a scripture, or set of beliefs, should be privileged and sanctioned as the only correct way of thinking.[17] When the emperor Justinian (527–565) passed a law that no one "infected with the madness of the unholy Hellenes" could teach, this led to the final disbanding of the school of philosophy at Athens, where Plato and Aristotle had lectured. Some of the faculty, including the philosopher Damascius, last head of the school, moved to the Sassanian Empire rather than subject themselves to Orthodox Christianity, and the Sassanian king Chosroes I (531–579) allowed them to resume their teaching.[18] Using Greek philosophical constructs, Damascius produced a book, *On First Beginnings*, in which he tries to explain the generations of the gods in the Babylonian *Creation Epic*:

> Among the barbarians, the Babylonians seem to be silent on the one principle of the universe and pose two principles, Tauthe [Tiamat] and Apason [Apsu], considering Apason as the husband of Tauthe, whom they call the mother of the gods. From Apason and Tauthe has been engendered, they say, an only child, Mooumis [Mummu], who is, I think, the intelligible world proceeding from these two principles. . . . Finally, . . . a son was born, Belos [Marduk], who, they say, is the maker of the world, the demiurge.[19]

By the Waters of Babylon: Judaism in Iraq

The Babylonian king Nebuchadnezzar II had followed the Assyrian practice of deporting defeated peoples. In 597 and 586 B.C.E., large numbers of Jews of all classes arrived in Iraq after his sack of Jerusalem and destruction of the Temple (see chapter 8). According to the prophet Jeremiah, God exhorted them not to pine in exile:

> Build homes and settle down. Plant gardens and eat their produce. Marry and beget sons and daughters, in order that you may increase in number rather than decrease. Seek the welfare of the country to which I have deported you, and pray on its behalf to God, for on its welfare your own depends.[20]

Little is known of the Jewish community under Babylonian rule, beyond a few private legal documents and administrative accounts recording issues of food to the former royal family.[21]

In 516 B.C.E., Cyrus the Great permitted Jews to return to Palestine if they so desired. Many accepted the offer, among other reasons to rebuild the Temple in Jerusalem; others preferred to stay in Babylonia, where they lived as subjects of the Persian and Seleucid kings. Aramaic and Hebrew literature tells of some Jews enjoying high positions at court, such as Esther (Hebrew Hadassah), the queen of Ahasuerus (Persian Xerxes). Most of the surviving Jewish historical sources, however, focus not on Babylonia but on events in Palestine and Jerusalem, culminating bitterly in the destruction of the city and its second Temple by the Romans in 70 C.E.[22]

The imposition of Roman rule over Palestine, the disintegration of the Seleucid state, and the incorporation of Babylonia and Assyria into the Parthian Empire meant that by the end of the first century a hostile border separated the Mesopotamian from the Palestinian Jews. Within the often loose administrative structure of the Parthian state, the Jewish communities in Mesopotamia became self-governing, under the leadership of rabbis learned in Jewish law and scholarship. In Babylonia, an official called the exilarch represented the community to their Parthian overlords. As productive, loyal peasants and merchants, the Jews experienced little interference with their affairs, sharing with the Parthians a detestation of Rome.[23]

With the Christianization of the Roman world, the gulf between Mesopotamia and Palestine widened, though the Jewish communities managed to keep in contact through scholars traveling back and forth between them. Babylonian Jews came to view their Judaism as purer than Palestinian Judaism, which had absorbed much Greco-Roman influence, whereas Parthian culture had had little or no impact.[24]

The rise of the Sassanian Empire affected the Jews both directly and indirectly. The intensified border wars with Rome ultimately led to the decimation of the large Jewish community in the upper Euphrates region, whose vitality may be gauged from the brilliantly painted synagogue at Dura Europas, a Roman garrison town near the frontier. In Babylonia, royal patronage of Zoroastrianism brought increased interference with Jewish life. Zoroastrian extremists insisted that the Jews expose rather than bury their dead, contrary to Jewish observance, and they objected to the use of fire in Jewish ceremonies, such as in lighting candles for

Passover. At the same time, under Sassanian centralization the Jews were no longer self-governing. The Sassanian kings, however, with a few exceptions, preferred to treat the prosperous and law-abiding Jewish community well, for, like the Parthians before them, they had in common a hatred of the Christian Roman Empire.[25]

The major legacy of the Sassanian Jewish community was the Babylonian Talmud, next to the Hebrew Bible the most important surviving body of Jewish writing. Written in Judeo-Aramaic and drawn from many sources, it consists of legal and ritual discussions, ethics, morals, magic, medicine, polemics, fables, stories, dream analysis, and scriptural commentary. The Talmud was probably compiled by teachers and sages for their colleagues, including those working in the Jewish academies (*yeshivot*) that began to develop in Babylonia during this period and would continue to flourish for centuries in Baghdad.[26]

The principal artifacts of Jewish life in Parthian and Sassanian Iraq are clay bowls with magic spells usually inked inside them in concentric spirals. Hundreds have been found at Nippur and other sites, buried upside down in private houses, often under thresholds. The spells addressed demons to prevent them from harming the family that lived there: "Go out in the form of birds who fly and go out and move from one place to another . . . like wax that melts in the fire—run away!"[27] Some bowls curse specific people and may have been hidden near their houses to harm them. Occasionally, there are crude drawings of demons, more rarely of the magicians themselves brandishing implements used in exorcism. Though most bowls are written in Judeo-Aramaic, some are written in Syriac, Mandaic, or Middle Persian, and a few in meaningless scribbles, perhaps passed off on illiterate buyers. Jewish magicians were evidently highly regarded, consulted by Jewish as well as Christian, Mandaean, and Persian clients.[28] So esteemed was Aramaic as a language of magic and mystery that one Greek philosopher of the fourth century considered it to be preferred by the gods, even more so than Greek:

As the gods have taught us, that the language of sacred peoples, such as the Assyrians and Egyptians, is appropriate for sacred rites, we believe that we should address the gods in the language that is congenial to them.[29]

Christianity in Iraq

The beginnings of Christianity in Iraq are shrouded in legend. Some communities attributed their initial conversion to the apostle Thomas, who was said to have journeyed through Iraq on his way to India.[30] In any case, Christianity was well established by the end of the first century, especially in cities and towns along the Tigris, including Assur (Christian Athor) and Arbela (Christian Adiabene). Whereas theologians in Rome and Constantinople might have seen uniformity of doctrine in the Middle East, Christian writers in Syria and Iraq saw diversity, distinguishing four main groups: the church of Syria (Beth Romaye), with its bishopric at Antioch; that of Assyria and Babylonia (Beth Aramaye), with its bishopric at Ctesiphon; the Christian Arabs of the mid-Euphrates region (Beth Arabaye); and the church in Iran (Beth Parsaye). These four groups held different beliefs and rites and spoke different languages, but by the fifth century they shared a Bible and liturgy in Syriac. This was a dialect of Aramaic spoken by Christians, which spread west of the Euphrates during the fourth century, gradually replacing both Greek and Latin in church usage in Syria and Palestine.[31]

The major reason for division among the Christian churches was dissension concerning the nature of Jesus, whether at his birth he was a human being or God, and whether or not his divine and human natures were divided or united. When one spoke of Jesus as the son of God, did that mean that Jesus was younger and subordinate to God? When one spoke of his being born of Mary in time and place, did that mean that he was human or partly human, thus imperfect and inferior to God? If he was purely divine, did his bodily suffering and earthly mission lose their immediacy? How could almighty God have been born of a woman and crucified? Successive church councils, the most important held at Nicaea in 325, Chalcedon in 410, Ephesus in 431, and Constantinople in 553, at none of which the churches of Iraq were represented, defined the Orthodox position on these matters: Jesus had both a human and a divine nature, inseparably joined in one person of one divine substance. Significant numbers of Christians, belonging to ancient and well-established Christian communities, especially in the Middle East, insisted that Jesus had but one nature, in which the human was absorbed by the divine. These Christians, called Monophysites, were condemned as heretics by the Orthodox church.[32]

Although Orthodoxy was strong among the Greek-speaking population along the Levantine coast, once one crossed the mountains, the East and West Syrian churches, the Christian Arabs, and the Iranian church tended to reject Orthodoxy, though with doctrinal disputes among themselves. In Egypt, many native non-Greeks belonged to the Monophysite Coptic church, which dated to the earliest Christianization of Egypt in the second century, and in Armenia, converted to Christianity in 301 by Gregory the Illuminator, a native of Edessa in Syria, an independent Monophysite church was formed in 551.[33]

A Syrian priest, Nestorius, a deeply religious man who was appointed patriarch of Constantinople in 428, taught that Jesus had been born as a human being, not as God, so it was wrong to call Mary "the Mother of God," as was done in the Orthodox church. He attracted many followers, but was condemned as a heretic in 431 and died of exposure in exile in the Egyptian desert. Many of his followers, referred to as Nestorians, fled to Sassanian territory, including Iraq, where they were allowed to practice their faith mostly unmolested. By the end of the sixth century, Christians in Iraq were considered Nestorian in doctrine because they followed his teaching about the Virgin Mary. Their rite was referred to as East Syrian or Chaldean; their church was sometimes called Assyrian, the name often used in modern times; and their church leadership was appointed by the Sassanian monarch. Other adherents to the East Syrian rite in Iraq, called the Chaldean Catholics, separated from the Assyrian Church, and since the sixteenth century have recognized the primacy of the pope.[34] In the mid-sixth century, Jacob Bardaeus, bishop of Edessa, revitalized the West Syrian Monophysite church, and his followers, referred to as Jacobites, spread his teachings into Iraq, treating the Assyrian church as heretical.[35]

As a result of these developments, the Christians of Iraq were increasingly divided from both the Orthodox church at Constantinople and the West Syrian church at Antioch. Compared to the West Syrian church, the Christian communities in Iraq produced fewer historians and theologians. The best known of these was Tatian (ca. 150), who wrote the earliest life of Jesus by combining the evidence of the four gospel accounts of the New Testament into one narrative.[36] Under some Sassanian rulers, the Zoroastrian church persecuted Christians without making distinctions, charging them with polluting fire, water, and the dead, and with blasphemy for claiming that God had created both good and evil.[37]

Sassanian Society, Statecraft, and Economy

Sassanian society crystallized into three classes: the priesthood; the nobility, including the ruling families; and the remainder of the population, which was obliged to support the first two classes, who claimed "the power of life and death over slaves and commons," according to a Roman historian.[38] Much of the peasantry worked land that was not theirs, but possessed in suzerainty by nobles or warriors. To the third class also belonged pastoralists, nomads, and professionals, such as craftsmen, administrators, and merchants.

The Sassanian state was more centralized than the Parthian, with a departmentalized bureaucracy headed by a vizier, or trusted advisory minister.[39] Sassanian treatises on government survived well into the Middle Ages in Arabic and Persian translations, and were widely studied in the Muslim world.[40] They held that a strong state depended on a strong army, which in turn depended on a prosperous citizenry, ruled by a just elite:

> When people have become poor, the royal treasury remains empty, the soldier receives no pay and the kingdom is lost. . . . To have many children is fitting for the populace, but kings and nobles take pride in the smallness of their families. The hedgerow bird has a numerous brood but the falcon contents herself with a small one.[41]

The most energetic and effective of the Sassanian rulers recognized that sound fiscal policy was crucial. Accordingly, they sought to predict revenues, to collect them systematically, and to project budgets based upon them. Since the main revenues of the state came from agricultural production, royal agents compiled cadasters, or lists of arable lands, and the income due from them. The Sassanians preferred not to extract revenue directly from producers, but rather to rely on local headmen, notables, or squires to assume the responsibility for tax collection in their area, the amounts determined from well-informed projections made by the central administration. The systematization of this practice was a major innovation, though aspects of it were known previously. It would lay the foundation for administration and revenue collection in Islamic Iraq and Iran, as well as throughout the Ottoman Empire. Finally, there was the traditional patchwork of military fiefs granted directly to soldiers by the crown or a great prince, a pattern familiar already in the Babylonian and Persian periods.[42]

The Sassanian monarchs also encouraged land and sea commerce. The desert caravan trade continued to be supported by tolls and fees and protected by caravanserais, large enclosures situated at regular stages of the journey, where the caravan could be brought into safety, the animals stabled in the courtyard, and the people lodged in suites of rooms facing on the courtyard, a design not dissimilar to a modern motel. As the Parthians had found, it was essential to control the head of the Gulf. From there, it was only a step for the Sassanians to develop a maritime policy and to consider the possibility of trading posts or client groups in South Arabia.[43]

The Sassanians invested heavily in the development of the Iraqi alluvial plains, from massive irrigation works to resettlement schemes, stimulated by the presence of the capital at Ctesiphon. The old cities of Babylon, Borsippa, Nippur, and Uruk flourished. New urban centers were founded, among them Veh Ardashir, sited on the Tigris between Seleucia and Ctesiphon. Across the river was Aspanabr, home of the royal stables, parks, and palaces.[44] To decorate one of the complexes there, the Byzantine historian Procopius tells us, the emperor Justinian sent "craftsmen skilled in ceilings."[45] According to one enthusiastic writer, the crops of southern Iraq grew so luxuriantly "that a squirrel need never touch the ground between Ctesiphon and the Gulf."[46] Iraq seemed poised to regain her role as the crossroads of Western Asia.

Again, this was not to be. The Jezira region and Armenia became the principal battlegrounds between the two colossal empires of the time—the Roman/Byzantine versus the Sassanian. The economic loss, destruction, suffering, and depopulation brought about when either one of them resolved to renew hostilities against the other left the Euphrates Valley a forlorn remnant of what it had been, a no-man's-land, as Procopius called it.[47] Joshua the Stylite, writing near Edessa at the beginning of the sixth century, described violence, starvation, cannibalism, continuous warfare, and cruelty:

> For the Magister had thus commanded all the generals, that if any one of the Greeks [Byzantine soldiers] was found saving a male [in Sassanian territory] from twelve years old and upwards, he should be put to death in his stead; and whatsoever village they entered, that they should not leave a single house standing in it.[48]

Without close links with the north and west, long-term prosperity in Iraq was not possible, nor could it sustain a central position in a successful larger state.

Arab Settlement in Iraq

The depredations in the Euphrates Valley opened the way, beginning perhaps in the late fourth century, for an influx of Arabic-speaking peoples from Arabia.[49] Previous contact between Iraq and Arabia had mainly taken place via the caravan routes crossing the desert and heading south along the Gulf and Red Sea, probably ultimately connecting with the urban and agricultural regions of South Arabia. The Assyrians had garnered considerable plunder from their Arabian forays, and were struck by the fact that the tribesmen were sometimes led by queenly women.[50] We may also recall the prolonged residence of the Babylonian king Nabonidus at Teima (see chapter 8).

Already in the Hellenistic period, Arabs had settled in the southern Jordan Valley, and by Roman times they had gone from pastoralism to an exuberant urbanism, deriving prosperity from the caravan trade skirting the western coast of Arabia and passing through Mecca and Medina. Goods transported included precious and semiprecious stones, metals, and leather products, but the most prized commodities were frankincense and myrrh. Both are resins harvested from trees growing principally in Yemen and South Arabia, home of the "Happy Arabs," as the Romans called them. The remoteness of the sources, the rarity of the trees, and the perpetually high demand for incense in public and private rituals made frankincense and myrrh among the costliest materials of the ancient world.[51]

The Arabs in north and central Arabia were predominantly nomadic, organized into tribes and smaller groupings that gave the individual his identity, community, family, and social hierarchy.[52] Against their incursions, it was probably Shapur II who built a line of forts, walls, and moats in southwestern Iraq.[53] The most important cultural expressions of these Arabs were verse and oratory. Poets were highly esteemed; their work brought special honor to their tribes, and their greatest achievements were treasured by later generations.

Arabs had also moved into Syria, especially in the plain south of Damascus. The Byzantine rulers gave tribal leaders titles and paid them to police the frontier and the desert east of the Jordan River. One group of these, the Ghassanids, converted to Christianity and established a ruling dynasty.[54] The Sassanians likewise found good reason to encourage the development of small Arab principalities along the Euphrates to guard the border on their behalf. Some of these were also Christian. Hira, a city just south of modern Kufa in Iraq, became the seat of the Lakhmid Dynasty, an Arab state politically dependent on the Sassanians, and particularly noted as a center of Arab culture.[55]

The Hira poet Adi ibn Zaid personifies the cultural diversity of the mid-Euphrates Valley in the early seventh century. A Christian Arab, bilingual in Persian, he grew up at the Zoroastrian court of Chosroes I at Ctesiphon, visited Constantinople and Damascus, then returned to his native city, where he intrigued to make his pagan father-in-law, Numan, king. Later, Adi himself fell victim to a palace conspiracy and died in prison. To avenge the poet, Chosroes II had Numan trampled to death by elephants.[56] The surviving fragments of his verse often reflect on the transitory nature of human life and accomplishment. Here, he imagines the musings of a roadside graveyard:

> He who sees us should tell himself he's about to pass away,
> For even the silent mountains abide not time's passage, nor
>   what that brings.
> Many are the riders who have made their halt hard by us,
>   to drink their wine, thinning it with a splash of crystal.
> Their jugs were ready to mix more, their splendid steeds
>   were prancing proud in their traces,
> They spent their hour here in the joy of living,
> They too marked by us their time, without a sense of haste.
> But time presses forward those who enjoy their moment,
>   from that, their state of being, to the other.[57]

Although the Arabs living in the Jordan Valley and Syria had learned to write a form of Aramaic, and the South Arabians had their own language and writing system, the Arabs in North Arabia and Iraq experimented, perhaps as early as the third century, with writing their own language, Arabic, in a cursive version of the alphabetic script used for Aramaic. This was the ancestor of the present-day Arabic script, which, tradition has it, was first used at Hira, not far from where writing had begun, nearly four thousand years before.[58]

Sassanian Art

In the art of the Sassanian period, we see the beginnings of what we may consider the Mesopotamian legacy. A common Sassanian motif, for example, is the mythical *senmurv*, a feline or canine creature with a fanned peacock tail and wings ending in an upturned curl. This beast appears on gilded silver bowls, seals, and architectural elements, and especially woven into fine silk textiles. While the senmurv might have been an independent invention, the long-standing Mesopotamian proclivity for fantastic but organically credible composite beings, such as the human-headed winged bulls guarding the entrances to the Assyrian palaces (see figure 16) or the dragons on the Ishtar Gate at Babylon, strongly suggests some degree of cultural transmission and continuity, likely via Persian intermediaries.[59]

Sassanian imagery came in turn to influence Byzantine and Western European art. As pilgrims visited the Christian Holy Land of Palestine, they acquired relics whose canny purveyors often packaged them in Sassanian silks to promote their genuineness. The fabrics' intricate patterns, interlaced roundel designs, and exotic and composite creatures, among them the elephant and senmurv, inspired various aspects of Western iconography, particularly as they offered a way to lend biblical subjects or referents an aura of authenticity.[60]

Knotted textiles from the region were in universal demand, as they had been previously and would continue to be until the present day. Historians of the Muslim conquest described a spectacular carpet or wall-hanging in the palace at Ctesiphon called "The Springtime of King Chosroes," which depicted garden beds framed by watercourses, with the trees and flowers picked out in gold and silver threads, the paths strewn with seed-pearls, the shrubs bejeweled with precious stones, and the streams sparkling with blue gems. When the Arabs took the capital in 636, they are said to have cut the rug into small pieces, distributing the fragments as war booty. Complementing such garden carpets were formal palace gardens, no doubt laid out in the four-quadrant plan known as the *chahar bagh*, for which our earliest archaeological evidence comes from the Persian palaces.[61] Ctesiphon also boasted marble and glass mosaics, brilliantly colored stuccowork tiles made in molds, and other luxurious fittings.[62]

Sassanian royal self-presentation drew heavily on Persian imperial imagery, which itself had taken much from Assyrian modes. As the kings of old had been shown, Sassanian monarchs triumph in battle and kill lions and other noble quarry, often in Assyrian- and Persian-style hunting parks called *paridaiza*, or "paradise," from a Persian term meaning "surrounded by a wall." The rulers also loom large on rock reliefs, sometimes carved near those of

Mesopotamian and Persian kings. But because the Sassanians are usually depicted frontally, this tends to result in an awkward disjunction between the royal personage and his heroic actions.[63]

In figure 21, we have a stucco bust of Shapur II (309–379) or Bahram V (420–438), one of fourteen apparently made to decorate the courtyard columns of the Sassanian palace at Kish. Although we may recognize in his elaborately rendered coiffure the long-standing Mesopotamian interest in the details of kingly beards and hair, the heavy crenellated crown, supported perforce by the massive neck and shoulders, is purely Sassanian. Normally, at least one new crown type was designed for each king; that of Chosroes II (590–628) weighed so much that it had to be hung from a golden chain above the throne, the king easing his head into it when he was seated.[64]

Shapur I and Shapur II

Of the two dozen Sassanian monarchs, Shapur I (241–271) and Shapur II (309–379) stand out for their significant roles in shaping the empire. Shapur I, son of Ardashir, ruled for several years as coregent with his father before assuming sole kingship. The new dynasty's military and administrative strength allowed him to focus on foreign affairs. He moved first to secure the eastern frontier, prevailing from the Indus to Bactria. Then he turned his attention westward, defeating the Romans in decisive battles in Syria and Iraq. He also laid siege to Hatra, which no Roman army had been able to take, but which had now allied with Rome against the Sassanians.[65] According to a traditional Iranian story, the impregnable city was betrayed by its ruler's daughter, who had fallen in love with Shapur. At their wedding, Shapur ordered his bride executed for her ingratitude to her father.[66]

Three Roman emperors would challenge Shapur and lose. After the Roman emperor Gordion III was killed near Ctesiphon in 244, his successor Philip the Arab had to pay 500,000 pieces of gold to ransom the army, and he was forced to cede much of Syria and Armenia to Shapur, who moved on to conquer the key Roman cities of Dura Europas and Antioch. A Roman counterattack in

Figure 21. Royal bust from Kish, stucco, height 51 cm, Field Museum of Natural History, Chicago. (© 1986 The Field Museum, A109938c, photographer Ron Testa) *Excavations at Kish, a site occupied continuously from the Ubaid to the Sassanian periods, were undertaken from 1923 to 1933 by a joint Oxford-Field Museum expedition, with a share of the finds distributed among several museums in England and America. Work in the latest levels yielded contextual evidence for the reuse of antique artifacts and materials, such as a brick of Samsuiluna, Hammurabi's son and successor, a Kassite boundary stone, and a marble slab inscribed "Palace of Nebuchadnezzar." In the Iraq War, a small U.S. military base was established at Kish, with attendant damage to the site.*

260 led to defeat and humiliation when the emperor Valerian was captured in battle near Edessa.[67]

Shapur commemorated his victories over the Romans in rock reliefs showing the emperors meekly kneeling or prostrate before the mounted, triumphant Sassanian king, as well as in monumental inscriptions "so that he who comes after us will recognize these glorious and heroic deeds and our reign."[68] Not only did Shapur I embody the Sassanian ideal of the divine warrior-king riding to victory, he commissioned numerous architectural and engineering projects (some using captive Roman specialists), as well as translations of Greek and Indian works on astrology, agriculture, philosophy, natural sciences, and physics, prefiguring the Baghdad translation movement of the ninth century.[69]

The Sassanian Empire reached its zenith during the seventy-year reign of Shapur II. To regain territory lost since the time of Shapur I, the king embarked on a series of military campaigns that earned him a reputation for exceptional brutality. He was said to have used elephants to trample the ruins of Susa, to have filled the wells used by Arab tribes with sand, and to have tied prisoners of war together by puncturing their shoulders. His reign saw the persecution of Christians, Jews, and Manichaeans, detailed accounts of which survive in the *Acts of Martyrs* from Ctesiphon and other centers.[70]

Hostilities against Rome resumed after Shapur II broke the fragile peace that had existed for several decades. In a haughty letter to the Roman emperor Constantius, about 355, he demanded that Armenia be handed over to him:

> I, Shapur, King of Kings, partner with the Stars, brother of the Sun and Moon . . . shall state my proposal in brief terms, recalling that what I am about to say I have often repeated. That my forefathers' empire reached as far as . . . Macedonia even your own ancient records bear witness; these lands it is fitting that I should demand, since (and may what I say not seem arrogant) I surpass the kings of old in magnificence and array of conspicuous virtues. . . . Therefore it is my duty to recover Armenia with Mesopotamia, which double-dealing wrested from my grandfather. . . . If you

wish to follow my sound advice, disregard this small tract, always a source of woe and bloodshed, so that you may rule the rest in security, wisely recalling that even expert physicians sometimes cauterize, lance, and even cut away some parts of the body, in order to save the rest sound for use. . . .[71]

In 363, the emperor Julian marched from Antioch to attack Ctesiphon, where he was killed.[72] The Roman military officer and historian Ammianus Marcellinus was an eyewitness to what it was like to face the Sassanian army:

. . . near daybreak a huge force of Persians appeared . . . all the companies were clad in iron. . . . Some, who were armed with pikes, stood so motionless that you would think them held fast by clamps of bronze. Hard by, the archers (for that nation has especially trusted in this art from the very cradle) were bending their flexible bows. . . . Behind them the gleaming elephants, with their awful figure and savage, gaping mouths, could scarcely be endured by the faint-hearted; and their trumpeting, their odor, and their strange aspect alarmed the horses still more.[73]

The Romans retreated, abandoning most of central Syria to the Sassanians and turning a deaf ear to the desperate pleas of the Christian population for protection.

The Sassanians and Byzantium

We may choose two wars of the sixth and seventh centuries as emblems of the titanic struggles between the Sassanians and Byzantium. The first pitted Chosroes I Anushirvan (531–579) against Justinian (527–565). Both were hard-working, calculating rulers with visions of reigning supreme in the world. Justinian was convinced he could rebuild the ancient Roman Empire. To retake its old western provinces in Italy, Spain, and North Africa from the Goths and Vandals, who had occupied them for a century or more, Justinian secured at no small expense a peace treaty with the Sassanians on his eastern frontier. This gave him a free hand in Italy against the Goths, though the campaign proved slow and discouraging. But when the beleaguered king of the Ostrogoths sought an alliance with the Sassanians in 539, the temptation proved too much for Chosroes to resist, especially since there was unrest in Armenia and among the Arab princes at Hira.[74]

Sassanian forces then poured into Syria and laid siege to Antioch, third city of the Byzantine empire after Constantinople and Alexandria. The garrison fled, leaving the city to the mercy of the Sassanian army, and the defenseless populace was put to the sword. The brilliant city, famous for its wealth, love of luxury, sophistication, and comfort, was destroyed, block by block.[75]

Chosroes may have dreamed next of a siege of Constantinople, but the city seemed too strong to be taken by land and the Sassanians lacked any appreciable Mediterranean naval power. As he hesitated, a severe outbreak of the plague in Constantinople and Turkey claimed hundreds of thousands of lives before it ran its course. The war ended with Justinian's achievements in shambles, while Chosroes had gained vast spoils and prestige. Yet the map of Western Asia remained essentially as it had been before the war, because the Sassanians showed no signs of following up their victory in Syria with a long-term occupation.

The second of these wars, which pitted Chosroes II (591–628) against Heraclius (575–641), was perhaps the closest thing to a world war in antiquity. Chosroes seized a moment of weakness in Byzantium to launch a major onslaught, evidently designed to destroy the Christian state and to reestablish the Persian Empire. The campaign at first proceeded brilliantly. Syria fell rapidly into Sassanian hands, and in 613 the army marched south to Jerusalem, capturing the city and making off with such sacred Christian relics as the true cross that Constantine's mother, Helen, had miraculously discovered in the early fourth century. The Sassanian armies pressed onward to Egypt, subjecting the Nile Valley to Iranian control for the first time in nearly a thousand years, and cutting off the primary source of grain for Constantinople. As the main Sassanian force advanced inexorably toward the capital, this time undaunted by its great walls, Heraclius despaired and even thought of abandoning the city and fleeing to Carthage. When the patriarch of the church offered its treasures to raise an army, he took courage.[76]

Heraclius devised a daring and unprecedented strategy. He sent his army on ships down the Bosphorus and along the southern coast of Turkey to Cilicia, thus outflanking the Sassanian force occupying his own territory. He then pushed east across Turkey, heading to Armenia, a region he knew well since it was the land of his forebears. The Sassanians were confident that the advent of winter would force him to retreat, but instead Heraclius spent the cold season in the mountains, so was ready to march in the following spring. Backed by Turkish allies, he emerged, defeated the Sassanians at Nineveh, and swept in triumph toward Ctesiphon. In 628, Chosroes was imprisoned and starved to death by his generals, who were obliged to sue for peace and withdraw their forces from Turkey, Syria, Palestine, and Egypt. Heraclius's victory left the Sassanians in serious disarray. As for the true cross and other sacred relics, they were brought to Constantinople and then returned to Jerusalem, amidst ceremony and rejoicing.[77]

Prelude to Conquest

Among other consequences, this war disrupted the network and allegiances of the vassal tribes and kingdoms in southern Syria and along the Euphrates. especially the Arabs long established in these regions. Many of their kingdoms, such as the Lakhmids, had been overwhelmed in the Sassanian advance toward Constantinople, as if Chosroes had expected that they would no longer be of import in his expanded empire. Nor did Heraclius take the Arabs seriously, although Arab auxiliaries had served him well in his campaigns against the Sassanians. From the perspective of Byzantium, the Arabs were merely quarrelsome tribes, with no tradition of statecraft or large-scale military power.[78]

The early seventh century also saw the Middle East still deeply fractured along confessional lines, since the imperial Orthodox church continued to condemn as heretics the majority of the Christians living in Syria, Palestine, Iraq, and Egypt. Heraclius tried to find a compromise solution, suggesting that perhaps one could agree that Jesus and God had a single energy or will, thus papering over the question of their joint or separate natures, but this ingenious effort satisfied militants on neither side and made little headway.[79]

With the wisdom of historical hindsight, we see that the way was left open for the Arabs—the people who had scarcely figured in either Byzantine or Sassanian strategic thinking—to expand their presence in the region. About 630, according to Arab historians, letters from Arabia went out to nine kings, Heraclius included, calling upon them to submit to a new faith, Islam, for there was but one God, and Muhammad was his messenger, to whom the angel Gabriel had revealed, in the Arabic language, the words of God.[80] To Heraclius, and in fact to some Christian scholars as late as the thirteenth century, Muhammad must have seemed one more heretic or false prophet in a realm beset by such persons.[81]

Upon Muhammad's death in 632, the Muslim Arabs, unified for the first time in their history under the banner of Islam, invaded and vanquished, in rapid succession, Syria and Palestine, Iraq, and Egypt, resolved to carry the religion and political order of Islam throughout the world. As Heraclius, defeated by a people "of sheep and camels,"[82] rode back over the mountains to Byzantium, he turned on his horse to bid a final farewell to Syria, saying, "What an excellent country this is for the enemy."[83]

In Iraq, the Sassanians fought bravely in two major battles near the Euphrates, but the heat, dust, and blinding sunlight told in favor of the Arab tribesmen. By 637, the last Sassanian king, Yezdigird III, had fled Ctesiphon for Iran, where he died in battle three years later, trying in vain to reconquer his kingdom. A new chapter in world history had begun.[84]

EPILOGUE. DISCOVERY AND DESTRUCTION OF ANCIENT IRAQ

> I am the Bull of Nineveh . . . guardian of the nation's history, the emblem of its power. . . . Now I stand in a strange land . . . in a city prouder, greater, more glorious than my native realm; but boast not ye vainglorious creatures of an hour. I have outlived many kingdoms.
>
> W. H. STONE, IN CHARLES DICKENS's *Household Words*, 1851

Exploration and Decipherment

Until the nineteenth century, European travelers to the Middle East seldom visited Iraq. The landscape had little to recommend it—monotonous desert, featureless alluvial plains, forbidding highlands. There were no impressive or picturesque ruins to warrant the difficult journey. Souvenir objects worthy of drawing-room display were not readily to hand, as they were in Egypt. The occasional small curiosities that had found their way to Europe and the United States, such as the Akkadian cylinder seal that a Crusader presented to the Capella Palatina in Palermo, or the Babylonian inscribed brick brought by a ship captain to New York in 1817, were just that.[1] Few places in Iraq were directly associated with the Bible; pilgrims to the Holy Land found the sites in Palestine more accessible and more overtly relevant. And among other deterrents, possibilities for commerce seemed limited, especially since rural Iraq was one of the least secure districts of the Ottoman Empire, which had held it since the sixteenth century.

Aspects of ancient Iraq did figure in medieval, Renaissance, and later illuminated manuscripts, stained glass, prints, paintings, and other media as imagined, generic backdrops for biblical narratives. Certain images, especially those of Babylon and the Tower of Babel, also conveyed a sense of fascinated disapproval of Mesopotamian places supposed to have been centers of immorality and pagan error. Renderings of the Garden of Eden, Noah's Ark, and the Hanging Gardens were Europeanized or exoticized, according to the tenets of the age.[2]

The growing interest of Renaissance and Enlightenment humanists in artifacts and inscriptions was piqued by the undeciphered scripts of the Middle East. They hoped that these mysterious writings would reveal the earliest wisdom of human civilization, which they thought dawned in this region, the "Orient." By the end of the eighteenth century, however, the European discovery of Sanskrit and Zend Avestan, the oldest known form of Persian, had inspired scholars to look farther east, for they reasoned that since Sanskrit and Persian had been shown to be related, and since both were related to Greek and Latin, the origins of European culture must lie in India and Iran.[3] This new conception was to have significant implications for the study of ancient Iraq.

Pietro della Valle, an Italian who traveled in Iraq and Iran between 1616 and 1620, was the first European to identify correctly the ruins of Babylon, although their location had been well known to medieval Arab geographers.[4] He was also the first European to describe cuneiform inscriptions, which he examined at Persepolis.[5] Unlike Egyptian writing, named "hieroglyphs" (sacred carving) by the ancient Greeks, the very existence of this script, which the Greeks called "Assyrian" or "Chaldean," had been forgotten in the Western world until della Valle reported on it. In 1634, an English traveler characterized the writing as "very faire and apparent to the eye, but so mysticall, so oddly framed as no Hieroglyphick no other deep conceit can be more difficultly fancied, more adverse to the intellect."[6] The term "cuneiform" (wedge-shaped) was given wide currency by Thomas Hyde in his encyclopedic work on the antiquities of Iran, published in 1700.[7]

In the early nineteenth century, the British diplomat Claudius Rich, among others, collected cuneiform bricks, tablets, and inscriptions on stone in Iraq and Iran, including some fakes. Carl Bellino, a friend of Rich, was the first to draw cuneiform tablets accurately, and Rich sent his work to would-be decipherers in Europe.[8] Once they realized that some of the inscriptions were written in Old Persian, scholars of Iranian languages made considerable progress toward reading them. They also recognized that the trilingual inscriptions of the Persian kings offered the best possibility for decipherment of the other languages written in cuneiform, just as the Rosetta Stone, a trilingual proclamation by Ptolemy V found in 1799 by Napoleon's expedition to Egypt, had provided the key to Egyptian hieroglyphs.

High on a cliff at Behistun in western Iran was an exceptionally long Old Persian inscription, together with two others in different languages, now known to be Babylonian and Elamite, all three commemorating the victory of Darius I over other claimants to his throne. The ancient stonecutters had smoothed the rock wall below their work to render it inviolate. Notwithstanding the difficulties, Henry Rawlinson, an officer in the British army in India, succeeded in copying nearly the entire text by 1847. Although little headway was made with the Elamite, since it was not related to any other known language, the Babylonian was soon shown to be related to Hebrew and Arabic, hence a member of the Semitic family.[9]

As with all decipherments, that of Babylonian cuneiform was met initially with scoffing and skepticism. The turning point came after Austen Henry Layard unearthed at Nineveh thousands of cuneiform tablets from the library of Assurbanipal (see chapter 7). Largely thanks to this find, sufficient advances in decipherment inspired the Royal Asiatic Society in 1857 to test its reliability by asking four scholars to submit to the Professor of Sanskrit at Oxford their independent translations of a section of the annals of Tiglath-Pileser I, newly found at Assur on a clay prism. The essential agreement among the four translations established the basic validity of their efforts.[10]

Once Babylonian could be read, a new window opened on peoples previously known mainly from biblical and Classical sources. Layard's work produced several spectacular discoveries, among them that the siege of Lachish by Sennacherib (2 Kings 18: 14–17, 19:8) was a historical event commemorated on the wall reliefs of his palace at Nineveh, confirmed by a cuneiform label stating, "Sennacherib, king of Assyria, sat on his throne and the spoil of the city of Lakisu passed before him." There on the slab was precisely the scene described—the enthroned king reviewing the booty brought to him by envoys from Lachish—while images of his siege of the city were carved on adjacent panels.[11]

Even more dramatic was the recovery of a version of the Flood story familiar from the Book of Genesis. In 1872, as George Smith was cataloguing the tablets Layard had shipped back to the British Museum, he chanced upon a fragment that told of the world covered by water, a boat coming to rest on a mountain, and a bird sent forth to find dry land. This "Chaldaean account of the Deluge," as he termed it, caused a public sensation. The *Daily Telegraph* newspaper financed an expedition to Nineveh, so that Smith could search for the rest of the tablet. Sorting through the rubbish heaps left by Layard and his successors at the site, Smith found in a few days many additional works from the great royal library, among them a fragment giving more of the Flood story, part of the *Epic of Gilgamesh*, as we now know (see chapter 5).[12]

Henceforth in European and American visions of history, ancient Iraq was incorporated into the Judeo-Christian "biblical world," inhabited by Semites, whereas Iran and India were linked to Europe and inhabited by Indo-European peoples. The Semites, named after one of the sons of Noah, included the Canaanites, Hebrews, and Arabs, and therefore, in terms of religion, Jews, Muslims, and the "Oriental Christians" of Syria, Iraq, Egypt, and Ethiopia. The Turks, who ruled the region, were excluded from the scheme and deemed invaders because they were not mentioned in the Bible nor in any Classical source.

Most European scholars regarded the Semites as nomads and monotheists incapable of philosophical thought, mythology, or sophisticated art. Discovery of the great cities and palaces of ancient Iraq, together with the abundant written evidence for polytheism, literature, and mythology jolted conventional wisdom and led to biased pronouncements and wrongheaded explanations.[13]

When Layard, for instance, challenged Rawlinson to justify his low opinion of the "Nineveh marbles," he replied, "You ask by what standard I compare them. Why of course, in any abstract matter we adopt the highest standard available—and I say therefore the Elgin marbles."[14] With the realization that Babylonian cuneiform was also used in Iraq to write the non-Semitic language now known as Sumerian, some argued that it must have been the Sumerians who invented the urban civilization of the Babylonians and Assyrians, just as others would later assert that contact with Indo-Europeans made the Assyrians more successful warriors.[15]

Still others felt that, whatever their origins, the cities and civilizations of ancient Iraq reflected barbaric Oriental splendor and Oriental despotism, an interpretation drawn from Herodotus and colored by contemporaneous views of the Ottoman Empire.[16] As such, they were inherently different from and inferior to their Indo-European counterparts. Pharaonic Egypt was exempt, neither Semitic nor Indo-European, but universally and perennially regarded with respect.

Certain Christian and Jewish scholars took yet another approach. They maintained that the cuneiform texts from Iraq, rather than corroborating the Hebrew Bible, showed that it was a collection of far older Babylonian myths adopted and retold by Jews and taken over by Christians and Muslims. The Flood Story was a case in point: if the Babylonians, long before the Jews, wrote of a Flood, then the Flood of Genesis must stem from a pagan myth. This debate, which reached its climax in the early twentieth century, ultimately challenged the authority of Judaism, Christianity, and Islam by asserting that the scripture each religion believed to be divine revelation, or at least the unique record of a people's relationship with God, had a common source in Babylonian myth. Extremists went so far as to say Moses was an astral deity and Jesus was a "mythic type" modeled on Marduk.[17]

Spurred on by further discoveries of palaces and tablets and by these religious and historical controversies, the pace of digging throughout Mesopotamia quickened. As much, if not more, potentially valuable information was lost as was gained. With archaeology still in its infancy, there was at best rudimentary knowledge of how to excavate the complex urban sites of ancient Iraq, or how to salvage the thousands of artifacts that were more fragile than those being found so well preserved in the arid, airless tombs of Egypt. For their part, excavators and sponsors were impatient for immediate results and museum displays. The rising empires in Europe, particularly England and France, saw acquiring and exhibiting the vestiges of these fallen empires of the past as new ways to enhance their own prestige, yet another arena for rivalry.[18]

In 1878, the Ottoman authorities granted permission for Hormuzd Rassam, an Iraqi Christian and Layard's former assistant, to work in a vast area, from Lake Van to the Gulf. His brief from the British Museum was to find as many tablets and to lay claim to as many sites as possible. Rassam rushed from place to place, hiring workers to dig unsupervised for months at a time. The French, meanwhile, were far from idle. The scramble for antiquities led to developments with long-lasting consequences for the illicit trade of artifacts from Iraq.[19]

Dismayed especially by Rassam's disregard for keeping even such records as met the standards of the day, the Ottoman government decided to tighten its formal regulation of the archaeological material emerging from its provinces. The Ottoman elite had traditionally evinced little interest in the pre-Islamic past of its territories, beyond protecting important religious monuments. In the mid-nineteenth century, however, the Ottomans began to view the collection and display of antiquities from throughout the empire as an effective means of promoting their ability to control and unite their European and Asian domains. Some of the spoils of war housed in the Byzantine church of Haghia Irene in Constantinople were reorganized in 1846 into a Magazine of Antiquities, later renamed the Imperial Museum and moved to the Tiled Pavilion, also within the Topkapı complex. To establish state authority over excavations and over the division of their finds, as well as to stanch the hemorrhage of objects to foreign lands, the Ottoman Antiquities Law was enacted in 1874 and revised in 1884 and 1906.[20]

These efforts were subverted, within and without. Covert diplomatic arrangements, for example, offered special division terms to curry favor with Germany. European and American demand for Mesopotamian artifacts, heightened in the face of Ottoman control, drove the development of the first substantial illicit antiquities trade in Iraq. Dealers in Baghdad sent out agents to buy salable objects, especially tablets, tens of thousands of which were shipped to Europe and the United States.[21] At the sites reserved by Rassam, the guards themselves often dug up and sold their finds to these agents. At ancient Lagash, the local Arab tribesmen knew where huge quantities of tablets were to be found and deceived the French excavator, de Sarzec, into digging elsewhere, so that the largest tablet archive ever discovered, still preserved in its original storerooms, was clandestinely unearthed, divided, and sold to collectors and museums in Europe and the United States.[22] The antiquities trade in Iraq, including a lively commerce in forged tablets and statuary, flourished up to the outbreak of World War I, continuing afterward on a more modest scale. During the war, the British seized as enemy goods the shipments of antiquities freshly excavated by the Germans at Babylon and Samarra and being legally exported, some of which were then stolen from the crates and sold on the market.[23]

Meanwhile, Arab villagers and tribesmen were wreaking another kind of havoc. By the mid-nineteenth century, the site of Babylon had been so heavily mined for bricks to construct houses in nearby Hillah that almost nothing was left of the remains of the great ziggurat and many of its major buildings. Countless tablets and other objects were tossed aside as debris by those ignorant even of their monetary value. The ruins at Ctesiphon were also mined for bricks. At Nineveh and Nimrud, reliefs were dug up and burned for lime.[24]

The emphasis on tablets widened a growing gap between the nascent disciplines of archaeology and Assyriology, as the new epigraphic and philological field was called. In his instructions to E. Wallis Budge of the British Museum, who made several expeditions to Iraq to purchase antiquities illegally, Rawlinson wrote, "The vitally important thing is to secure the tablets . . . once gone into the Museums of other countries, they are, so far as the British Museum is concerned, gone for ever."[25] The British Museum was, in fact, the first institution to begin publishing its tablets, initially in cuneiform type, then in facsimile drawings. Others eventually followed suit, so that several hundred tablets, such as the Babylonian inscription of Antiochus I from Borsippa (see chapter 9), were available in print by 1900. But the sheer quantity of tablets (the group sent back by Layard included more than 15,000 pieces; another group from Sippar more than 70,000), not to mention the time required for reading, copying, and translating each document, means that today all collections still contain large numbers of unpublished and in some cases uncatalogued holdings, as well as fragments that often are found to join other broken tablets. In recent years, previously unknown pieces of the *Epic of Gilgamesh*, for instance, have come to light as scholars have identified them in the British Museum, or among the tablets excavated at Assur more than fifty years ago and now housed in Berlin.[26]

The very richness of the written records from Mesopotamia encouraged Assyriologists to focus almost exclusively on the texts themselves. In this, they were following the example of both Classicists and biblical scholars, who, especially in the German university system of the nineteenth century, viewed language and texts as independent artifacts to be studied only in conjunction with other languages and texts. To them, archaeology seemed at best a subfield of the history of art, useful for producing objects illustrating textual subjects, at worst not an academic field at all.[27] Thus the tablets from ancient Iraq were read for their own sake, just as were the *Iliad* or the Book of Isaiah. Well over a century later, many Assyriologists are still in general agreement with Rawlinson's insistence on the primacy of cuneiform tablets for advancing knowledge, without regard to how and where they are obtained.

Archaeology Past and Present

Notwithstanding the disdain of philologists, the end of the nineteenth century saw archaeology evolve into a professional scientific discipline.[28] With every passing decade, thanks to collaborative research ventures with other fields, such as geophysics, ethnobotany, analytical chemistry, and genetics, new methodologies have augmented our ability to reconstruct the human past. The heart of archaeology is the conscientious retrieval and accurate recording of data from artifacts, features, and ecofacts, which, taken as a whole, shed light on behaviors and developments specific to a site

Figure 22 and frontispiece. Tablet of the *Epic of Gilgamesh*, height 23 cm, Yale Babylonian Collection, New Haven. (Yale Photographic Services) *Purchased about 1914 from a New York dealer, this tablet came from illicit excavations, possibly at Uruk. The text preserves major episodes from the Old Babylonian version of the epic (see chapter 5), but sections were destroyed by the digger's pick.*

in time and space. This, in a word, is context. Once a site has been excavated, context is preserved only in the documentary records of the expedition; if it is looted or carelessly dug, context is lost forever.[29]

A cuneiform tablet, illicitly acquired on the antiquities market, floats in a contextual void (figure 22). Specialists may read and date it more or less precisely, and can often determine where it was written. But without context there is much more we will never know. What other artifacts were associated with it? Where exactly was it, in a temple foundation deposit, an independent merchant's establishment, a schoolroom, or a royal library? Had it had been stacked with other tablets in a basket or on a shelf, a clue to the thought patterns that structured the storage of information millennia ago? Was it an heirloom, kept by a scholarly family, or had it been collected by an antiquarian king?

The sites of ancient Iraq present exceptional challenges to the archaeologist.[30] The lack of readily available stone resources meant that mud-brick was the usual construction material. As settlements tended to occupy the same locations for several thousand years, successive levels of mud-brick structures, built and rebuilt dozens of times over the millennia, formed enormous mounds called *tell*s, or "ruin-hills" in Babylonian, just as they are in Arabic. Consequently, the stratigraphy and chronological interrelationships of such sites are extremely complex, requiring careful clearance and recording by well-trained personnel. Further, it is quite difficult for any but the most experienced eye to determine the plans of buildings, since degraded mud-brick walls are nearly indistinguishable from their matrix of soil and debris, and only one or two courses may be preserved. Many an early excavator dug straight through walls without seeing that they were there.

The excavations at Babylon, directed from 1899 on by Robert Koldewey, and at Assur, directed from 1903 on by Walter Andrae, both projects under the auspices of the German Oriental Society, demonstrated for the first time that despite these challenges it was possible to carry out scrupulous archaeological work in Iraq. The German reports showed that a wealth of information could be obtained if archaeological methods of the highest order were applied, and if experts in various disciplines collaborated toward common objectives. At many sites, down to modern times, the core labor force has included men called Sherqati, descendants of those who had dug with Andrae at Assur (modern Qalat Sherqat) and who had passed on their knowledge and skills, especially in the tracing of mud-brick walls, to their sons and grandsons. A visiting archaeologist, used to the old methods, remarked to one of the German excavators, "Why look, you have walls!"[31]

Projects undertaken before and after World War I by German and other foreign teams generally followed this lead. At Ur, for example, the Englishman Leonard Woolley, working on behalf of the British Museum and the University of Pennsylvania Museum of Archaeology and Anthropology, held off excavating the Royal

Graves he found in 1922 for four years, so that he could train his foremen and workers sufficiently in the techniques he knew would be needed.

The decades during and after World War II saw a proliferation of foreign missions, as well as the first projects directed by Iraqis.[32] The scramble for biblical validation and for prestige artifacts and sites was replaced by a desire to understand more fully such matters as social and economic history, connections between core and peripheral areas, and the origins and growth of the world's earliest agriculture, writing, and urbanization, as well as prehistoric and Islamic Iraq. Several institutions, notably the University of Chicago, launched ambitious surveys, which have generated detailed maps of ancient sites in a given region, based on analyses of surface finds and geomorphological features.

The Nation of Iraq and Cultural Heritage

The course of archaeology in Iraq was decisively influenced by the British occupation and mandate in the aftermath of World War I, particularly by the vision of Gertrude Bell. Serving as Oriental Secretary to the first British administrator of the conquered territory, she was one of the few members of the new government with a working knowledge of Arabic. Bell was crucial in the effort to persuade Winston Churchill to create a single kingdom, under British control, combining the former Ottoman provinces of Basra, Baghdad, and Mosul, as well as certain areas of Kurdistan and the Arabian desert.[33]

In her travels throughout the region before the war, Bell had familiarized herself with what was known at the time of the sites, monuments, and cultural interconnections of the region's past, as well as the application of the latest scientific methods to archaeological investigation. Faisal I, an Arabian from Mecca whom the British installed in 1921 as king of Iraq, had some interest in archaeology himself, having been introduced to its principles by T. E. Lawrence "of Arabia," who had begun his career in the Middle East as a young archaeologist with Woolley at Carchemish. By one of his first royal acts, Faisal appointed Bell honorary Director of Archaeology.

Bell believed that the remains of ancient Iraq could play a critical role in the emergence of the modern state, if the nation were to manage its own cultural resources. With Faisal's support, but without the backing of key British authorities, who blamed her for not foreseeing the 1920 uprising, she initiated a three-part program. First, she founded the Iraqi Department of Antiquities, emphasizing the importance of preparing Iraqi scholars for the responsibilities of directing and staffing it, of issuing permits and superintending foreign excavation projects, and of sustaining an Iraqi program of field research.

Second, she wrote an antiquities law for the new nation, which reserved all exceptional finds for Iraq, as well as half of any other material recovered during an excavation season. Henceforth, Iraq would have the legal authority to retain objects found within her borders.

Third, Bell began planning for a national museum in Baghdad, convinced that displays of Mesopotamian achievements from prehistoric to Islamic periods would bolster Iraqi confidence in the future of their nation. She had to build the collections from nothing. As luck would have it, the 1920s saw major discoveries, whose excavators usually cooperated with the new antiquities policies, since Bell was both firm and scrupulous, making it clear that she put Iraqi interests first. At the conclusion of the 1923 season at Ur, for instance, Bell wrote that she and Woolley had come to an excellent understanding on the division of the finds: "The best object is a hideous Sumerian statue of a King of Lagash, about three feet high but headless. . . it will go back to London to be completely deciphered and then return to us."[34] This is the Enmetena of figure 8.

Until her death in 1926, Bell worked to establish the museum on a sound footing. In addition to supervising the division of excavated objects, she trained Iraqi cataloguers and label writers, ordered exhibit cases to be made, and sought a permanent home for the collections, initially kept in two rooms in a former Ottoman administrative building. Bell was ever more certain that the Iraq Museum was destined to be a locus of both nationalistic and archaeological importance. In June 1926, the museum opened with more than three thousand objects installed in the former Government Press building. Bell reported that Iraqis visited their new museum with enthusiasm and pride, from the start.

Foreign institutes opened in Iraq as well, including French, German, American, and British schools for archaeological research. Some of the excavation permits Bell issued reflected old Anglo-French rivalries, as when she ignored prior French claims at Kish, or tried to punish the Germans, as when she offered the site of Uruk to Yale University. The Baghdad School of the American Schools of Oriental Research, inaugurated in 1923 by the Yale Assyriologist Albert T. Clay, contained the first research library in archaeology and Assyriology in the country, surviving today as the library of the Iraq Museum.[35]

Bell's bequest of £50,000 to the Iraq Museum enabled it to move in the directions she had envisioned. By the 1930s, the collections were outgrowing their quarters. A large tract of land near the Tigris was chosen and reserved by erecting in 1939 a repro-duction Assyrian gateway, guarded by winged bulls removed from Dur-Sharrukin, an architectural style considered more culturally fitting than the Beaux-Arts structure the museum then occupied. A new museum, of more generic design, was inaugurated in 1966 and expanded in the 1980s, though the rapid influx of new mate-rials meant that, as before, the storerooms were soon overflowing with expedition files and study collections.

The Department of Antiquities in Iraq had become one of the strongest in the Middle East, with professional standards of cura-torship and conservation and an active research program. As Bell had hoped, the Iraq Museum ranked among the world's major re-positories for ancient artifacts, including cuneiform tablets, seals, and coins, with a Heritage Section for material from more recent periods, in addition to thousands of Islamic, Christian, and Jew-ish manuscripts. A children's museum was in constant use by school groups. Elsewhere, there were thirteen regional museums, explanatory panels at archaeological sites, and 1,600 site guards.

Since achieving independence in 1932, Iraq had also made a successful transition to controlling her own cultural heritage. Al-though the government asked the British archaeologist Seton Lloyd to serve as special advisor from 1939 to 1949, it named Sati' al-Husri in 1934 the first Iraqi Director-General of Antiquities.

Iraqis were sent for advanced degrees to American and European universities. In the years during and after World War II, Fuad Safar and Taha Baqir, both trained at the University of Chicago, directed excavations throughout Iraq, spanning all periods, from the prehistoric settlement at Hassuna to the early Islamic city of Wasit. To train future generations, they established in 1952 a Faculty of Archaeology at the University of Baghdad, which gave rise to programs at other Iraqi universities. A scholarly periodical, *Sumer*, began publication in 1945, with articles in Arabic and in European languages. After the establishment of the Republic, the burgeoning oil wealth of Iraq financed numerous excavations and ambitious restoration projects of ancient sites, such as the ziggurat at Ur (figure 10).

The most significant development was the virtual suppression of the illicit antiquities trade, a situation that lasted from the 1958 revolution to the Gulf War. Punishment for smuggling was swift and severe, including public execution. Foreign archaeological missions were still permitted to take home a share of their finds, but some protested the diminishing portion and withdrew from work in Iraq. Division ceased altogether in 1967, and was codified in the 1974 law, with only study and scientific materials allowed to leave the country thereafter. As a result, for nearly half of the twentieth century, there was no market in Mesopotamian antiquities.

After Saddam Hussein came to power in 1979, the government adopted increasingly contradictory archaeological policies. On the one hand, Ba'th party ideology embraced the ancient history of Iraq and supported Iraqi and foreign excavations. Hussein, comparing himself to Nebuchadnezzar II, restored large areas of Babylon and commemorated his projects with bricks inscribed in Arabic. On the other hand, he built new palaces and artificial lakes over sections of the ancient city. His public works projects included dams on the Tigris and Diyala rivers, which, like dams built at the same time in Turkey and Syria and the earlier Aswan High Dam in Egypt, flooded hundreds of archaeological sites. He also granted the elite large private domains, closed to supervision by the Department of Antiquities. One-party, dictatorial rule soon made professional and personal life difficult for Iraqi scholars who were not party loyalists. Some fled the country; those who stayed found that maintaining connections with foreign colleagues was dangerous.[36]

The Gulf War and Cultural Destruction

The 1991 Gulf War and its aftermath dealt the archaeological situation in Iraq a grievous blow. Military operations for the most part avoided ancient and Islamic sites, but damage inevitably occurred, notably to Ur (see figure 10), to the great iwan at Ctesiphon, and to the medieval university complex in Baghdad. Before the war began, curators at the Iraq Museum had taken the precaution of placing certain objects, among them the gold from Nimrud and Ur, in boxes deep in the vaults of the Central Bank. Their concerns were justified; nine of the regional museums were looted.[37]

The more serious cultural losses occurred after the war, as a direct consequence of the staggering human toll exacted by the sanctions imposed by the United Nations. Even after the oil-for-food program began in 1996, the economic plight of most people outside the ruling elite was desperate. A civil administrator, for example, who might already have sold the doors and fixtures of his dwelling for food, needed a month's salary to buy 3 kilograms of flour.

Under these circumstances, and when a well-preserved tablet could be sold on the spot for $100 or more in hard currency, it is hardly surprising that the looting of archaeological sites and the selling of artifacts began again. Many became actively involved in the lucrative trade, from high-ranking members of the regime to mid-level functionaries to impoverished villagers. Most of the regional museums were broken into and robbed of whatever antiquities they still contained. Severely hampered by a slashed budget, the staff of the Department of Antiquities struggled to protect cultural heritage, to employ some site guards, and to conduct salvage digs. Capital punishment was still meted out to antiquities thieves.[38]

All to little avail. Dealers and collectors, based mainly in the United States, Europe, and Japan, were willing to pay large sums for antiquities from Iraq. Major factors were the novelty of this material, the first on the market since the 1950s, and the high prices realized in 1988 at the Christie's auction of the Erlenmeyer collection of Mesopotamian art objects and tablets. Buyers were still often seduced by the hardy notions of biblical substantiation, ever present in popular concepts of ancient Mesopotamia. Most private purchasers either knew little of modern archaeology and cared nothing for context, or rationalized that the objects were better off out of Iraq. Museums, well aware of the issues, appear to have decided that being able to exhibit new acquisitions in Mesopotamian art outweighed any archaeological or ethical costs, and they claimed that this prevented items from vanishing into private possession, where they might never be viewed by the public, properly cared for, or published.

Cuneiform tablets and seals were, and continue to be, particularly desirable. With this material, the divergent philosophies of Assyriologists and archaeologists have come once again to the fore. As archaeologists see it, scholarly attention and publication confer legitimacy on artifacts and enhance their monetary value, which in turn drive up prices and demand. But by arguing that the textual significance transcends other considerations, some Assyriologists and specialists in seals have read, translated, and published inscribed works of unknown or dubious provenance. The divide extends to the editorial policies of professional journals: although numerous archaeological journals refuse to accept primary articles treating material of this ilk obtained since the 1970 UNESCO Convention on Cultural Property, as well as advertising from firms dealing in illicit antiquities, other publications continue to do both. But once this material is published, what are the ethics of using it in secondary studies? And what are the legal risks for individuals and institutions under current laws and practices?[39]

The Iraq War and Cultural Devastation

By January 2003, it was evident to many in the archaeological community that the imminent war posed a serious threat to cultural heritage in Iraq. American scholars supplied the Pentagon and the State Department with considerable background information. They also warned of the consequences if the U.S.-led coalition failed to uphold international legal regimes regarding the protection of cultural property in time of war, reminding planners of the laudatory role the military's Monuments, Fine Arts, and Archives section had played in World War II in safeguarding and recovering cultural property in Europe.

Officials in Washington paid scant heed, instead meeting more regularly with a group called the American Council for Cultural Policy, composed mainly of antiquities dealers, museum curators, and private collectors, who supported a "sensible, post-Saddam cultural administration" and revision of Iraq's antiquities law, which the council's treasurer, an attorney who represented the National Association of Dealers in Ancient, Oriental, and Primitive Art, characterized as "retentionist." Already in 1991, the "art-rich" nations were being advised that the illicit trade in antiquities would all but stop if only they would reinstate a division of finds.[40]

During February and March, the Iraq Museum undertook intensive preparations for war. A five-person team transferred over 8,000 objects to an ultra-secure, secret bunker within the museum compound, whose precise location is even now known only to a trusted few. The many boxes still in the vaults of the Central Bank were left there. Using sandbags and foam-rubber padding, staff members attempted to forestall any damage to immovable pieces. They also took nearly 40,000 medieval manuscripts to a bomb shelter in western Baghdad. New inner walls and barriers were built to strengthen existing ones.[41]

Meanwhile, the Office of Reconstruction and Humanitarian Assistance (later renamed the Coalition Provisional Authority) sent a list to the Coalition Forces Land Component command of buildings to be secured immediately after the taking of Baghdad. At the top were the Central Bank and the Iraq Museum, deemed "a prime target for looters."[42] Yet the overall attitude of war planners before and after the events of April leads to the conclusion that the protection of cultural property was never a priority. No mechanism was in place to safeguard cultural heritage, nor was any military unit assigned the specific mission of protecting the museum.

As troops entered this part of Baghdad on 8 April, a few curators and other personnel, some of whom had stayed in the museum for several previous nights, were in the building, expecting to welcome an American unit. By mid-morning, they were obliged to evacuate; later that day, U.S. soldiers holding the bridges over the Tigris would not let them pass to return. Iraqi soldiers took up positions in the museum compound, but there are conflicting reports on when they arrived and how many there were.

On 10 April, successive waves of looters poured into the museum, smashing or seizing everything from office equipment and electrical wire to exhibited artifacts and museum shop souvenirs. The looters included local residents, opportunists, and professional thieves. There are accounts of Iraqis early on beseeching the crew of a nearby American tank to swing its turret toward the museum as a deterrent, and of their not being given orders to do so, but these have not been verified by the U.S. military. The looting and destruction continued into the following day. At some point, the Iraqi soldiers left, shedding uniforms and weaponry, having engaged U.S. forces on several occasions.[43]

Staff members managed to reach the museum again on the 12th. They hung a handmade sign outside, claiming falsely but effectively that U.S. troops were now on the premises. On the 13th, senior museum officials made their way to an American headquarters to plead for protection. They were stunned to be asked such questions as where the museum was. An American tank platoon (four tanks, sixteen men, plus additional support) was finally sent to the museum on the morning of the 16th, in the words of one investigator for the American military, an "inexcusable delay."[44]

Photographs, video footage, and eyewitness reports of the fate of the museum immediately captured worldwide attention. Rumors, contradictions, accusations, and conspiracy theories abounded. Less coverage was given to the equally grave damage inflicted on other cultural institutions in Baghdad, Mosul, and other cities.[45] U.S. authorities tried at first to trivialize and denigrate the situation. In a news briefing on 11 April, Secretary of Defense Donald Rumsfeld said the television images were simply showing repeatedly "the same picture of someone walking out of some building with a vase," and, he quipped, "Is it possible that there were that many vases in the whole country?"[46] On 15 April, U.S. Marine

Colonel Matthew Bogdanos, already in Iraq as part of an investigative group, initiated the organization and deployment of a special team focused on the museum, which began its work a week later and stayed until November 2003.[47]

Media reports during this period concentrated on the number of objects missing, the "scorecard" as one magazine called it,[48] giving wildly fluctuating figures based on unreliable information or misapprehensions. As a result, there was little public understanding of the archaeological implications of what had occurred. The pieces kept in the study collections, for example, were not mass-produced items in a warehouse inventory, but they represented multiple seasons of painstaking excavation, yet to be fully catalogued, analyzed, and published, many now smashed and commingled on the storeroom floors, or gone. And how could the damage to register books, excavation notes, file cards, and other documentation—the sole records of context—be quantified?

Meanwhile, far greater, but seldom reported, devastation was taking place elsewhere.[49] From the moment the war began, there has been systematic looting on an enormous scale, especially in southern Iraq, often with two or three hundred diggers journeying daily by coordinated shuttle service back and forth to sites, accompanied by men armed with Kalashnikovs and grenade launchers. Many of them have been working at previously excavated mounds, deepening old trenches or tunneling beneath them, while others have been digging in new locations.

In their search for the most lucrative pieces, looters cast aside the unprofitable: potsherds, broken sculptures, tablet fragments, cracked cylinder seals, and the like. Archaeologists estimate that for every whole object, two thousand sherds and a thousand small finds are discarded onto vast rubbish heaps. Furnished with published archaeological survey maps and aided by former site guards and workmen, looters can be highly responsive to market demands for antiquities of particular periods.

For the diggers, this is often their sole and safest source of income in today's Iraq. A small tablet fetches them $7 to $10, a more impressive one $100, a figurine $50 to $60, a cylinder seal $200, a plaque with the goddess Ishtar $500. The prices and profits rise with every step of the journey to the final buyer, who may pay

$1,000 for an interesting tablet, $50,000 for a group of related tablets, $12 million for an Assyrian relief sawed down to salable size. Cylinder seals start at $5,000; in 2001, a seal sold at Christie's in New York for $424,000. The record for any sculpture ever sold at auction—$57.1 million at Sotheby's in 2007—belongs to a small limestone leonine figure of about 3000 B.C.E., which emerged decades ago from an unknown provenance, probably Iran.[50] To put this in perspective, the 2007 net assets of the British School of Archaeology in Iraq were $695,000.[51]

Some archaeological sites have become military bases. At Babylon, American forces established Camp Alpha, headquarters of the Multinational Division Central-South, in a 150-hectare compound. Heavy vehicular traffic, helicopter rotor wash, leveling and paving operations, fuel leakage, and contextual contamination from the many thousands of bags and wire-mesh baskets stuffed with material bulldozed at Babylon or brought in from other locations to form berms have caused irreparable damage.[52]

The U.S. military has belatedly begun or collaborated on several projects designed to acquaint troops deployed to Iraq and Afghanistan with cultural heritage, archaeological considerations, and antiquities issues. One is a lecture series offered by the Archaeological Institute of America in cooperation with the U.S. Central Command.[53] Another is the distribution to troops of decks of Heritage Resource Preservation playing cards produced by the Legacy Resource Management Program of the Department of Defense. Each suit depicts captioned images within a cultural theme, while the card backs feature a cuneiform tablet and the messages "Support the Mission, Show Respect" and "Respect Iraqi and Afghan Heritage," the latter written also in Arabic, Pushtu, and Dari.[54]

Despite these and other national and international efforts, the cultural heritage of Iraq is vanishing at a rate without precedent or parallel. Numerous important sites have been utterly destroyed, records and artifacts lost forever. But the devastation affects far more than ancient Iraq alone, for what is gone beyond recovery is our common human past.

NOTES

Chapter 1. In the Beginning

Epigraph source: *Muses*, 488.
1. *Muses*, 726.
2. Heimpel 1987b; Jacobsen 1987: 245; K. Foster 2000.
3. Postgate 1992: 3–21; Potts 1997: 1–42.
4. Roaf 1990: 19–23; Butzer 1995.
5. *Muses*, 792.
6. Glassner 1984; Michalowski 1999.
7. Kraus 1970; Steinkeller 1993: 112–3; Rubio 2005.
8. Wensinck 1927: 513; Miquel 1986: 1250–3; Bernhardsson 2005: 97–100.
9. Segal 1955; Finkelstein 1962.
10. Layard 1853, 1:29.
11. Matthews 2003: 19–26.
12. Price and Gebauer, eds. 2003.
13. Childe 1951: 59–86; Hole 1984; Liverani 2001: 5–7.
14. Mellaart 1975.
15. Ucko and Dimbleby, eds. 1969; Streuver 1971; J. Oates 1973; Smith 1995: 50–89; Sherratt 1997; Matthews 2003: 67–92.
16. Price and Gebauer, eds. 2003.
17. Renfrew, Dixon, and Cann 1966; G. Wright 1969.
18. Potts 1997: 138–63.
19. Civil 1964: 74, lines 71–7; Milano, ed. 1994; McGovern 2003.
20. Oates and Oates 1976: 38–48, 53; Moorey 1994: 141–53.
21. Young, Smith, and Mortensen, eds. 1983.
22. Mellaart 1967.
23. Oates and Oates 1976: 70–86; Nissen 1988: 15–38; Huot 1994.
24. Adams 1981: 59; Nissen 1988: 39–64.
25. Civil 1961: 156–7, lines 14–23.
26. Steinkeller 1981; B. Foster 1982a: 107.

211

27. Lloyd 1978: 37–47; Henrickson and Thuesen, eds. 1989; Frangipane 1996: 105–46.

28. Diakonoff 1966: 49–50; Weiss 1986; Zarins 1990.

29. Moorey 1994: 153–5.

30. Forest 1987; Stein 1994: 41–3.

Chapter 2. The Birthplace of Civilization

Epigraph source: A. Berlin 1979, *Enmerkar and Ensuḫkešdanna: A Sumerian Narrative Poem*. *Occasional Publications of the Babylonian Fund* 2, 38, lines 1–5. Philadelphia: University Museum of Archaeology and Anthropology.

1. *Muses*, 488.

2. Moorey 1994: 148, 155–6.

3. B. Foster 2001: 3.

4. Oates and Oates 1976: 110–8; Nissen 1988: 95–103; Boehmer 1997; Forest 1999: 57–87.

5. Dhorme 1945; Römer 1969; Van Dijk 1971; Jacobsen 1976, 1987; Bottéro 2001a; Bahrani 2003: 121–48.

6. Oppenheim 1961, 1977: 183–98; Postgate 1992: 109–36.

7. *Muses*, 873; Joannès 2004: 183.

8. Edzard 1965; Lambert 1975; Beaulieu 2004; B. Foster 2007a.

9. Black and Green 1992.

10. Bottéro and Kramer 1989: 165–88; B. Foster 2007b: 76–7.

11. Harris 1991; Bahrani 2000.

12. Hallo and Van Dijk 1968: 14, lines 9–10.

13. *Muses*, 167.

14. *Muses*, 283.

15. Sjöberg 1969: 29, lines 199–201.

16. Adams and Nissen 1972: 9–33; Nissen 1988: 67–73; Richardson 2007.

17. Frankfort 1970: 24–37; Roaf 1990: 71; Hansen 2003a: 21–6.

18. Frankfort 1970: 31–2.

19. Heinrich 1936: 15–7; Nissen 1988: 103–5; Bahrani 2002.

20. Frankfort 1939; Collon 1987; Nissen 1988: 76–9.

21. Dittmann 1986; Matthews 1993.

22. H. Wright 2001.

23. Liverani 2006: 15–6.

24. B. Foster and Robson 2004.

25. Frangipane 1996: 143–6; Liverani 2006: 15–24.

26. Gelb 1965; Liverani 1986: 115–25; Nissen 1988: 84–5.
27. Liverani 2006: 18.
28. Liverani 1988a: 135–40; Diakonoff 1991: 36–7; Pollock 1999: 90–1, 173–95.
29. Falkenstein 1959, 1: 11, line 11.
30. *Muses*, 492.
31. Algaze 1993, 2001; Butterlin 2003.
32. Frankfort 1941; Kantor 1992, 1: 17–9; Sieverstein 1992; Pittman 1996.
33. Frangipane 2001.
34. Edzard 1976/80a; Green 1981.
35. Jacobsen 1987: 312; Glassner 2003b: 11–25; Vanstiphout 2003: 84–5, lines 502–4.
36. *Muses*, 1023; Michalowski 1994.
37. Cooper 1996; Michalowski 1996; Glassner 2003b.
38. Nissen 1986; Michalowski 1990; Schmandt-Besserat 2007.
39. Damerow 1988: 275–97; Schmandt-Besserat 1996.
40. Friberg 1994; Englund 1998: 46–9.
41. Oppenheim 1959; Lebrun and Vallat 1978.
42. Nissen, Damerow, and Englund 1993; Englund 1998: 82–106.
43. Benito 1969: 96, lines 192–6; Bottéro and Kramer 1989: 165–88.

CHAPTER 3. EARLY CITY-STATES

Epigraph source: C. J. Gadd and S. N. Kramer 1966, *Ur Excavations, Texts* VI/2, Nos. 340–1. London: British Museum; Alster 1997, 1: 74.

1. B. Foster 1986; Steinkeller 1988.
2. Postgate 1992: 32–4; Matthews 1993; Steinkeller 2002.
3. H. Wright 1969; Charvát 1979, 1982; Visicato and Westenholz 2005.
4. Woolley 1934; Moorey 1982; Zettler and Horne, eds. 1998; Reade 2003; Marchesi 2004; A. Cohen 2005.
5. Cavigneaux and Al-Rawi 2000: 59.
6. Stauder 1972/5; Kilmer 1993/7; Hansen 1998: 52–9; de Schauensee 2002.
7. Collon 1992; Hansen 1998; A. Cohen 2005: 117–44.
8. Glassner 2004: 117–27.
9. *Muses*, 552.

10. Jacobsen 1957; Edzard 1974; Steinkeller 1999; Glassner 2004: 121.
11. Hallo 1963.
12. Gelb 1981; Nissen 1988: 129–64.
13. Nissen 1988: 145.
14. Biggs 1974: 35; Mander 1984; Pomponio and Visicato 1994; B. Foster 2005a.
15. Archi 1992.
16. Charvát 1986; Pomponio and Visicato 1994: 21–4; B. Foster 2005a: 81, note 28.
17. Pomponio and Visicato 1994: 16, 10–20.
18. Matthews 1991.
19. B. Foster 2005a: 83.
20. Green 1978: 151.
21. Pomponio and Visicato 1994: 19–20.
22. Cooper 1983b.
23. Cooper 1986: 55.
24. Winter 1985.
25. Civil 1994: 31, lines 46–51.
26. Hruška 1983: 83–5; Potts, ed. 1983; B. Foster 1997.
27. Alster 1983: 63.
28. Moorey 1994: 242–78.
29. K. Foster 1979: 3–9, 15–31, 44–6; Moorey 1994: 166–86.
30. Hansen 2003a: 27–37.
31. Bauer 1998: 475–93.
32. Cooper 1986: 72.
33. Maekawa 1973/4; B. Foster 1981.
34. Cooper 1986: 94–5.
35. Ellis 1992.
36. *Muses*, 247.
37. *Muses*, 249.
38. B. Foster 2001: 88.

CHAPTER 4. KINGS OF THE FOUR QUARTERS OF THE WORLD

Epigraph source: *Muses*, 110.
1. Lewis 1980; Cooper and Heimpel 1983; Van De Mieroop 1999; A. Westenholz 1999: 34–40; *Muses*, 912–3.
2. J. Westenholz 1983, 1992, 1997; *Muses*, 107–14, 338–43.
3. B. Foster 1986; Steinkeller 1993; A. Westenholz 1999: 98–100; Van De Mieroop 2002.

4. Harmand 1973: 150–3, 160; Huot 1989: 221–8; Frayne 1993: 29; A. Westenholz 1999: 65–8; Civil 2003; *Muses*, 341.

5. Frayne 1993: 14–5; A. Westenholz 1999: 3–4.

6. Cooper 1983a: 50–1, lines 25–8.

7. Winter 1987.

8. Wilcke 1972; J. Westenholz 1992.

9. Hallo and Van Dijk 1968: 1–11; J. Westenholz 1992.

10. Hallo and Van Dijk 1968: 33, lines 138–40.

11. B. Foster 1982a: 40–51; A. Westenholz 1999: 41–3.

12. Amiet 1976; Heimpel 1982, 1987a; Frayne 1993: 76; Moorey 1994: 26–8; A. Westenholz 1999: 44–6.

13. Gelb 1979; B. Foster 1985, 2000.

14. King 1907, 2: 32.

15. A. Westenholz 1999: 46–55.

16. B. Foster 1982a, 1986, 1993a.

17. Hansen 2003b.

18. Amiet 1976: 29–32; Winter 1999.

19. Ghirshman 1954: 53–6; Laessøe 1959: 14–15; Strommenger 1963.

20. Frayne 1993: 113–4; *Muses*, 63.

21. Koenig 1965: 76, no. 22; Bourgeois 1992; Harper and Amiet 1992.

22. Gelb and Kienast 1990: 262; Franke 1995.

23. Oates and Oates 1989; B. Foster 1993b.

24. A. Westenholz 1987.

25. Cooper 1983a: 54–5, lines 102–5.

26. A. Westenholz 1979, 1999: 55; B. Foster 1980.

27. A. Westenholz 1999: 51–4; *Muses*, 59–62.

28. *Muses*, 63.

29. Weiss and Courty 1993; Weiss 1997; A. Westenholz 1999: 56–9.

30. Cooper 1983a: 62–3, lines 245–53.

31. *Muses*, 355.

32. Kienast and Volk 1995: 135.

33. Winter 1989; Evans 2003.

34. Edzard 1997: 78, lines xv 6–10.

35. Frayne 1993: 284–7.

36. Glassner 2004: 144–9.

37. Sallaberger 1999.

38. Canby 2001.

39. Sjöberg 1960: 81–2, lines 19–21.

40. Roaf 1990: 104–7; Glassner 2003a: 136–75; George 2005/6.

41. Flückiger-Hawker 1999: 138, lines 213–5.

42. Klengel, ed. 1989: 92–143; Klein 1995.

43. Klein 1981: 196–9, lines 62–74.

44. According to the interpretation of Jacobsen 1987: 318–9, though the passage is obscure.

45. Vanstiphout 2003: 86, lines 537–41.

46. K. Foster 1999; Vanstiphout 2003: 23–48.

47. Vanstiphout 1990/2.

48. Vanstiphout in Hallo 1997: 579, lines 93–9.

49. Michalowski 1987: 63–6; Black 1998; Veldhuis 2004: 39–44, 58–66.

50. Falkenstein 1959, 1: 22–3, lines 68–73.

51. Neumann 1987: 35–91.

52. Winter 1987; Frayne 1997: 92–110, 236–41, 285–94, 361–6.

53. Gelb 1965.

54. Maekawa 1984, 1987: 62–70; Robson 1999: 138–66.

55. Sallaberger 1999: 338–9; Sharlach 2004.

56. Snell 1982; Neumann 1992; Sallaberger 1999: 200–336.

57. Sallaberger 1999: 159–61.

58. Sollberger 1951.

59. Roth 1997: 16.

60. Renger 1995: 287–8.

61. B. Foster 1986.

62. Maekawa 1981.

63. Hallo 1978.

64. Buccellati 1966; Steinkeller 1987; Maeda 1992.

65. Michalowski 1989: 40–1, lines 65–71.

66. Wilcke 1970.

67. Michalowski 1989: 58–9, lines 366–8.

CHAPTER 5. THE AGE OF HAMMURABI

Epigraph source: *Muses*, 132.

1. Buccellati 1992; Heimpel 2003: 14–25; Stol 2004: 645–53.

2. Charpin 1992a; Edzard 2004: 491–4.

3. Edzard 1976/80b: 174–5; Sollberger 1976/80; Michalowski 1984.

4. Charpin 1986, 1996, 2004: 123–4; Stone 1987; Van De Mieroop 1987; Dyckhoff 1998.

5. Finkelstein 1966.

6. Lafont 2001: 214, 229.
7. Eidem and Laessøe 2001: 70–1.
8. Frayne 1989; Van De Mieroop 1993; Charpin 2004: 119–27; Brisch 2007: 53–69.
9. Oppenheim 1954; Leemans 1960: 23–56; Diakonoff 1990: 112–25; Van De Mieroop 1992: 188–203; Stol 2004: 876–8.
10. Leemans 1960: 39.
11. Durand 1987: 155–6.
12. Charpin 2004: 147–88.
13. Durand 1997, 1: 138.
14. Parrot 1974; Margueron 1982, 1995; Dalley 1984; Gates 1984.
15. Durand 1997, 1: 256.
16. Durand 2000, 1: 347–8.
17. Charpin 2003; Van De Mieroop 2005.
18. *Muses*, 131.
19. Kraus 1968: 5.
20. Collon 1995: 99; André-Salvini 2003a.
21. Frayne 1990: 334.
22. Roth 1997: 108 (§ 142–3).
23. Westbrook 2003: 361–430; Charpin 2004: 305–16.
24. B. Foster 1995: 173.
25. Roth 1995; Joannès, ed. 2000; Lévy, ed. 2000.
26. Dombradi 1996; Charpin in Joannès, ed. 2000.
27. Stol 2004: 910–8.
28. Michel 2001: 507.
29. Bottéro 1995: 28.
30. Bottéro 1980/3; Dalley 1984: 78–95; Bottéro 2001b: 43–83.
31. Musche 1999; *Muses*, 165–9.
32. *Muses*, 169.
33. Cooper 1972/5.
34. Grayson 1973: 149; Bottéro 2001b: 90–111.
35. *Muses*, 201.
36. George 2000, 2003; B. Foster 2001, 2007b: 67–73.
37. B. Foster 2001: 75.
38. B. Foster 2001: 95.
39. B. Foster 2001: 95.
40. Charpin 1992b.
41. Yoffee 1988; Pientka 1998; Charpin 2004: 365–71.
42. Sassmannshausen 1999.
43. Charpin 2004: 382–3.

CHAPTER 6. BABYLONIA IN THE FAMILY OF NATIONS

Epigraph source: P. Michalowski 1981, "An Old Babylonian Literary Fragment concerning the Kassites," *Annali dell'Istituto Orientale di Napoli* 41: 385–9.

1. Brinkman 1967, 1976/80.
2. Limet 1971; Sommerfeld 1995; Van Lerberghe 1995; Sassmannshausen 1999.
3. Baqir 1944, 1945, 1946; Tomabechi 1983; Meyer 1999.
4. McDonald 2005.
5. Moorey 1994: 302–22.
6. Seidl 1989; Slanski 2003.
7. Collon 1987: 58–61.
8. Edzard 1976/80a: 546–7; Studevent-Hickman 2007.
9. Waschow 1936: 46–8; Brinkman 1980.
10. B. Foster 1987; Jursa 2004: 55–8.
11. Cassin 1966; Brinkman 1974; Ellis 1976: 109–32, 148–66; Oelsner 1982; Sassmannshausen 1999; figure for royal land grants courtesy S. Paulus.
12. Yadin 1963; Littauer and Crouwel 1979, 2002; Darnell and Manassa 2007: 77–80.
13. Ebeling 1951: 25, G, lines 3–7.
14. Moorey 1970; Littauer and Crouwel 1979, 2002; Meadow 1986.
15. Gurney 1983: 41–5.
16. *Muses*, 767.
17. Zaccagnini 1973; R. Cohen and Westbrook 2000; Liverani 2001; Feldman 2006; Van De Mieroop 2007.
18. Moran 1992; Liverani 1998.
19. Moran 1992: 13, with slight changes.
20. Moran 1992: 9.
21. Goldberg 2004.
22. Moran 1992: 18.
23. Goetze 1947; Bottéro 1974, 1992; B. Foster 1982b: 113.
24. Durand 1998: 95–117.
25. Durand 2000, 3: 403–4.
26. Goetze 1957: 103 no. 21, lines 4–7.
27. Bottéro 1974: 124–43; Jeyes 1980.
28. Goetze 1947; Glassner 1983.
29. Freedman 1998: 199, lines 83–6.

30. Bottéro 1977: 15–28; Krecher 1976/80; Hallo 1996; Seminara 2001; Radner 2005: 16–7.
31. Alster 1997, 1: 54, 2.47.
32. Landsberger 1937.
33. Waschow 1936: 33–4.
34. Biggs 1987/90; Scurlock 2005.
35. *Muses*, 397.
36. *Muses*, 400.
37. Sitzler 1995.
38. Wilhelm 1989.
39. Cassin 1974; Lacheman 1974; Maidman 1995.
40. Cassin 1938: 16–32.
41. Moorey 1994: 159–62, 189–215; Paynter and Tite 2001; Robson 2001.
42. *Muses*, 375.
43. B. Foster 2007b: 21–2.
44. *Muses*, 370.
45. Brinkman 1968: 90–148; *Muses*, 376–80.
46. *Muses*, 383.
47. *Muses*, 472.
48. Brinkman 1968: 148–66; Zettler 1989.

Chapter 7. The Assyrian Achievement

Epigraph source: W. G. Lambert 1960, *Babylonian Wisdom Literature*, 282. Oxford: Clarendon Press.

1. D. Oates 1968: 19; Postgate 1989: 141–2; Arnaud 2007: 43.
2. Lambert 1983.
3. Charpin and Durand 1997.
4. Moorey 1994: 297–301.
5. Larsen 1976.
6. Collon 1995: 90–4; Michel 2001.
7. Michel 2001: 419–511.
8. Michel 2001: 302.
9. Glassner 2004: 136–45.
10. *Muses*, 334; Garelli 1981.
11. Liverani 1988b.
12. Moran 1992: 39.
13. Eickhoff 1976/80.
14. Frankfort 1970: 131–42; Collon 1987: 65–9.

15. Frankfort 1970: 132; Grayson 1972: 126.
16. Grayson 1972: 108.
17. *Muses*, 318–23.
18. *Muses*, 298–317.
19. Glassner 2004: 281.
20. Wapnish 1995.
21. Grayson 1976: 29.
22. Grayson 1972: 46–7; Grayson 1976: 43.
23. Lipin 1960/1.
24. Diakonoff 1949: 44–58; Postgate 1982.
25. Sandars 1985; Zettler 1989.
26. Sader 1989.
27. Beaulieu 2005: 54.
28. Brinkman 1984; Frame 1992.
29. Luckenbill 1927, 2: 310.
30. *Muses*, 794; Luckenbill 1927, 2: 352; Tadmor 1999.
31. Oded 1979.
32. Oded 1979: 20; De Odorico 1995: 170–6.
33. Tadmor 1982; Rosenthal 1987.
34. Olmstead 1918; Liverani 2004.
35. Oates and Oates 2001.
36. Grayson 1976: 176.
37. Lion and Michel, eds. 2006.
38. Porada 1989; Matthiae 1996; Reade 1998: 34–41; Russell 1999: 9–63; Albenda 2005.
39. Giovino 2007.
40. Grayson 1976: 164–7, quotation from 166 with slight changes.
41. Grayson 1976: 165–7; Reade 1980.
42. Oates and Oates 2001: 78–90.
43. Zimansky 1985.
44. Van De Mieroop 1999.
45. *Muses*, 796.
46. Albenda 1986; Russell 1999: 99–123.
47. Luckenbill 1927, 2: 42.
48. Brinkman 1964.
49. Frahm 1999; B. Foster 2001: 138.
50. Dalley 1994; Bagg 2000.
51. Russell 1991.
52. Luckenbill 1924: 97, line 84.
53. K. Foster 1998; Thomason 2005.

54. Luckenbill 1924: 115, line 57; 124, line 44.
55. Luckenbill 1924: 111, line 56.
56. Clayton and Price, eds. 1988; Romer and Romer 1995.
57. Dalley 1994, 2002.
58. K. Foster 2005.
59. Russell 1991: 191–222.
60. Luckenbill 1924: 82–4.
61. Luckenbill 1924: 84; Brinkman 1984; Glassner 2004: 23–5.
62. Glassner 2004: 199.
63. Villard 1997; Livingstone 2007.
64. Livingstone 2007.
65. B. Foster 2007a: 83–4.
66. Black and Tait 1995; Potts 2000.
67. Veenhof 1986; Pedersén 1998.
68. Krecher 1976/80.
69. Weidner 1952/3; *Muses*, 324; Pedersén 1998: 134; Maul 2003.
70. Frame and George 2005.
71. Oppenheim 1977: 16–8.
72. Reade 1986.
73. Lanfranchi, Roaf, and Rollinger, eds. 2003.
74. Pickworth 2005.
75. Glassner 2004: 222–3.
76. Nylander 1980.
77. Temple 1999.
78. Mallowan 1978; Oates and Oates 2001.
79. Glassner 2004: 223.

CHAPTER 8. THE GLORY OF BABYLON

Epigraph source: *Muses*, 847.
1. Porter 1993: 41–61.
2. Parpola and Watanabe 1988: 35, lines 162–9 (§ 14).
3. Brinkman 1984: 93–104; Melville 1999: 79–90; Diodorus Siculus, *History*, II 21.
4. Arnaud 2004; Joannès 2004: 123–5.
5. Ezekiel 17: 11–21.
6. J. Oates 1979; Wiseman 1985; Clayton and Price, eds. 1988; Romer and Romer 1995.
7. Pongratz-Leisten 1994.
8. Rollinger 1993; Dalley 1996; Nesselrath 1999.
9. Grayson 1975: 88–9, lines 11–2.

10. Daniel 4: 33; Sack 1972, 1978.
11. *Muses*, 854.
12. Sack 1972, 1978; Finkel 1999.
13. Schaudig 2001: 506.
14. Beaulieu 1989; Braun-Holzinger and Frahm 1999.
15. *Muses*, 864.
16. Beaulieu 1989: 203.
17. Beaulieu 1989: 215–8.
18. Schaudig 2001: 519.
19. *Muses*, 870–3.
20. Glassner 2004.
21. Glassner 2004: 268–9.
22. J. Oates 1979: 108–9; Collon 1995: 168–9; Woods 2004.
23. Schaudig 2001: 457–60.
24. Frayne 1993: 197–8.
25. B. Foster 2007b: 115.
26. Dandamayev 1983; Beaulieu 2007: 475–6.
27. Aaboe 1974; Klengel 1989: 399–403; Britton and Walker 1996; Depuydt 2008.
28. Bottéro 2001b: 194.
29. Dandamayev 1988; Slotsky 1997.
30. Rochberg 1998.
31. B. Foster 2007b: 104–9.
32. *Muses*, 699.
33. *Muses*, 949.
34. *Muses*, 880–911.
35. *Muses*, 907.
36. Joannès 2004: 154–64.
37. Joannès 2004: 187–90.
38. Jursa 2004.
39. Dandamayev 1984.
40. Dandamayev 1971: 70–8; Dercksen 1999; Wunsch 2000.
41. Joannès 1989; Wunsch 1993, 1999; Abraham 2004; Jursa 2007.
42. Cocquerillat 1968; Joannès 2004: 154.
43. Liverani 1976; Oppenheim 1978; Favaro 2007.
44. Jursa 2003; Liverani 2003.
45. Cogan in Hallo 2000: 314–6.
46. Briant 2002.
47. Grélot 1972: 297–327; Rosenthal 1987.
48. Briant 2002: 484.

49. Dalley 1993; Kuhrt 1995; Bartl and Hauser, eds. 1996; J. Curtis 2003.
50. Ebeling 1930/4: 4–7.
51. Briant 1994; Joannès 2004: 203–11.
52. Joannès 2004: 211–5.
53. Stolper 1985.
54. Joannès 2004: 153.
55. Roth 1989, 1989/90.
56. *Muses*, 369.
57. Kuhrt and Sherwin-White 1987; Van Driel 1987; Joannès 2004: 205.
58. Glassner 2004: 238–43.
59. Stronach 1978; Root 1979; Harper, Aruz, and Tallon, eds. 1992.

CHAPTER 9. MESOPOTAMIA BETWEEN TWO WORLDS

Epigraph source: Pausanias, *Guide to Greece*, IV 32, 4. Translated with an introduction by Peter Levi. Harmondsworth, UK: Penguin Books.

1. Marsden 1964.
2. Wilcken 1967: 144–5; Briant 1980; Sancisi-Weerdenberg 1993.
3. Kuhrt 1990; Briant 2002: 862–4; Boiy 2004: 110–2; Glassner 2004: 248–9.
4. Depuydt 1997; Boiy 2004: 116–7.
5. Briant 1990; Boiy 2004: 127–34; Glassner 2004: 246–7.
6. Sherwin-White 1987; Kuhrt and Sherwin-White 1994.
7. Peters 1970: 87.
8. Bickerman 1966; Frye 1984: 191–7.
9. Briant 1990, 1994.
10. *Muses*, 866; Sherwin-White 1987: 27–9; Horowitz 1991; Kuhrt and Sherwin-White 1991.
11. Burstein 1978; Kuhrt 1987.
12. Verbrugghe and Wickersham 2001: 44.
13. Reiner 1961.
14. Black and Green 1992: 82–3.
15. Bowman 1986: 22–5.
16. Verbrugge and Wickersham 2001: 95–120.
17. Invernizzi, Mancini, and Valtz 1985.
18. Sherwin-White 1987: 18–21; S. Downey 1997; Boiy 2004: 135–7.

19. Van der Spek 2001; Boiy 2004: 73–98.
20. Doty 1977: 150–69; Sherwin-White 1987: 29–30; Van der Spek 2005.
21. Doty 1977: 308–35.
22. Fino 2005: 255–7.
23. Krückmann 1931: 14, note 3.
24. Van der Spek 1986: 144–7; 1993.
25. Van der Spek 2000.
26. Millar 1998b; Parker 2000.
27. Walker, ed. 1996; Slotsky 1997: 105–6; Vargyas 1997; Boiy 2004: 238–9.
28. Boiy 2004: 13–39.
29. Burstein 1978.
30. Momigliano 1975: 7–8.
31. Neusner 1969a: 10.
32. Van der Spek 2005: 405–6.
33. Pingree 1998; Boiy 2004: 307–14.
34. Friberg 2007.
35. Nougayrol 1955; Ammianus Marcellinus, *History*, XXIII 6, 25.
36. André-Salvini 2003b.
37. Fino 2005.
38. Peters 1970: 43; Bar-Kochva 1976: 75–83.
39. Pingree 1998.
40. Wolski 1956/8; Wiesehöfer 2001: 130–6.
41. Rostovtzeff 1943; Junkelmann 1990, 3: 163–9.
42. Plutarch, *Crassus*.
43. Wiesehöfer 2001: 136–44.
44. Polybius, *Histories*, XXIX 27.
45. Polybius, *Histories*, XXXI 9; 2 Maccabees 8:7; Bevan 1902, 2: 160–1.
46. Verstandig 2001: 57–79.
47. Simpson 1997.
48. Harmatta 1981.
49. Kurz 1983: 562.
50. Widengren 1956.
51. Nodelman 1960; Justin, *History*, XXXVIII 9.
52. Nissen 1971; Bartl and Hauser, eds. 1996; Hauser 1999.
53. Isidore of Charax, *Parthian Stations*.
54. Hirth 1885: 35–40; Tao 2007.

55. Fino 2005: 161–8.
56. Colledge 1967: 115–42; V. Curtis 2007; Wiesehöfer 2007: 127–30.
57. Kirkbride 1975.
58. D. Oates 1973; Gibson, Sanders, and Mortensen 1981.
59. Colledge 1967: 143–65; Colledge 1977; Schlumberger 1983.
60. Justin, *History*, XLI 3.
61. Ingholt 1954; V. Curtis 2000.
62. Minorsky 1944; Boyce 1983: 1158–9; V. Curtis 1993: 62–5.
63. Brunner 1980.
64. Justin, *History*, XXXII 2, 12; Diodorus Siculus, *History*, XX-VIII 3, XXIX 5; Bevan 1902, 2: 120; Bar-Kochva 1976: 163–73.
65. Wiesehöfer 2001: 123–5; Ammianus Marcellinus, *History*, XXIII 6, 76–80.
66. Plutarch, *Crassus*, XXXIII.
67. Horace, *Odes*, 3, 2; Wissemann 1982.
68. Schneider 2007: 54.
69. Verstandig 2001: 275–92.
70. Joannès 2004: 253.
71. Sachs 1976: 395.
72. Geller 1995; Dalley, ed. 1998; Boiy 2004: 304–16.

CHAPTER 10. SASSANIAN IRAQ

Epigraph source: Babylonian Talmud, ʿAbodah zarah 11b, *Hebrew-English Edition of the Babylonian Talmud*. Translated by A. Mishcon and A. Cohen; ed. I. Epstein. London: Soncino Press.

1. Yarshater 1983; B. Robinson 2002.
2. Frye 1983: 116–7.
3. Boyce 1968: 67; Yarshater 1971.
4. Simpson 1997.
5. Christensen 1944, 2: 392–3; Hadi Muhy al-Khafaji, in al-Khaqani, ed., 1987, 12: 400–1.
6. Dvornik 1966, 2: 611–40.
7. Barnes 1981: 245–50.
8. Boyce 1975: 181–91; Frye 1984: 57–8.
9. Bickerman 1983: 786–90; Duchesne-Guillemin 1983; Frye 1984: 59.
10. Insler 1975; de Menasce 1983: 1170–6; Kellens 1989.

11. Boyce 1968: 33–4; Colpe 1983: 826–31.
12. Hoyland 2001: 139–66.
13. Dirven 1997; Butcher 2003: 335–70.
14. Müller-Kessler 2004.
15. Brown 1969; Widengren 1983; Lieu 1992, 1994; Millar 1993: 501–3.
16. Bivar 1975; Daniels 1975; Colpe 1983: 853–6; Turcan 1993: 31–43, 81–92.
17. MacMullen 1997.
18. Bury 1923, 2: 369–71.
19. Talon 2001: 272–3.
20. Jeremiah 29: 5–7.
21. Weidner 1939; Jursa 2005: 151.
22. Swartz 2006.
23. Newman 1932; Neusner 1969a; Gafni 2006; Goodblatt 2006a.
24. Neusner 1969a: 44–6.
25. Neusner 1966: 1–125; 1968: 1–40; 1969b: 1–72; 1970: 1–132.
26. Gafni 2002; Goodblatt 2006b; Kalmin 2006.
27. Naveh and Shaked 1985: 181.
28. Naveh and Shaked 1985; Harper 2006: 24–7; Swartz 2006.
29. Iamblichus of Chalcis, *De Mysteriis*, VII 256, 4–8.
30. Labourt 1904: 10; Fiey 1979: X, 24.
31. Vööbus 1987: 8; Millar 1998c: 384–94.
32. Butcher 2003: 335–70.
33. Frend 1972; Butcher 2003: 389–90.
34. Amann 1931; Tisserant 1931.
35. Hitti 1951: 272.
36. Bruns 2000.
37. Wigram 1910: 64–5; Wiessner 1967: 203–4.
38. Ammianus Marcellinus, *History*, XXIII 6, 80; Frye 1984: 2–4; Tafazzoli 2000: 2–3.
39. Lambton 2000.
40. Gutas 2006.
41. Boyce 1968: 49.
42. Christensen 1944, 2: 366–7; Lukonin 1983: 744–6; Tafazzoli 2000: 41.
43. Begley and De Puma 1991; Whitehouse 1996; Tomber 2007.
44. Simpson 2000: 61.
45. Simpson 2000: 62.

46. Wigram 1929: 48. We are unable to identify an ancient source for this quotation.
47. Segal 1955.
48. Joshua the Stylite, *Chronicle*, 63.
49. Bowersock 1983; Millar 1993: 387–90; Hoyland 2001; Briquel Chatonnet 2004.
50. Eph'al 1982.
51. Heck 2003.
52. Hoyland 2001: 58–83.
53. Tisserant 1931: 166–9; Frye 1983: 138; Whitehouse 1996: 340.
54. Shahid 1965.
55. Kister 1968; Shahid 1986.
56. Nicholson 1907: 45–8; Horovitz 1930.
57. Adi ibn Zaid, 441–2.
58. Gruendler 1993: 1–2, 128.
59. Harper 2006.
60. Collon 1995: 212–27.
61. K. Foster 2005; Kennedy 2007: 122.
62. Fino 2005: 168–71.
63. Harper 1978; Shepherd 1983; Demange, ed. 2006.
64. Christensen 1944, 2: 397–8; Frye 1983: 134–5; Ibn Ishaq, *Life of Muhammad*, 30.
65. Maricq 1957; Sommer 2005: 355–90.
66. Yarshater 1983: 380, 401.
67. Back 1978: 313.
68. Sprengling 1953; Back 1978: 327–8; Wiesehöfer 2001: 155.
69. Gutas 1998: 25–6.
70. Labourt 1904: 43–82; Wiessner 1967; Frye 1983: 136–8; Hoyland 2001: 29.
71. Ammianus Marcellinus, *History*, XVII 5, 3.
72. Browning 1976.
73. Ammianus Marcellinus, *History*, XXV 1, 12–4.
74. Bury 1923, 2: 89–123; Baker 1931: 228–31; Browning 1987: 115–20.
75. G. Downey 1963: 248–55.
76. Ostrogorsky 1957: 84–6; Stratos 1972, 1: 124–5; Treadgold 1997: 287–93; Kaegi 2003: 88–9, 111, 122–55.
77. Stratos 1972, 1: 248–55; Treadgold 1997: 293–300; Kaegi 2003: 156–91.
78. Howard-Johnston 1999; Kaegi 2003: 208.

79. Stratos 1972, 1: 286–304; Treadgold 1997: 300–1, 305.
80. Ibn Ishaq, *Life of Muhammad*, 654–7; Bashear 1997; Kaegi 2003: 236.
81. Meyendorff 1964; Lamoureux 2001.
82. Ibn Ishaq, *Life of Muhammad*, 654.
83. al-Baladhuri, *Kitâb Futûh al-Buldân*, 1: 210; Stratos 1972, 2: 73.
84. Hitti 1964: 155–9; Donner 1981: 157–220; Kennedy 2007: 98–138.

Epilogue. Discovery and Distruction of Ancient Iraq

Epigraph source: B. Foster 2008, "Assyriology and English Literature." In: M. Ross, ed., *From the Banks of the Euphrates: Studies in Honor of Alice Louise Slotsky*, 63. Winona Lake, Ind.: Eisenbrauns.

1. Dinsmoor 1943: 100; Pallis 1956: 70–87; Collon 1995: 19.
2. Roaf 1990: 222–3; Glassner 2003a; K. Foster 2005.
3. Schwab 1984.
4. Pallis 1956: 48–53; Janssen 1995.
5. Budge 1925: 15–6; Pallis 1956: 56.
6. Budge 1925: 17; Pallis 1956: 57–61.
7. Budge 1925: 19; Pallis 1956: 63.
8. Stolper 2004.
9. Pallis 1956: 132–59; A. Robinson 1995: 70–9.
10. Pallis 1956: 160–4.
11. Larsen 1996; Russell 1997.
12. Budge 1925: 113–5.
13. Carena 1989.
14. Bernhardsson 2005: 43.
15. Frahm 2006: 85–6.
16. Frahm 2006.
17. Frahm 2006: 82–3.
18. Lloyd 1980; Maisels 1993.
19. Postgate 1977: 43.
20. Shaw 2003.
21. Postgate 1977: 43.
22. Budge 1925: 199–202.
23. Bernhardsson 2005: 73–92.
24. Budge 1925: 12, 101, 133, 136–7, 139, 142.
25. Budge 1925: 138.
26. Maul 2005.

27. Hanisch 2003: 18–20.
28. Daniel 1981.
29. Brodie, Doole, and Renfrew, eds. 2001; Brodie and Tubb, eds. 2002; Atwood 2004.
30. Kramer 1967: 17–29; Roaf 1990: 14–6.
31. Albright 1960: 20.
32. Oates and Oates 1976: 34–68; J. Curtis, ed. 1982; Foster, Foster, and Gerstenblith 2005: 193–5, 204–5.
33. Batatu 1978: 13–9; Wallach 1996; Howell 2007.
34. Bell 1953: 324.
35. B. Foster 2007c: 32, 35.
36. Fales 2004; Damrosch 2006: 254–72; Gibson 2006: 247.
37. Gibson and McMahon 1992; Baker, Matthews, and Postgate 1993.
38. Farchakh 2001; Alnasrawi 2003.
39. Tubb, ed. 1995; Foster, Foster, and Gerstenblith 2005: 245–73; Hoffman 2006; Robson, Treadwell, and Gosden, eds. 2006.
40. Lawler 2003a; Eakin 2007: 68.
41. Farchakh 2003a, 2003b.
42. Bogdanos 2005: 202–3.
43. Gibson, Russell, Biggs, Paley, and Nofziger 2003; Bogdanos 2005; Polk and Schuster 2005; Emberling and Hanson, eds. 2008.
44. Bogdanos 2005: 211.
45. Nashef 2004; Foster, Foster, and Gerstenblith 2005: 275–7.
46. http://www.defenselink.mil/transcripts/transcript.aspx?.trans criptid=2367.
47. Bogdanos 2005.
48. Lawler 2003b: 584.
49. Bianco 2004; Flandrin 2004; Nashef 2004; Rothfield, ed. 2008.
50. Farchakh 2003c; 2004; Atwood 2004: 1–9; Vogel 2007.
51. Statement of Financial Activities for the year ended 31 March 2007, British School of Archaeology in Iraq, pp. 14–5.
52. Olbrys, Dolatowska, and Burda 2004.
53. Waldbaum 2005.
54. Schlesinger 2007.

BIBLIOGRAPHY

CLASSICAL AND MEDIEVAL AUTHORS

Adi ibn Zaid. Edited by Louis Cheikho. *Šuʿarāʾ al-Naṣrāniyyah, qabla al-Islām,* pp. 439–74. Beirut: Dar al-Mashriq, 1927 [reprint 1967].

Ammianus Marcellinus. *History.* Translated by John C. Rolfe. *Loeb Classical Library.* Cambridge, Mass.: Harvard University Press, 1940.

al-Baladhuri. *Kitâb Futûh al-Buldân.* Translated by Philip Khouri Hitti. *The Origins of the Islamic State. Studies in History, Economic and Public Law* 68. New York: Columbia University Press, 1916 [reprint 1968].

Diodorus Siculus. *History.* Translated by C. H. Oldfather. New York: Putnams, 1933.

Horace. *Odes.* Translated by James Michie. *The Odes of Horace.* New York: Washington Square Press, 1963.

Iamblichus of Chalcis. *De Mysteriis.* Translated by Edouard des Places. *Jamblique: Les Mystères d'Egypte.* Paris: Les Belles Lettres, 1966.

Ibn Ishaq. *Sīrat Rasūl Allāh.* Translated by A. Guillaume. *The Life of Muhammad.* Oxford: Oxford University Press, 1955.

Isidore of Charax. *Parthian Stations.* Translated by Wilfred H. Schoff. Philadelphia: Commercial Museum, 1914.

Joshua the Stylite. *Chronicle.* Translated by W. Wright. *The Chronicle of Joshua the Stylite, composed in Syriac* A.D. *507.* Cambridge, UK: Cambridge University Press, 1882.

Justin. *History.* Translated by John Selby Watson. London: Henry G. Bohn, 1853.

Plutarch. *Lives. Plutarch's Lives: The Translation called Dryden's, corrected from the Greek and revised by A. H. Clough.* New York: Bigelow, Brown, no date.

Polybius. *Histories.* Translated by W. R. Paton. Loeb Classical Library. Cambridge, Mass.: Harvard University Press, 1960.

OTHER WORKS CITED

Aaboe, Asger. 1974. "Scientific Astronomy in Antiquity." In: D. G. Kendall, ed., *The Place of Astronomy in the Ancient World*, pp. 21–42. Oxford: Oxford University Press.

Abraham, Kathleen. 2004. *Business and Politics under the Persian Empire: The Financial Dealings of Marduk-nasir-apli of the House of Egibi (521–487 B.C.E.).* Bethesda, Md.: CDL Press.

Adams, Robert McC. 1981. *Heartland of Cities: Surveys of Ancient Settlement and Land Use on the Central Floodplain of the Euphrates.* Chicago: University of Chicago Press.

Adams, Robert McC. and Hans J. Nissen. 1972. *The Uruk Countryside: The Natural Setting of Urban Societies.* Chicago: University of Chicago Press.

Albenda, Pauline. 1986. *The Palace of Sargon, King of Assyria.* Paris: CNRS Editions.

———. 2005. *Ornamental Wall Painting in the Art of the Assyrian Empire.* Leiden: E. J. Brill.

Albright, William F. 1960. *The Archaeology of Palestine.* London: Pelican Books.

Algaze, G. 1993. *The Uruk World System: The Dynamics of Expansion of Early Mesopotamian Civilization.* Chicago: University of Chicago Press.

———. 2001. "The Prehistory of Imperialism: The Case of Uruk Period Mesopotamia." In: M. S. Rothman, ed., *Uruk Mesopotamia and Its Neighbors: Cross-cultural Interactions and Their Consequences in the Era of State Formation*, pp. 27–84. Santa Fe: School of American Research.

Alnasrawi, Abbas. 2003. "Sanctions and the Iraqi Economy." In: Shams C. Inati, ed., *Iraq: Its History, People, and Politics*, pp. 215–31. Amherst, N.Y.: Humanity Books.

Alster, Bendt. 1983. "Dilmun, Bahrein, and the Alleged Paradise in Sumerian Myth and Literature." In: Daniel T. Potts, ed., *Dilmun: New Studies in the Archaeology and Early History of Bahrein*, pp. 39–74. *Berliner Beiträge zum Vorderen Orient* 2. Berlin: Dietrich Reimer Verlag.

———. 1997. *Proverbs of Ancient Sumer: The World's Earliest Proverb Collections.* Bethesda, Md.: CDL Press.

Amann, E. 1931. "Nestorius." *Dictionnaire de Théologie Catholique*, 11: 76–157. Paris: Letouzay.

Amiet, Pierre. 1976. *L'art d'Agadé au Musée du Louvre*. Paris: Edition des Musées Nationaux.

André-Salvini, Béatrice. 2003a. *Le Code de Hammurabi*. Paris: Réunion des Musées Nationaux.

———. 2003b. "The Rediscovery of Gudea Statuary in the Hellenistic Period." In: Joan Aruz, ed., *Art of the First Cities: The Third Millennium B.C. from the Mediterranean to the Indus*, pp. 424–5. New York: Metropolitan Museum of Art.

Archi, Alfonso. 1992. "Transmission of the Mesopotamian Lexical and Literary Texts from Ebla." *Quaderni di Semitistica* 18: 1–39.

Arnaud, Daniel. 2004. *Nabuchodnossor II, roi de Babylone*. Paris: Fayard.

———. 2007. *Assurbanipal, roi d'Assyrie*. Paris: Fayard.

Atwood, Roger. 2004. *Stealing History: Tomb Raiders, Smugglers, and the Looting of the Ancient World*. New York: St. Martin's Press.

Back, Michael. 1978. *Die Sassanidischen Staatsinschriften*. *Acta Iranica* 18. Leiden: E. J. Brill.

Bagg, Ariel M. 2000. *Assyrische Wasserbauten: Landschaftliche Wasserbauten im Kernland Assyriens zwischen der 2. Hälfte des 2. und der 1. Hälfte des 1. Jahrtausends v. Chr.* Mainz: von Zabern.

Bahrani, Zainab. 2002. "Performativity and the Image: Narrative, Representation, and the Uruk Vase." In: E. Ehrenberg, ed., *Leaving No Stones Unturned: Essays on the Ancient Near East and Egypt in Honor of Donald P. Hansen*, pp. 15–22. Winona Lake, Ind.: Eisenbrauns.

———. 2003. *The Graven Image: Representation in Babylonia and Assyria*. Philadelphia: University of Pennsylvania Press.

Baker, G. P. 1931. *Justinian, the Last Roman Emperor*. New York: Cooper Square Press [reprint 2002].

Baker, H. D., R. J. Matthews, and J. N. Postgate. 1993. *Lost Heritage: Antiquities Stolen from Iraq's Regional Museums*, fascicle 2. London: British School of Archaeology in Iraq.

Baqir, Taha. 1944. "Iraq Government Excavations at ʿAqar Quf, 1942–43." *Iraq Supplement*. London: British School of Archaeology in Iraq.

———. 1945. "Iraq Government Excavations at ʿAqar Quf, Second Interim Report, 1943–44." *Iraq Supplement*. London: British School of Archaeology in Iraq.

———. 1946. "Iraq Government Excavations at ʿAqar Quf, Third Interim report, 1944–1945." *Iraq* 8: 73–93.

Bar-Kochva, Bezalel. 1976. *The Seleucid Army: Organization and Tactics in the Great Campaigns.* Cambridge, UK: Cambridge University Press.

Barnes, Timothy. 1981. *Constantine and Eusebius.* Cambridge, Mass.: Harvard University Press.

Bartl, Karin and Stefan Hauser, eds. 1996. *Continuity and Change in Northern Mesopotamia from the Hellenistic to the Early Islamic Period: Proceedings of a Colloquium held at the Seminar für Vorderasiatische Altertumskunde, Freie Universität Berlin, 6–9 April 1994. Berliner Beiträge zum Vorderen Orient* 17. Berlin: Dietrich Reimer Verlag.

Bashear, Suleiman. 1997. "The Mission of Diḥya al-Kalbī," *Der Islam* 74: 64–91.

Batatu, Hanna. 1978. *The Old Social Classes and the Revolutionary Movements of Iraq: A Study of Iraq's Old Landed and Commercial Classes and of Its Communists, Baʿthists, and Free Officers.* Princeton: Princeton University Press.

Bauer, Josef. 1998. "Der Vorsargonische Abschnitt der mesopotamischen Geschichte." In: Pascal Attinger and Markus Wäfler, eds., *Mesopotamien: Späturuk-Zeit und Frühdynastische Zeit,* pp. 431–585. *Orbis Biblicus et Orientalis* 160/1. Göttingen: Vandenhoeck & Ruprecht.

Beaulieu, Paul-Alain. 1989. *The Reign of Nabonidus, King of Babylon 556–539 B.C. Yale Near Eastern Researches* 10. New Haven: Yale University Press.

———. 2004. "History of Mesopotamian Religion." In: S. I. Johnston, ed., *Religions of the Ancient World: A Guide,* pp. 165–72. Cambridge, UK: Cambridge University Press.

———. 2005. "World Hegemony, 900–300 BCE." In: Daniel C. Snell, ed., *A Companion to the Ancient Near East,* pp. 48–61. Malden, Mass.: Blackwell Publishing.

———. 2007. "Late Babylonian Intellectual Life." In: Gwendolyn Leick, ed., *The Babylonian World,* pp. 473–84. London: Routledge.

Begley, V. and R. D. De Puma. 1991. *Rome and India: The Ancient Sea Trade.* Madison: University of Wisconsin Press.

Bell, Gertrude. 1953. *Selected Letters,* edited by Florence Bell. Harmondsworth, UK: Penguin.

Benito, C. A. 1969. *"Enki and Ninmah" and "Enki and the World Order."* Ph.D. dissertation, University of Pennsylvania.

Bernhardsson, Magnus. 2005. *Reclaiming a Plundered Past: Archaeology and Nation Building in Modern Iraq.* Austin: University of Texas Press.

Bevan, E. R. 1902. *The House of Seleucus*. London: E. Arnold [reprint 1966].

Bianco, Pialuisa. 2004. *Iraq prima e dopo la guerra: I siti archeologici*. Rome: l'Erma di Bretschneider.

Bickerman, E. J. 1966. "The Seleucids and the Achaemenids." In: *Atti del convegno sul tema: La Persia e il mondo Greco-Romano (Roma 11–14 aprile 1965)*, pp. 87–117. Rome: Accademia Nazionale dei Lincei.

————. 1983. "Time-Reckoning." In: Ehsan Yarshater, ed., *The Cambridge History of Iran*, 3(2): 778–91. Cambridge, UK: Cambridge University Press.

Biggs, Robert D. 1974. *Inscriptions from Tell Abū-Ṣalābīkh. Oriental Institute Publications* 98. Chicago: University of Chicago Press.

————. 1987/90. "Medizin A." *Reallexikon der Assyriologie*, 7: 623–9. Berlin: De Gruyter.

Bivar, A.D.H. 1975. "Mithra and Mesopotamia." In: John R. Hinnells, ed., *Mithraic Studies: Proceedings of the First International Congress of Mithraic Studies*, 2: 275–89. Manchester: Manchester University Press.

Black, Jeremy. 1998. *The Literature of Ancient Sumer*. Oxford: Oxford University Press.

Black, Jeremy and Anthony Green. 1992. *Gods, Demons and Symbols of Ancient Mesopotamia: An Illustrated Dictionary*. London: British Museum Press.

Black, Jeremy and W. J. Tait. 1995. "Archives and Libraries in the Ancient Near East." In: Jack M. Sasson, ed., *Civilizations of the Ancient Near East*, 2: 2197–209. New York: Scribner's.

Boehmer, Rainer Michael. 1997. "Uruk-Warka." In: Eric M. Meyers, ed., *The Oxford Encyclopedia of Archaeology in the Near East*, 5: 294–8. Oxford: Oxford University Press.

Bogdanos, Matthew, with William Patrick. 2005. *Thieves of Baghdad*. New York: Bloomsbury Press.

Boiy, T. 2004. *Late Achaemenid and Hellenistic Babylon. Orientalia Lovaniensia Analecta* 136. Leuven: Peeters.

Bottéro, Jean. 1974. "Symptômes, signes, écritures." In: Remo Guideri, ed., *Divination et Rationalité*, pp. 70–197. Paris: Editions du Seuil.

————. 1977. "Les Noms de Marduk, l'écriture et la 'logique' en Mésopotamie ancienne." In: Maria de Jong Ellis, ed., *Essays on the Ancient Near East in Memory of Jacob Joel Finkelstein*, pp. 5–28. *Memoirs of the Connecticut Academy of Arts & Sciences* 19. Hamden, Conn.: Shoestring Press.

Bottéro, Jean. 1980/3. "Küche." *Reallexikon der Assyriologie,* 6: 277–98. Berlin: De Gruyter.

———. 1995. *Textes culinaires Mésopotamiens. Mesopotamian Civilizations* 6. Winona Lake, Ind.: Eisenbrauns.

———. 2001a. *Religion in Ancient Mesopotamia.* Translated by T. L. Fagan. Chicago: University of Chicago Press.

———. 2001b. *Everyday Life in Ancient Mesopotamia.* Translated by Antonia Nevill. Baltimore: Johns Hopkins University Press.

Bottéro, Jean and Samuel Noah Kramer. 1989. *Lorsque les dieux faisaient l'homme: Mythologie mésopotamienne.* Paris: Gallimard.

Bourgeois, Brigitte. 1992. "Conservation of Other Materials." In: Prudence O. Harper, Joan Aruz, and Françoise Tallon, eds., *The Royal City of Susa: Ancient Near Eastern Treasures in the Louvre,* pp. 285–6. New York: Metropolitan Museum of Art.

Bowersock, G. W. 1983. *Roman Arabia.* Cambridge, Mass.: Harvard University Press.

Bowman, Alan K. 1986. *Egypt after the Pharaohs, 332 BC–AD 642.* Berkeley: University of California Press.

Boyce, Mary. 1968. *The Letter of Tansar. Literary and Historical Texts from Iran* 1. Roma: Istituto Italiano per il Medio ed Estremo Oriente.

———. 1975. *A History of Zoroastrianism, Volume 1. Handbuch der Orientalistik,* Erste Abteilung, Band 8 Abschnitt 1, Lieferung 2 Heft 2A. Leiden: E. J. Brill.

———. 1983. "Parthian Writings and Literature." In: Ehsan Yarshater, ed., *The Cambridge History of Iran,* 3(2): 1151–65. Cambridge, UK: Cambridge University Press.

Braun-Holzinger, Eva and Eckart Frahm. 1999. "Liebling des Marduk— König der Blasphemie. Große babylonische Herrscher in der Sicht der Babylonier und in der Sicht anderer Völker." In: Johannes Renger, ed., *Babylon: Focus mesopotamischer Geschichte, Wiege früher Gelehrsamkeit, Mythos in der Moderne: 2. Internationales Colloquium der Deutschen Orient-Gesellschaft 24–26. März in Berlin,* pp. 131–56. Saarbrücken: Saarbrückener Druckerei und Verlag.

Briant, Pierre. 1980. "Conquête territoriale et conquête idéologique: Alexandre le Grand et l'idéologie monarchique achéménide." In: Pierre Briant, *Rois, tributs et paysans: Etudes sur les formations tributaires du Moyen-Orient ancien,* pp. 357–403. Paris: Les Belles Lettres.

———. 1990. "The Seleucid Kingdom, the Achaemenid Empire and the History of the Near East in the First Millennium B.C." In: Per Bilde, ed., *Religion and Religious Practice in the Seleucid Kingdom,* pp. 40–90. Aarhus: Aarhus University Press.

————. 1994. "De Samarkand à Sardes et de la ville de Suse au pays des Hanéens." *Topoi* 4/2: 455–67.

————. 2002. *From Cyrus to Alexander: A History of the Persian Empire.* Translated by Peter T. Daniels. Winona Lake, Ind.: Eisenbrauns.

Brinkman, John. 1964. "Merodach-Baladan II." In: *From the Workshop of the Chicago Assyrian Dictionary: Studies Presented to A. Leo Oppenheim, June 7, 1964*, pp. 6–53. Chicago: Oriental Institute of the University of Chicago.

————. 1967. "The Tribal Organization of the Kassites." In: Denis Sinor, ed., *Proceedings of the 27th International Congress of Orientalists, Ann Arbor, Michigan, 13th–19th August 1967*, pp. 55–6. Wiesbaden: Harrassowitz.

————. 1968. *A Political History of Post-Kassite Babylonia, 1158–722 B.C. Analecta Orientalia* 43. Rome: Pontificium Institutum Biblicum.

————. 1974. "The Monarchy in the Time of the Kassite Dynasty." In: Paul Garelli, ed., *Le palais et la royauté: Archéologie et civilisation: XIXᵉ Rencontre Assyriologique Internationale, 1971*, pp. 395–408. Paris: Librairie Orientaliste Paul Geuthner.

————. 1976/80. "Kassiten." *Reallexikon der Assyriologie,* 5: 464–73. Berlin: De Gruyter.

————. 1980. "Forced Laborers in the Middle Babylonian Period." *Journal of Cuneiform Studies* 32: 17–22.

————. 1984. *Prelude to Empire: Babylonian Society and Politics, 747–626 BC. Occasional Publications of the Babylonian Fund* 7. Philadelphia: University Museum of Archaeology and Anthropology.

Briquel Chatonnet, Françoise. 2004. *Les Araméens et les premiers Arabes.* Aix-en-Provence: Edisud.

Brisch, Nicole Maria. 2007. *Tradition and the Poetics of Innovation: Sumerian Court Literature of the Larsa Dynasty (c. 2003–1763 B.C.E).* Alter Orient und Altes Testament 339. Münster: Ugarit Verlag.

Britton, John and Christopher B. F. Walker. 1996. "Astronomy and Astrology in Mesopotamia." In: Christopher B. F. Walker, ed., *Astronomy before the Telescope,* pp. 42–67. London: British Museum Press.

Brodie, Neil, Jennifer Doole, and Colin Renfrew, eds. 2001. *Trade in Illicit Antiquities: The Destruction of the World's Archaeological Heritage.* Cambridge, UK: McDonald Institute for Archaeological Research.

Brodie, Neil and Kathryn W. Tubb, eds. 2002. *Illicit Antiquities: The Theft of Culture and the Extinction of Archaeology.* London: Routledge.

Brown, Peter. 1969. "The Diffusion of Manichaeism in the Roman Empire." In: Peter Brown, *Religion and Society in the Age of Saint Augustine*, pp. 94–118. London: Faber and Faber.

Browning, Robert. 1976. *The Emperor Julian*. Berkeley: University of California Press.

———. 1987. *Justinian and Theodora*. London: Thames and Hudson.

Brunner, Christopher J. 1980. "The Fable of the Babylonian Tree." *Journal of Near Eastern Studies* 39: 191–202, 291–302.

Bruns, Peter. 2000. "Tatian der Syrer." *Lexikon für Theologie und Kirche*, 9: 1274–5. Freiburg: Herder.

Buccellati, Giorgio. 1966. *The Amorites of the Ur III Period*. Naples: Istituto di Studi del Vicino Oriente.

———. 1992. "Ebla and the Amorites." In: Cyrus Gordon and Gary A. Rendsburg, eds., *Eblaitica: Essays on the Ebla Archives and Eblaite Language*, 3: 83–104. Winona Lake, Ind.: Eisenbrauns.

Budge, E. Wallis. 1925. *The Rise & Progress of Assyriology*. London: Martin Hopkinson & Co.

Burstein, S. M. 1978. *The Babyloniaca of Berossus. Sources from the Ancient Near East* 1.5. Malibu: Undena Publications.

Bury, John. 1923. *History of the Later Roman Empire, from the Death of Theodosius I. to the Death of Justinian*. New York: Dover Publications [reprint 1958].

Butcher, Kevin. 2003. *Roman Syria and the Near East*. Los Angeles: Getty Museum.

Butterlin, Pascal. 2003. *Les temps proto-urbains de Mésopotamie: Contacts et acculturation à l'époque d'Uruk au Moyen-Orient*. Paris: CNRS Editions.

Butzer, Karl W. 1995. "Environmental Change in the Near East and Human Impact on the Land." In: Jack M. Sasson, ed., *Civilizations of the Ancient Near East*, 1: 123–51. New York: Scribner's.

Canby, Jenny Vorys. 2001. *The "Ur-Nammu" Stela*. Philadelphia: University Museum of Archaeology and Anthropology.

Carena, Omar. 1989. *History of the Near Eastern Historiography and Its Problems, 1852–1985. Alter Orient und Altes Testament* 218. Neukirchen-Vluyn: Butzon und Bercker.

Cassin, Elena. 1938. *L'Adoption à Nuzi*. Paris: Maisonneuve.

———. 1966. "Babylonien unter den Kassiten." In: *Fischer Weltgeschichte 3, Die Altorientalischen Reiche* II, pp. 9–70. Frankfurt am Main: Fischer Bücherei.

———. 1974. "Le palais de Nuzi et la royauté d'Arrapha." In: Paul Garelli, ed., *Le palais et la royauté: Archéologie et civilisation: XIXᵉ*

Rencontre Assyriologique Internationale, 1971, pp. 373–92. Paris: Librairie Orientaliste Paul Geuthner.

Cavigneaux, Antoine and Farouk N. H. Al-Rawi. 2000. *Gilgameš et la mort: Textes de Tell Haddad* VI. Groningen: Styx.

Charpin, Dominique. 1986. *Le Clergé d'Ur au siècle d'Hammurabi (XIXᵉ–XVIIIᵉ siècles av. J.-C.)*. Geneva: Librairie Droz.

————. 1992a. "Les malheurs d'un scribe ou l'inutilité du sumérien loin de Nippur." In: Maria de Jong Ellis, ed., *Nippur at the Centennial: Papers Read at the 35ᵉ Rencontre Assyriologique Internationale, Philadelphia, 1988*, pp. 7–27. *Occasional Publications of the Samuel Noah Kramer Fund* 14. Philadelphia: University Museum of Archaeology and Anthropology.

————. 1992b. "Immigrés, réfugiés et déportés en Babylonie sous Hammu-rabi et ses successeurs." In: Dominique Charpin and Francis Joannès, eds., *La circulation des biens, des personnes et des idées dans le Proche-Orient ancien: Actes de la XXXVIIIᵉ Rencontre Assyriologique Internationale (Paris, 8–10 juillet 1991)*, pp. 207–18. Paris: Editions Recherche sur les Civilisations.

————. 1996. "Maisons et maisonnées en Babylonie ancienne de Sippar à Ur: Remarques sur les grandes demeures des notables paléobabyloniens." In Klaas R. Veenhof, ed., *Houses and Households in Ancient Mesopotamia: Papers Read at the 40ᵉ Rencontre Assyriologique Internationale, Leiden, July 5–8, 1993*, pp. 221–8. Leiden: Nederlands Instituut voor het Nabije Oosten.

————. 2003. *Hammu-rabi de Babylone*. Paris: Presses Universitaires de France.

————. 2004. "Histoire politique du Proche-Orient Amorrite (2002–1595)." In: Pascal Attinger, Walther Sallaberger, and Markus Wäfler, eds., *Mesopotamien: Die altbabylonische Zeit*, pp. 25–480. *Orbis Biblicus et Orientalis* 160/4. Göttingen: Vandenhoeck & Ruprecht.

Charpin, Dominique and Jean-Marie Durand. 1997. "Assur avant l'Assyrie." *MARI* 8: 367–91.

Charvát, Petr. 1979. "Early Ur." *Archiv Orientální* 47: 15–20.

————. 1982. "Early Ur—War Chiefs and Kings of Early Dynastic III." *Altorientalische Forschungen* 9: 43–59.

————. 1986. "The Name Anzu-ᵈSùd in the Texts from Fara." In: Karl Hecker and Walter Sommerfeld, eds., *Keilschriftliche Literaturen: Ausgewählte Vorträge der XXXII. Rencontre Assyrologique Internationale, Münster, 8.—12.7.1985*, pp. 45–53. *Berliner Beiträge zum Vorderen Orient* 6. Berlin: Dietrich Reimer Verlag.

Childe, V. Gordon. 1951. *Man Makes Himself.* New York: Mentor Books.

Christensen, Arthur. 1944. *L'Iran sous les Sassanides,* second edition. Copenhagen: Ejnar Munksgaard.

Civil, Miguel. 1961. "The Home of the Fish: A New Sumerian Literary Composition." *Iraq* 23: 154–75.

———. 1964. "A Hymn to the Beer Goddess and a Drinking Song." In: *From the Workshop of the Chicago Assyrian Dictionary: Studies Presented to A. Leo Oppenheim, June 7, 1964,* pp. 67–89. Chicago: Oriental Institute of the University of Chicago.

———. 1994. *The Farmer's Instructions: A Sumerian Agricultural Manual. Aula Orientalis Supplementa* 5. Barcelona: Editorial AUSA.

———. 2003. "Of Bows and Arrows." *Journal of Cuneiform Studies* 55: 49–54.

Clayton, Peter and Martin Price, eds. 1988. *The Seven Wonders of the Ancient World.* London: Routledge.

Cocquerillat, Denise. 1968. *Palmeraies et cultures de l'Eanna d'Uruk (559–520). Ausgrabungen der Deutschen Forschungsgemeinschaft in Uruk-Warka* 8. Berlin: Mann Verlag.

Cohen, Andrew C. 2005. *Death Rituals, Ideology, and the Development of Early Mesopotamian Kingship: Toward a New Understanding of Iraq's Royal Cemetery of Ur: Ancient Magic and Divination* 7. Leiden: E. J. Brill.

Cohen, Raymond and Raymond Westbrook. 2000. *Amarna Diplomacy: The Beginnings of International Relations.* Baltimore: Johns Hopkins University Press.

Colledge, Malcolm A. R. 1967. *The Parthians.* London: Thames and Hudson.

———. 1977. *Parthian Art.* Ithaca: Cornell University Press.

Collon, Dominique. 1987. *First Impressions: Cylinder Seals in the Ancient Near East.* Chicago: University of Chicago Press.

———. 1992. "Banquets in the Art of the Ancient Near East." In: R. Gyselen, ed., *Banquets d'Orient,* pp. 23–30. *Res Orientales* 4. Bures-sur-Yvette: Groupe pour l'Etude de la Civilisation du Moyen-Orient.

———. 1995. *Ancient Near Eastern Art.* Berkeley: University of California Press.

Colpe, Carsten. 1983. "Development of Religious Thought." In: Ehsan Yarshater, ed., *The Cambridge History of Iran,* 3(2): 819–865. Cambridge, UK: Cambridge University Press.

Cooper, Jerrold S. 1972/5. "Heilige Hochzeit B." *Reallexikon der Assyriologie*, 4: 259–69. Berlin: De Gruyter.

———. 1983a. *The Curse of Agade*. Baltimore: The Johns Hopkins University Press.

———. 1983b. *Reconstructing History from Ancient Inscriptions: The Lagash-Umma Border Conflict. Sources from the Ancient Near East* 2/1. Malibu: Undena Publications.

———. 1986. *Sumerian and Akkadian Royal Inscriptions, I. Presargonic Inscriptions. The American Oriental Society Translation Series* 1. New Haven: American Oriental Society.

———. 1996. "Mesopotamian Cuneiform, Sumerian and Akkadian." In: William Bright, ed., *The World's Writing Systems*, pp. 37–57. Oxford: Oxford University Press.

Cooper, Jerrold S. and Wolfgang Heimpel. 1983. "The Sumerian Sargon Legend." In: Jack M. Sasson, ed., *Studies in Literature from the Ancient Near East by Members of the American Oriental Society. American Oriental Series* 65 = *Journal of the American Oriental Society* 103: 67–82.

Curtis, John. 2003. "The Assyrian Heartland in the Period 612–539 BC." In: Giovanni B. Lanfranchi, Michael Roaf, and Robert Rollinger, eds., *Continuity of Empire(?): Assyria, Media, Persia*, pp. 157–67. *History of the Ancient Near East/Monographs* 5. Padua: S.A.R.G.O.N.

———, ed. 1982. *Fifty Years of Mesopotamian Discovery: The Work of the British School of Archaeology in Iraq 1932–1982*. London: British School of Archaeology in Iraq.

———. 2000. *Mesopotamia and Iran in the Parthian and Sasanian Periods: Rejection and Revival c. 238 BC–AD 642*. London: British Museum Press.

Curtis, Vesta Sarkhosh. 1993. *Persian Myths*. London: British Museum Press.

———. 2000. "Parthian Culture and Costume." In: John Curtis, ed., *Mesopotamia and Iran in the Parthian and Sasanian Periods: Rejection and Revival c. 238 BC–AD 642*, pp. 23–34. London: British Museum Press.

———. 2007. "The Iranian Revival in the Parthian Period." In: Vesta Sarkhosh Curtis and Sarah Stewart, eds., *The Age of the Parthians: The Idea of Iran*, 2: 7–25. London: I. B. Tauris.

Dalley, Stephanie. 1984. *Mari and Karana: Two Old Babylonian Cities*. London: Longman.

———. 1993. "Nineveh after 612 B.C." *Altorientalische Forschungen* 20: 143–7.

Dalley, Stephanie. 1994. "Nineveh, Babylon and the Hanging Gardens: Cuneiform and Classical Sources Reconciled." *Iraq* 56: 45–58.

————. 1996. "Herodotus and Babylon." *Orientalistische Literaturzeitung* 91: 525–32.

————. 2002. "More about the Hanging Gardens." In: Lamia al-Gailani Werr, ed., *Of Pots and Plans: Papers Presented to David Oates on the Archaeology and History of Mesopotamia and Syria*, pp. 67–73. London: NABU.

————, ed. 1998. *The Legacy of Mesopotamia*. Oxford: Oxford University Press.

Damerow, Peter. 1988. "The First Representation of Numbers and the Development of the Number Concept." In: Peter Damerow, ed., *Abstraction and Representation: Essays on the Evolution of Thinking*, pp. 275–97. *Boston Studies in the Philosophy of Science* 175. New York: Humanities Press.

Damrosch, David. 2006. *The Buried Book: The Loss and Rediscovery of the Great Epic of Gilgamesh*. New York: Henry Holt & Co.

Dandamayev, Muhammad A. 1971. "Die Rolle des *tamkārum* in Babylonien im 2. und 1. Jahrtausend v. u. Z." In: H. Klengel, ed., *Beiträge zur sozialen Struktur des alten Vorderasien*, pp. 69–78. Deutsche Akademie der Wissenschaften zu Berlin, Zentralinstitut für alte Geschichte und Archäologie, *Schriften zur Geschichte und Kultur des Alten Orients* 1. Berlin: Akademie Verlag.

————. 1983. *Vavilonskie Piscy*. Moscow: Nauka.

————. 1984. *Slavery in Babylonia from Nabopolassar to Alexander the Great (626–331 B.C.)*. Translated by Victoria A. Powell. No place: Northern Illinois University Press.

————. 1988. "Wages and Prices in Babylonia in the 6th and 5th Centuries B.C." *Altorientalische Forschungen* 15: 53–8.

Daniel, Glyn. 1981. *A Short History of Archaeology*. New York: Thames and Hudson.

Daniels, C. M. 1975. "The Role of the Roman Army in the Spread and Practice of Mithraism." In: John R. Hinnells, ed., *Mithraic Studies: Proceedings of the First International Congress of Mithraic Studies*, 2: 249–74. Manchester: Manchester University Press.

Darnell, John C. and Colleen Manassa. 2007. *Tutankhamun's Armies: Battle and Conquest during Ancient Egypt's Late 18th Dynasty*. New York: John Wiley & Sons.

de Menasce, J. P. 1983. "Zoroastrian Pahlavi Writings." In: Ehsan Yarshater, ed., *The Cambridge History of Iran*, 3(2): 1166–95. Cambridge, UK: Cambridge University Press.

Demange, Françoise, ed. 2006. *Les Perses sassanides: Fastes d'un empire oublié (224–642)*. Paris: Paris-Musées.

De Odorico, M. 1995. *The Use of Numbers and Quantifications in the Assyrian Royal Inscriptions*. State Archives of Assyria, Studies 3. Helsinki: Neo-Assyrian Text Corpus.

Depuydt, Leo. 1997. "The Time of Death of Alexander the Great: 11 June 323 B.C. (−322), ca. 4:00–5:00 P.M." *Welt des Orients* 28: 117–35.

———. 2008. "Ancient Chronology's Alpha and Egyptian Chronology's Debt to Babylonia." In: Micah Ross, ed., *From the Banks of the Euphrates: Studies in Honor of Alice Louise Slotsky*, pp. 35–50. Winona Lake, Ind.: Eisenbrauns.

Dercksen, J. G., ed. 1999. *Trade and Finance in Ancient Mesopotamia. MOS Studies* 1. Leiden: Nederlands Instituut voor het Nabije Oosten.

de Schauensee, Maude. 2002. *Two Lyres from Ur*. Philadelphia: University Museum of Archaeology and Anthropology.

Dhorme, Eduard. 1945. *Les religions de Babylonie et d'Assyrie*. Paris: Presses Universitaires de France.

Diakonoff, Igor. 1949. *Razvitie zemel'nyh otnošeniy v Assirii*. Leningrad: Lenin Universitet.

———. 1966. "Osnovnye čerty ėkonomiki v monarkiah drevnej Zapadnoj Azii." *Narody Azii i Afriki* No. 1: 44–58.

———. 1990. *Lyudi Goroda Ura*. Moscow: Nauka.

———. 1991. *Early Antiquity*. Translated by Alexander Kirjanov. Chicago: University of Chicago Press.

Dinsmoor, William B. 1943. "Early American Studies of Mediterranean Archaeology." *Proceedings of the American Philosophical Society* 87: 70–104.

Dirven, L. 1997. "The Exaltation of Nabû: A Revision of the Relief Depicting the Battle against Tiamat from the Temple of Bel in Palmyra." *Welt des Orients* 28: 96–116.

Dittmann, R. 1986. "Seals, Sealing and Tablets." In: U. Finkbeiner and W. Röllig, eds., *Jamdet Nasr: Period or Regional Style?* pp. 132–66. *Beiheft zur Tübinger Atlas des Vorderen Orients, B* 62. Wiesbaden: Rudolf Habelt.

Dombradi, E. 1996. *Die Darstellung des Rechtsaustrags in den altbabylonischen Prozessurkunden. Freiburger Altorientalische Studien* 20. Stuttgart: Franz Steiner Verlag.

Donner, Fred M. 1981. *The Early Islamic Conquests*. Princeton: Princeton University Press.

Doty, L. Timothy. 1977. *Cuneiform Archives from Hellenistic Uruk.* Ph.D. dissertation, Yale University.

Downey, Glanville. 1963. *Ancient Antioch.* Princeton: Princeton University Press.

Downey, Susan. 1997. "Seleucia on the Tigris." In: Eric M. Meyers, ed., *The Oxford Encyclopedia of Archaeology in the Near East,* 4: 513–4. Oxford: Oxford University Press.

Duchesne-Guillemin, J. 1983. "Zoroastrian Religion." In: Ehsan Yarshater, ed., *The Cambridge History of Iran,* 3(2): 866–906. Cambridge, UK: Cambridge University Press.

Durand, Jean-Marie. 1987. "Documents pour l'histoire du royaume de Haute-Mésopotamie, I." MARI 5: 155–98.

———. 1997. *Documents épistolaires du Palais de Mari, Tome I. Littératures anciennes du Proche-Orient* 16. Paris: Les Editions du Cerf.

———. 1998. *Archives épistolaires de Mari* I/1. *Archives Royales de Mari* XXVI. Paris: Editions Recherche sur les Civilisations.

———. 2000. *Documents épistolaires du Palais de Mari, Tome III. Littératures anciennes du Proche-Orient* 18. Paris: Les Editions du Cerf.

Dvornik, Francis. 1966. *Early Christian and Byzantine Political Philosophy: Origins and Background. Dumbarton Oaks Studies* 9. Washington, D.C.: Dumbarton Oaks.

Dyckhoff, C. 1998. "Balamunamḫe von Larsa, eine altbabylonische Existenz zwischen Ökonomie, Kultus und Wissenschaft." In: Jiří Prosecký, ed., *Intellectual Life of the Ancient Near East: Papers Presented at the 43rd Rencontre Assyriologique Internationale Prague, July 1–5, 1996,* pp. 117–24. Prague: Academy of Sciences of the Czech Republic.

Eakin, Hugh. 2007. "Treasure Hunt: The Downfall of the Getty Curator Marion True." *The New Yorker,* 17 December, 62–75.

Ebeling, Erich. 1930/4. *Neubabylonische Briefe aus Uruk. Beiträge zur Keilschriftforschung und Religionsgeschichte des Vorderen Orients* 1–4. Berlin: Selbtsverlag.

———. 1951. *Bruchstücke einer mittelassyrischen Vorschriftensammlung für die Akklimatisierung und Trainierung von Wagenpferden.* Deutsche Akademie der Wissenschaften zu Berlin, Institut für Orientforschung, *Veröffentlichung* 7.

Edzard, Dietz O. 1965. "Mesopotamien, die Mythologie der Sumerer und Akkader." In: H. Haussig, ed., *Mythen im Vorderen Orient. Wörterbuch der Mythologie,* 1: 19–139. Stuttgart: Ernst Klett Verlag.

———. 1974. "Problèmes de la royauté dans la période présargonique." In: Paul Garelli, ed., *Le palais et la royauté: Archéologie et civilisa-*

tion: XIXᵉ Rencontre Assyriologique Internationale, 1971, pp. 141–9. Paris: Librairie Paul Geuthner.

———. 1976/80a. "Keilschrift." *Reallexikon der Assyriologie*, 5: 544–68. Berlin: De Gruyter.

———. 1976/80b. "Išbi-Erra." *Reallexikon der Assyriologie*, 5: 174–5. Berlin: De Gruyter.

———. 1997. *Gudea and His Dynasty. The Royal Inscriptions of Mesopotamia, Early Periods* 3/1. Toronto: University of Toronto Press.

———. 2004. "Altbabylonische Literatur und Religion." In: Pascal Attinger, Walther Sallaberger, and Markus Wäfler, eds., *Mesopotamien: Die altbabylonische Zeit*, pp. 485–640. *Orbis Biblicus et Orientalis* 160/4. Göttingen: Vandenhoeck & Ruprecht.

Eickhoff, T. 1976/80. "Kār-Tukulti-Ninurta." *Reallexikon der Assyriologie*, 5: 456–9. Berlin: De Gruyter.

Eidem, Jesper and Jørgen Laessøe. 2001. *The Shemshara Archives 1: The Letters. Det Kongelige Danske Videnskabernes Selskab, Historisk-filosofiske Skrifter* 23. Copenhagen: Det Kongelige Danske Videnskabernes Selskab.

Ellis, Maria de Jong. 1976. *Agriculture and the State in Ancient Mesopotamia. Occasional Publications of the Babylonian Fund* 1. Philadelphia: University Museum of Archaeology and Anthropology.

———, ed. 1992. *Nippur at the Centennial: Papers Read at the 35ᵉ Rencontre Assyriologique Internationale, Philadelphia, 1988. Occasional Publications of the Samuel Noah Kramer Fund* 14. Philadelphia: University Museum of Archaeology and Anthropology.

Emberling, Geoff and Kathryn Hanson, eds. 2008. *Catastrophe! The Looting and Destruction of Iraq's Past*. Chicago: Oriental Institute of the University of Chicago.

Englund, Robert. 1998. "Texts from the Late Uruk Period." In: Pascal Attinger and Markus Wäfler, eds., *Mesopotamien: Akkade-Zeit und Ur III-Zeit*, pp. 15–233. *Orbis Biblicus et Orientalis* 160/3. Göttingen: Vandenhoeck & Ruprecht.

Eph'al, Israel. 1982. *The Ancient Arabs: Nomads on the Borders of the Fertile Crescent 9th–5th Centuries B.C.* Jerusalem: Magnes Press.

Evans, Jean M. 2003. "Approaching the Divine: Mesopotamian Art at the End of the Third Millennium B.C." In: Joan Aruz, ed., *Art of the First Cities: The Third Millennium B.C. from the Mediterranean to the Indus*, pp. 417–24. New York: Metropolitan Museum of Art.

Fales, Frederick Mario. 2004. *Saccheggio in Mesopotamia*. Udine: Editrice Universitaria Udinese.

Falkenstein, Adam. 1959. *Sumerische Götterlieder, I. Teil. Abhandlungen der Heidelberger Akademie der Wissenschaften, Philosophisch-historische Klasse* Jahrgang 1959, 1. Abhandlung. Heidelberg: Carl Winter Verlag.

Farchakh, Joanne. 2001. "Irak, 10 ans d'archéologie sous embargo." *Archéologia* 374: 22–41.

———. 2003a. "The Specter of War." *Archaeology,* May/June: 14–5.

———. 2003b. "Comment protéger l'archéologie en Irak juste avant la guerre?" *Archéologia* 397: 20–33.

———. 2003c. "Le massacre du patrimoine irakien." *Archéologia* 402: 14–31.

———. 2004. "Irak: Témoignages d'une archéologie héroïque." *Archéologia* 411: 14–27.

Favaro, Sabina. 2007. *Voyages et voyageurs à l'époque néo-assyrienne. State Archives of Assyria, Studies* 18. Helsinki: The Neo-Assyrian Text Corpus Project.

Feldman, Marian H. 2006. *Diplomacy by Design: Luxury Arts and an "International Style" in the Ancient Near East, 1400–1200 BCE.* Chicago: University of Chicago Press.

Fiey, J. 1979. *Communautés syriaques en Iran et Irak des origines à 1552.* London: Variorum Reprints.

Finkel, Irving. 1999. "The Lament of Nabû-šuma-ukîn." In: Johannes Renger, ed., *Babylon: Focus mesopotamischer Geschichte, Wiege früher Gelehrsamkeit, Mythos in der Moderne: 2. Internationales Colloquium der Deutschen Orient-Gesellschaft 24.—26. März in Berlin,* pp. 323–42. Saarbrücken: Saarbrückener Druckerei und Verlag.

Finkelstein, Jacob J. 1962. "Mesopotamia." *Journal of Near Eastern Studies* 21: 73–92.

———. 1966. "The Genealogy of the Hammurapi Dynasty." *Journal of Cuneiform Studies* 20: 95–118.

Fino, Elisabeth Valtz. 2005. "In the Wake of Alexander the Great." In: Milbry Polk and Angela M. H. Schuster, eds., *The Looting of the Iraq Museum, Baghdad: The Lost Legacy of Ancient Mesopotamia,* pp. 141–71. New York: Abrams.

Flandrin, Philippe. 2004. *Le pillage de l'Irak.* Paris: Editions Du Rocher.

Flückiger-Hawker, E. 1999. *Urnamma of Ur in Sumerian Literary Tradition. Orbis Biblicus et Orientalis* 166. Göttingen: Vandenhoeck & Ruprecht.

Forest, Jean-Daniel. 1987. "La grande architecture obeidienne: Sa forme et sa fonction." In: J.-L. Huot, ed., *Préhistoire de la Mésopotamie,* pp. 385–423. Paris: CNRS.

————. 1999. *Les premiers temples de Mésopotamie (4ᵉ et 3ᵉ millénaires)*, *BAR International Series* 765. Oxford: Archaeopress.

Foster, Benjamin R. 1980. "Notes on Sargonic Royal Progress." *Journal of the Ancient Near Eastern Society of Columbia University* 12: 29–42.

————. 1981. "A New Look at the Sumerian Temple State." *Journal of the Economic and Social History of the Orient* 24: 224–41.

————. 1982a. *Administration and Use of Institutional Land in Sargonic Sumer*. *Mesopotamia* 9. Copenhagen: Akademisk Forlag.

————. 1982b. *Umma in the Sargonic Period*. *Memoirs of the Connecticut Academy of Arts & Sciences* 20. Hamden, Conn.: Shoestring Press.

————. 1985. "The Sargonic Victory Stele from Telloh." *Iraq* 47: 15–30.

————. 1986. "Agriculture and Accountability in Ancient Mesopotamia." In: H. Weiss, ed., *The Origins of Cities in Dry-Farming Syria and Mesopotamia in the Third Millennium B.C.*, pp. 109–28. Guilford, Conn.: Four Quarters.

————. 1987. "The Late Bronze Age Palace Economy: A View from the East." In: Robin Hägg and Nanno Marinatos, eds., *The Function of the Minoan Palaces: Proceedings of the Fourth International Symposium at the Swedish Institute in Athens, 10–16 June, 1984*, pp. 11–6. *Skrifter utgivna av Svenska Institutet i Athen* 4, XXXV. Stockholm: Paul Åströms Förlag.

————. 1993a. "Management and Administration in the Sargonic Period." In: Mario Liverani, ed., *Akkad, The First Universal Empire: Structure, Ideology, Traditions*, pp. 25–38. *History of the Ancient Near East/Studies* 5. Padua: Sargon.

————. 1993b. "'International' Trade at Sargonic Susa." *Altorientalische Forschungen* 20: 98–102.

————. 1995. "Social Reform in Ancient Mesopotamia." In: K. D. Irani and Morris Silver, eds., *Social Justice in the Ancient World*, pp. 165–77. Westport, Conn.: Greenwood.

————. 1997. "A Sumerian Merchant's Account of the Dilmun Trade." *Acta Sumerologica* 19: 53–62.

————. 2000. "The Forty-nine Sons of Agade." In: Simonetta Graziani, ed., *Studi sul Vicino Oriente Antico dedicati alla memoria di Luigi Cagni*, pp. 309–18. Dipartimento di Studi Asiatici, *Series Minor* 61. Naples: Istituto Universitario Orientale.

————. 2001. *The Epic of Gilgamesh*. Norton Critical Editions. New York: W. W. Norton & Company.

Foster, Benjamin R. 2005a. "Shuruppak and the Sumerian City State." In: L. Kogan, N. Koslova, S. Loesov, and S. Tishenko, eds., *Orientalia et Classica: Papers of the Institute of Oriental and Classical Studies* 8, *Memoriae Igor M. Diakonoff*, pp. 71–88. *Babel und Bibel* 2.

————.2005b. *Before the Muses: An Anthology of Akkadian Literature.* Third edition. Bethesda, Md.: CDL Press.

————. 2007a. "Mesopotamia." In: John R. Hinnells, ed., *A Handbook of Ancient Religions*, pp. 161–213. Cambridge, UK: Cambridge University Press.

————. 2007b. *Akkadian Literature of the Late Period. Guides to the Mesopotamian Textual Record* 2. Münster: Ugarit-Verlag.

————. 2007c. "On the Formal Study of Near Eastern Languages in America, 1770–1930." In: Abbas Amanat and Magnus T. Bernhardsson, eds., *U.S.–Middle East Historical Encounters: A Critical Survey*, pp. 10–44. Gainesville: University of Florida Press.

Foster, Benjamin R., Karen Polinger Foster, and Patty Gerstenblith. 2005. *Iraq Beyond the Headlines: History, Archaeology, and War.* Singapore: World Scientific.

Foster, Benjamin R. and Eleanor Robson. 2004. "A New Look at the Sargonic Mathematical Corpus." *Zeitschrift für Assyriologie* 94: 1–15.

Foster, Karen Polinger. 1979. *Aegean Faience of the Bronze Age.* New Haven: Yale University Press.

————. 1998. "Gardens of Eden: Exotic Flora and Fauna in the Ancient Near East." In: Jeff Albert, Magnus Bernhardsson, and Roger Kenna, eds., *Transformations of Middle Eastern Natural Environments: Legacies and Lessons*, pp. 320–9. New Haven: Yale University Press.

————. 1999. *The City of Rainbows: A Tale from Ancient Sumer.* Philadelphia: University Museum of Archaeology and Anthropology.

————. 2000. "Volcanic Landscapes in Lugal-e." In: L. Milano, S. de Martino, F. M. Fales, and G. B. Lanfranchi, eds., *Landscapes, Territories, Frontiers and Horizons in the Ancient Near East: Papers Presented to the XLIV Rencontre Assyriologique Internationale Venezia, 7–11 July 1997*, 3: 23–39. Padua: Sargon srl.

————. 2005. "The Hanging Gardens of Nineveh." *Iraq* 66: 207–20.

Frahm, Eckart. 1999. "Nabû-zuqup-kēnu, das Gilgameš-Epos und der Tod Sargons II." *Journal of Cuneiform Studies* 51: 73–90.

————. 2006. "Images of Assyria in Nineteenth- and Twentieth-Century Western Scholarship." In: Steven W. Holloway, ed., *Orientalism, Assyriology, and the Bible*, pp. 74–94. Sheffield: Phoenix Press.

Frame, Grant. 1992. *Babylonia 689–627 BC: A Political History.* Leiden: Nederlands Historisch-Archaeologisch Instituut.

Frame, Grant and Andrew George. 2005. "The Royal Libraries of Nineveh: New Evidence for King Ashurbanipal's Tablet Collecting." *Iraq* 67: 265–84.

Frangipane, Marcella. 1996. *La nascita dello Stato nel Vicino Oriente, dai lignaggi all burocrazia nella Grande Mesopotamia*. Bari: Laterza.

———. 2001. "Centralization Processes in Greater Mesopotamia: Uruk 'Expansion' as the Climax of Systemic Interactions among Areas of the Greater Mesopotamian Region." In: M. S. Rothman, ed., *Uruk Mesopotamia and Its Neighbors: Cross-cultural Interactions and Their Consequences in the Era of State Formation*, pp. 307–48. Santa Fe: School of American Research.

Franke, Sabina. 1995. *Königsinschriften und Königsideologie: Die Könige von Akkade zwischen Tradition und Neuerung*. Münster: Lit Verlag.

Frankfort, Henri. 1939. *Cylinder Seals: A Documentary Essay on the Art and Religion of the Ancient Near East*. London: Macmillan.

———. 1941. "The Origins of Monumental Architecture in Egypt." *American Journal of Semitic Languages and Literatures* 58: 329–58.

———. 1970. *The Art and Architecture of the Ancient Orient*. The Pelican History of Art, Harmondsworth, UK: Penguin Books.

Frayne, Douglas. 1989. "A Struggle for Water: A Case Study from the Historical Records of the Cities Isin and Larsa (1900–1800 BC)." *Bulletin of the Canadian Society for Mesopotamian Studies* 17: 17–28.

———. 1990. *Old Babylonian Period (2003–1595 BC)*. *The Royal Inscriptions of Mesopotamia, Early Periods* 4. Toronto: University of Toronto Press.

———. 1993. *Sargonic and Gutian Periods (2334–2113 BC)*. *The Royal Inscriptions of Mesopotamia, Early Periods* 2. Toronto: University of Toronto Press.

———. 1997. *Ur III Period (2112–2004 BC)*. *The Royal Inscriptions of Mesopotamia, Early Periods* 3/2. Toronto: University of Toronto Press.

Freedman, Sally Moren. 1998. *If a City Is Set on a Height: The Akkadian Omen Series Šumma Alu ina Mēlê Šakin, Volume 1: Tablets 1–21*. *Occasional Publications of the Samuel Noah Kramer Fund* 17. Philadelphia: University Museum of Archaeology and Anthropology.

Frend, W.H.C. 1972. *The Rise of the Monophysite Movement: Chapters in the History of the Church in the Fifth and Sixth Centuries*. Cambridge, UK: Cambridge University Press.

Friberg, J. 1994. "Preliterate Counting and Accounting in the Middle East." *Orientalistische Literaturzeitung* 89: 477–502.

Friberg, J. 2007. *Amazing Traces of a Babylonian Origin in Greek Mathematics.* Singapore: World Scientific.

Frye, Richard N. 1983. "The Political History of Iran under the Sasanians." In: Ehsan Yarshater, ed., *The Cambridge History of Iran,* 3(1): 116–80. Cambridge, UK: Cambridge University Press.

———. 1984. *The History of Ancient Iran. Handbuch der Altertumswissenschaft,* Abteilung 3, Teil 7. Munich: C. H. Beck.

Gafni, Isaiah M. 2002. "Babylonian Rabbinic Culture." In: David Biale, ed., *Cultures of the Jews: A New History,* pp. 223–65. New York: Schocken Books.

———. 2006. "The Political, Social, and Economic History of Babylonian Jewry, 224–638 CE." In: Steven T. Katz, ed., *The Cambridge History of Judaism,* 4: 792–820. Cambridge, UK: Cambridge University Press.

Garelli, Paul. 1981. "La conception de la royauté en Assyrie." In: F. M. Fales, ed., *Assyrian Royal Inscriptions: New Horizons in Literary, Ideological, and Historical Analysis: Papers of a Symposium held in Cetona (Siena) June 26–28, 1980,* pp. 1–11. *Orientis Antiqvi Collectio* 17. Roma: Istituto per l'Oriente, Centro per le Antichità e la Storia dell'Arte del Vicino Oriente.

Gates, Marie-Henriette. 1984. "The Palace of Zimri-Lim at Mari." *Biblical Archaeologist* 47: 70–87.

Gelb, I. J. 1965. "The Ancient Mesopotamian Ration System." *Journal of Near Eastern Studies* 24: 230–43.

———. 1979. "Household and Family in Early Mesopotamia." In: E. Lipiński, ed., *State and Temple Economy in the Ancient Near East* 1: 1–97. *Orientalia Lovaniensia Analecta* 5. Leuven: Peeters.

———. 1981. "Ebla and the Kish Civilization." In: Luigi Cagni, ed., *La Lingua di Ebla: Atti del Convegno Internazionale (Napoli, 21–23 aprile 1980),* pp. 9–73. Seminario di Studi Asiatici, *Series Minor* 14. Naples: Istituto Universitario Orientale.

Gelb, I. J. and Burkhart Kienast. 1990. *Die altakkadischen Königsinschriften des dritten Jahrtausends v. Chr. Freiburger Altorientalische Studien* 7. Stuttgart: Franz Steiner Verlag.

Geller, Markham J. 1995. "The Influence of Ancient Mesopotamia on Hellenistic Judaism." In: Jack M. Sasson, ed., *Civilizations of the Ancient Near East,* 1: 43–54. New York: Scribner's.

George, Andrew. 2000. *The Epic of Gilgamesh, a New Translation: The Babylonian Epic Poem and Other Texts in Akkadian and Sumerian.* London: Penguin Books.

————. 2003. *The Babylonian Gilgamesh Epic: Introduction, Critical Edition and Cuneiform Texts*. Oxford: Oxford University Press.

————. 2005/6. "The Tower of Babel: Archaeology, History and Cuneiform Texts." *Archiv für Orientforschung* 51: 75–95.

Ghirshman, Roman. 1954. *Iran: From the Earliest Times to the Islamic Conquest*. Baltimore: Penguin.

Gibson, McGuire. 2006. "Archaeology and Nation-Building in Iraq." *Journal of the American Oriental Society* 126: 245–52.

Gibson, McGuire and Augusta McMahon. 1992. *Lost Heritage: Antiquities Stolen from Iraq's Regional Museums*, fascicle 1. Chicago: American Association for Research in Baghdad.

Gibson, McGuire, John Malcolm Russell, Robert Biggs, Samuel M. Paley, and James A. R. Nofziger. 2003. "Art Loss in Iraq." *IFAR Journal* 6: 30–61.

Gibson, McGuire, John C. Sanders, and Bodil Mortensen. 1981. "Tell Razuk: Stratigraphy, Architecture, Finds." In: McGuire Gibson, ed., *Uch Tepe I: Tell Razuk, Tell Ahmed al-Mughir, Tell Ajamat*, pp. 28–87. Chicago: Oriental Institute of the University of Chicago.

Giovino, Mariana. 2007. *The Assyrian Sacred Tree: A History of Interpretation*. Orbis Biblicus et Orientalis 230. Göttingen: Vandenhoeck & Ruprecht.

Glassner, Jean-Jacques. 1983. "Narām-Sin Poliorcète, les avatars d'une sentence divinatoire." *Revue d'Assyriologie* 57: 3–10.

————. 1984. "La division quinaire de la terre." *Akkadica* 40: 17–34.

————. 2003a. *La Tour de Babylone: Que reste-t-il de la Mésopotamie?* Paris: Editions du Seuil.

————. 2003b. *The Invention of Cuneiform: Writing in Sumer*. Translated by Zainab Bahrani and Marc Van De Mieroop. Baltimore: The Johns Hopkins University Press.

————. 2004. *Mesopotamian Chronicles*. SBL Writings from the Ancient World Series 19. Atlanta: Scholars Press.

Goetze, Albrecht. 1947. "Historical Allusions in Old Babylonian Omen Texts." *Journal of Cuneiform Studies* 1: 253–65.

————. 1957. "Reports on Acts of Extispicy from Old Babylonian and Kassite Times." *Journal of Cuneiform Studies* 11: 89–105.

Goldberg, Jeremy. 2004. "The Berlin Letter, Middle Elamite Chronology and Šutruk-Nahhunte I's Genealogy." *Iranica Antiqua* 39: 33–42.

Goodblatt, David. 2006a. "The Jews in Babylonia, 66–c. 235 CE." In: Steven T. Katz, ed., *The Cambridge History of Judaism* 4: 82–92. Cambridge, UK: Cambridge University Press.

Goodblatt, David. 2006b. "The History of the Babylonian Academies." In: Steven T. Katz, ed., *The Cambridge History of Judaism* 4: 821–39. Cambridge, UK: Cambridge University Press.

Grayson, Albert Kirk. 1972. *Assyrian Royal Inscriptions I: From the Beginning to Ashur-resha-ishi I*. Wiesbaden: Harrasowitz.

———. 1973. "'They Embraced One Another': Mesopotamian Attitudes toward Sex." In: A. K. Grayson and Donald B. Redford, *Papyrus and Tablet*, pp. 140–52. Englewood Cliffs, N.J.: Prentice-Hall.

———. 1975. *Babylonian Historical-Literary Texts*. Toronto: University of Toronto Press.

———. 1976. *Assyrian Royal Inscriptions II: From Tiglath-Pileser I to Ashur-nasir-apli II*. Wiesbaden: Harrassowitz.

Green, Margaret W. 1978. "The Eridu Lament." *Journal of Cuneiform Studies* 30: 127–67.

———. 1981. "The Construction and Implementation of the Cuneiform Writing System." *Visible Language* 15: 345–72.

Grélot, Pierre. 1972. *Documents araméens d'Egypte. Littératures anciennes du Proche-Orient*. Paris: Les Editions du Cerf.

Gruendler, Beatrice. 1993. *The Development of the Arabic Scripts from the Nabataean Era to the First Islamic Century According to Dated Texts. Harvard Semitic Studies* 43. Atlanta: Scholars Press.

Gurney, Oliver. 1983. *The Middle Babylonian Legal and Economic Texts from Ur*. London: British School of Archaeology in Iraq.

Gutas, Dimitri. 1998. *Greek Thought, Arabic Culture: The Graeco-Arabic Translation Movement in Baghdad and Early ʿAbbāsid Society (2nd–4th/8th–10th Centuries)*. London: Routledge.

———. 2006. "The Greek and Persian Background of Early Arabic Encyclopedism." In: Gerhard Endress, ed., *Organizing Knowledge: Encyclopaedic Activities in the Pre-Eighteenth Century Islamic World*, pp. 91–101. *Islamic Theology and Science, Texts and Studies* 61. Leiden: E. J. Brill.

Hallo, William W. 1963. "Beginning and End of the Sumerian King List in the Nippur Recension." *Journal of Cuneiform Studies* 17: 52–71.

———. 1978. "Simurrum and the Hurrian Frontier." *Revue Hittite et Asianique* 36: 31–73.

———. 1996. "Bilingualism and the Beginnings of Translation." In: M. Fox, V. Hurowitz, A. Hurvitz, M. Klein, B. Schwartz, and N. Shupak, eds., *Texts, Temples, and Traditions: A Tribute to Menahem Harran*, pp. 345–57. Winona Lake, Ind.: Eisenbrauns.

———. 1997. *The Context of Scripture 1: Canonical Compositions from the Biblical World*. Leiden: E. J. Brill.

————. 2000. *The Context of Scripture 2: Monumental Inscriptions from the Biblical World*. Leiden: E. J. Brill.

Hallo, William W. and J.J.A. Van Dijk. 1968. *The Exaltation of Inanna. Yale Near Eastern Researches* 3. New Haven: Yale University Press.

Hanisch, Ludmila. 2003. *Die Nachfolger der Exegeten: Deutschsprachige Erforschung des Vorderen Orients in der ersten Hälfte des 20. Jahrhunderts*. Wiesbaden: Harrassowitz.

Hansen, Donald P. 1998. "Art of the Royal Tombs of Ur: A Brief Interpretation." In: Richard L. Zettler and Lee Horne, eds., *Treasures from the Royal Tombs of Ur*, pp. 43–72. Philadelphia: University Museum of Archaeology and Anthropology.

————. 2003a. "Art of the Early City-States." In: Joan Aruz, ed., *Art of the First Cities: The Third Millennium B.C. from the Mediterranean to the Indus*, pp. 21–37. New York: Metropolitan Museum of Art.

————. 2003b. "Art of the Akkadian Dynasty." In: Joan Aruz, ed., *Art of the First Cities: The Third Millennium B.C. from the Mediterranean to the Indus*, pp. 189–98. New York: Metropolitan Museum of Art.

Harmand, Jacques. 1973. *La guerre antique de Sumer à Rome*. Paris: Presses Universitaires de France.

Harmatta, J. 1981. "Mithridates and the Rise of the Parthian Writing System." *Acta Antiqua Academia Scientiarum Hungaricae* 29: 219–25.

Harper, Prudence O. 1978. *The Royal Hunter: Art of the Sassanian Empire*. New York: The Asia Society.

————. 2006. *In Search of a Cultural Identity: Monuments and Artifacts of the Sasanian Near East, 3rd to 7th Century A.D.* New York: Bibliotheca Persica.

Harper, Prudence O. and Pierre Amiet. 1992. "Mesopotamian Monuments Found at Susa." In: Prudence O. Harper, Joan Aruz, and Françoise Tallon, eds., *The Royal City of Susa: Ancient Near Eastern Treasures in the Louvre*, pp. 159–82. New York: Metropolitan Museum of Art.

Harper, Prudence O., Joan Aruz, and Françoise Tallon, eds. 1992. *The Royal City of Susa: Ancient Near Eastern Treasures in the Louvre*. New York: Metropolitan Museum of Art.

Harris, Rivkah. 1991. "Inanna-Ishtar as Paradox and a Coincidence of Opposites." *History of Religions* 30: 261–78.

Hauser, S. R. 1999. "Babylon in arsakidischer Zcit." In: Johannes Renger, ed., *Babylon: Focus Mesopotamischer Geschichte, Wiege früher Gelehrsamkeit, Mythos in der Moderne: 2. Internationales Colloquium der Deutschen Orient-Gesellschaft 24.–26. März in Berlin*, pp. 207–39. Saarbrücken: Saarbrückener Druckerei und Verlag.

Heck, Gene W. 2003. "'Arabia without Spices': An Alternate Hypothesis." *Journal of the American Oriental Society* 123: 547–76.

Heimpel, Wolfgang. 1982. "A First Step in the Diorite Question." *Revue d'Assyriologie* 76: 65–7.

————. 1987a. "Ein zweiter Schritt in der Dioritfrage." *Zeitschrift für Assyriologie* 77: 69–70.

————. 1987b. "The Natural History of the Tigris According to the Sumerian Composition *Lugal.*" *Journal of Near Eastern Studies* 46: 309–17.

————. 2003. *Letters to the King of Mari: A New Translation, with Historical Introduction, Notes, and Commentary. Mesopotamian Civilizations* 12. Winona Lake, Ind.: Eisenbrauns.

Heinrich, Ernst. 1936. *Kleinfunde aus den archaischen Tempelschichten in Uruk. Ausgrabungen der Deutschen Forschungsgemeinschaft in Uruk-Warka* 1. Leipzig: Harrassowitz.

Henrickson, E. F. and I. Thuesen, eds. 1989. *Upon This Foundation: The 'Ubaid Reconsidered.* Copenhagen: Museum Tusculaneum Press.

Hirth, F. 1885. *China and the Roman Orient: Researches into the Ancient and Medieval Relations as Represented in Old Chinese Records.* Leipzig: Georg Hirth.

Hitti, Philip K. 1951. *History of Syria, Including Lebanon and Palestine.* New York: Macmillan.

————. 1964. *History of the Arabs, from the Earliest Times to the Present,* eighth edition. London: Macmillan.

Hoffman, Barbara T., ed. 2006. *Art and Cultural Heritage: Law, Policy, and Practice.* Cambridge, UK: Cambridge University Press.

Hole, Frank. 1984. "A Reassessment of the Neolithic Revolution." *Paléorient* 10/2: 49–60.

Horovitz, Josef. 1930. "'Adi ibn Zeid, the Poet of Hira." *Islamic Culture* 4: 31–69.

Horowitz, Wayne. 1991. "Antiochus I, Esagil, and a Celebration of the Ritual for Renovation of Temples." *Revue d'Assyriologie* 85: 75–7.

Howard-Johnston, James. 1999. "Heraclius' Persian Campaigns and the Revival of the East Roman Empire, 622–630." *War in History* 6: 1–44.

Howell, Georgina. 2007. *Gertrude Bell, Queen of the Desert, Shaper of Nations.* New York: Farrar, Straus and Giroux.

Hoyland, Robert G. 2001. *Arabia and the Arabs from the Bronze Age to the Coming of Islam.* London: Routledge.

Hruška, Blahoslav. 1983. "Dilmun in den vorsargonischen Wirtschaftstexten aus Šuruppak und Lagaš." In: Daniel T. Potts, ed., *Dilmun: New Studies in the Archaeology and Early History of Bahrein*, pp. 83–5. *Berliner Beiträge zum Vorderen Orient.* Berlin: Dietrich Reimer Verlag.

Huot, Jean-Louis. 1989. *Les Sumériens, entre le Tigre et l'Euphrate.* Paris: Editions Errance.

———. 1994. *Les premiers villageois de Mésopotamie, du village à la ville.* Paris: Colin.

Ingholt, Harald. 1954. *Parthian Sculptures from Hatra: Orient and Hellas in Art and Religion.* New Haven: Connecticut Academy of Arts and Sciences.

Insler, Stanley. 1975. *The Gāthās of Zarathustra.* Leiden: E. J. Brill.

Invernizzi, Antonio, Maria Magdalena Negro Ponzi Mancini, and Elisabeta Valtz. 1985. "Seleucia on the Tigris." In: Giorgio Gullini, ed., *The Land between Two Rivers: Twenty Years of Italian Archaeology in the Middle East, the Treasures of Mesopotamia*, pp. 87–99. Turin: Il Quadrante Edizioni.

Jacobsen, Thorkild. 1957. "Early Political Development in Mesopotamia." *Zeitschrift für Assyriologie* 52: 91–140.

———. 1976. *The Treasures of Darkness: A History of Mesopotamian Religion.* New Haven: Yale University Press.

———. 1987. *The Harps That Once. . . .* New Haven: Yale University Press.

Janssen, C. 1995. *Babil, the City of Witchcraft and Wine: The Name and Fame of Babylon in Medieval Arabic Geographical Texts. Mesopotamian History and Environment, Memoirs* 2. Ghent: Peeters.

Jeyes, Ulla. 1980. "The Act of Extispicy in Ancient Mesopotamia: An Outline." *Assyriological Miscellanies* 1: 13–32. Copenhagen: Institute of Assyriology.

Joannès, Francis. 1989. *Archives de Borsippa: La famille Ea-ilûta-bâni: Etude d'un lot d'archives familiales en Babylonie du VIIIᵉ au Vᵉ siècle av. J.-C.* Geneva: Droz.

———. 2004. *The Age of Empires: Mesopotamia in the First Millennium BC.* Translated by Antonia Nevill. Edinburgh: Edinburgh University Press.

———, ed. 2000. *Rendre la justice en Mésopotamie: Archives judiciaires du Proche-Orient ancien (IIIᵉ–1ᵉʳ millénaires avant J.-C.).* Saint-Denis: Presses Universitaires de Vincennes.

Junkelmann, Marcus. 1990. *Die Reiter Roms*. Mainz: von Zabern.

Jursa, Michael. 2003. "Observations on the Problem of the Median 'Empire' on the Basis of Babylonian Sources." In: G. B. Lanfranchi, M. Roaf, and R. Rollinger, eds., *Continuity of Empire(?): Assyria, Media, Persia*, pp. 169–79. *History of the Ancient Near East/ Monographs* 5. Padua: S.A.R.G.O.N.

————. 2004. *Die Babylonier: Geschichte, Gesellschaft, Kultur*. Munich: Verlag C. H. Beck.

————. 2005. *Neo-Babylonian Legal and Administrative Documents: Typology, Contents and Archives*. Guides to the Mesopotamian Textual Record 1. Münster: Ugarit-Verlag.

————. 2007. "The Babylonian Economy in the First Millennium BC." In: Gwendolyn Leick, ed., *The Babylonian World*, pp. 224–35. London: Routledge.

Kaegi, Walter E. 2003. *Heraclius, Emperor of Byzantium*. Cambridge, UK: Cambridge University Press.

Kalmin, Richard. 2006. "The Formation and Character of the Babylonian Talmud." In: Steven T. Katz, ed., *The Cambridge History of Judaism*, 4: 840–76. Cambridge, UK: Cambridge University Press.

Kantor, Helene J. 1992. "The Relative Chronology of Egypt and Its Foreign Correlations before the Late Bronze Age." In: Robert W. Ehrich, ed., *Chronologies in Old World Archaeology*, 1: 1–46. Chicago: University of Chicago Press.

Kellens, J. 1989. "Avesta." *Encyclopaedia Iranica*, 3: 35–44. London: Routledge & Kegan Paul.

Kennedy, Hugh M. 2007. *The Great Arab Conquests: How the Spread of Islam Changed the World We Live In*. London: Weidenfeld & Nicholson.

al-Khaqani, Ali, ed. 1987. *Šu'ara' al-Ghari*. Qom: Bahram.

Kienast, Burkhart and Konrad Volk. 1995. *Die sumerischen und akkadischen Briefe des III. Jahrtausends aus der Zeit vor der III. Dynastie von Ur. Freiburger Altorientalische Studien* 7. Stuttgart: Franz Steiner Verlag.

Kilmer, A. D. 1993/7. "Musik." *Reallexikon der Assyriologie*, 8: 463–82. Berlin: De Gruyter.

King, Leonard W. 1907. *Chronicles Concerning Early Babylonian Kings, Including Records of the Early History of the Kassites and the Country of the Sea*. London: Luzac.

Kirkbride, Diana. 1975. "Umm Dabaghiyah 1974: A Fourth Preliminary Report." *Iraq* 33: 3–10.

Kister, M. J. 1968. "Al-Hira: Some Notes on Its Relations with Arabia." *Arabica* 15: 143–69.

Klein, Jacob. 1981. *Three Šulgi Hymns: Sumerian Royal Hymns Glorifying King Šulgi of Ur.* *Bar-Ilan Studies in Near Eastern Languages and Cultures.* Ramat-Gan: Bar-Ilan University.

———. 1995. "Shulgi of Ur: King of a Neo-Sumerian Empire." In: Jack M. Sasson, ed., *Civilizations of the Ancient Near East,* 2: 843–57. New York: Scribner's.

Klengel, Horst, ed. 1989. *Kulturgeschichte des alten Vorderasien.* Berlin: Akademie Verlag.

Koenig, Friedrich W. 1965. *Die Elamischen Königsinschriften. Archiv für Orientforschung* Beiheft 16.

Kraay, Colin M. 1966. *Greek Coins.* New York: Abrams.

Kramer, Samuel Noah. 1967. *Cradle of Civilization.* New York: Time-Life Books.

Kraus, Fritz Rudolf. 1968. *Briefe aus dem Archiv des Šamaš-ḫāzir in Paris und Oxford (TCL 7 und OECT 3). Altbabylonische Briefe in Umschrift und Übersetzung* 4. Leiden: E. J. Brill.

———. 1970. *Sumerer und Akkader: Ein Problem der altmesopotamischen Geschichte. Mededelingen der Koninklijke Nederlandse Akademie van Wetenschappen, AFD. Letterkunde, Nieuwe Reeks* 33 No. 8. Amsterdam: North-Holland Publishing Company.

Krecher, Joachim. 1976/80. "Kataloge, literarische." *Reallexikon der Assyriologie,* 5: 478–85. Berlin: De Gruyter.

Krückmann, Oluf. 1931. *Babylonische Rechts- und Verwaltungsurkunden aus der Zeit Alexanders und der Diadochen.* Weimar: Hof-Buchdruckerei.

Kuhrt, Amélie. 1987. "Berossus' Babyloniaka and Seleucid Rule in Babylonia." In: Amélie Kuhrt and Susan Sherwin-White, eds., *Hellenism in the East: The Interaction of Greek and Non-Greek Civilizations from Syria to Central Asia after Alexander,* pp. 32–56. Berkeley: University of California Press.

———. 1990. "Alexander and Babylon." *Achaemenid History* 5: 121–30.

———. 1995. "The Assyrian Heartland in the Achaemenid Period." In: P. Briant, ed., *Dans les pas des Dix-Mille: Peuples et pays du Proche-Orient vus par un Grec,* pp. 239–54. *Actes de la Table Ronde, Toulouse, 3–4 février 1995. Pallas* 43.

Kuhrt, Amélie and Susan Sherwin-White. 1987. "Xerxes' Destruction of Babylonian Temples." *Achaemenid History* 2: 69–78.

———. 1991. "Aspects of Royal Seleucid Ideology: The Cylinder of Antiochus I from Borsippa." *Journal of Hellenic Studies* 111: 71–86.

Kuhrt, Amélie and Susan Sherwin-White. 1994. "The Transition from the Achaemenid to the Seleucid Rule in Babylonia: Revolution or Evolution?" *Achaemenid History* 8: 311–27.

Kurz, Otto. 1983. "Cultural Relations between Parthia and Rome." In: Ehsan Yarshater, ed., *The Cambridge History of Iran*, 3(1): 559–67. Cambridge, UK: Cambridge University Press.

Labourt, J. 1904. *Le Christianisme dans l'Empire Perse sous la dynastie sassanide (224–632)*. Paris: Victor Lecoffre.

Lacheman, Ernest. 1974. "Le palais et la royauté de la ville de Nuzi: Les rapports entre les données archéologiques et les données épigraphiques." In: Paul Garelli, ed., *Le palais et la royauté: Archéologie et civilisation: XIXe Rencontre Assyriologique Internationale, 1971*, pp. 359–71. Paris: Librairie Orientaliste Paul Geuthner.

Laessøe, Jørgen. 1959. *The Shemshāra Tablets: A Preliminary Report. Det Kongelige Danske Videnskabernes Selskab 4/3, Arkaeologisk-kunsthistoriske Meddelelser*. Copenhagen: Ejnar Munksgaard.

Lafont, Bertrand. 2001. "Relations internationales, alliances et diplomatie au temps des royaumes amorrites: Essai de synthèse." In: J.-M. Durand and Dominique Charpin, eds., *Mari, Ebla et les Hourrites. Amurru* 2: 213–328.

Lambert, W. G. 1975. "The Cosmology of Sumer and Babylon." In: C. Bleecker and M. Loewe, eds., *Ancient Cosmologies*, pp. 42–65. London: Allen and Unwin.

———. 1983. "The God Aššur." *Iraq* 45: 82–6.

Lambton, Ann K. S. 2000. "Wazīr." *Encyclopaedia of Islam*, second edition, 11: 185–94.

Lamoureaux, J. C. 2001. "Early Eastern Christian Responses to Islam." In: John Tolan, ed., *Medieval Christian Views of Islam*, pp. 3–31. New York: Routledge.

Landsberger, Benno. 1937. *Die Serie ana ittišu. Materialien zum Sumerischen Lexikon* 1. Rome: Pontificium Institutum Biblicum.

Lanfranchi, Giovanni B., Michael Roaf, and Robert Rollinger, eds. 2003. *Continuity of Empire(?): Assyria, Media, Persia. History of the Ancient Near East/Monographs* 5. Padua: S.A.R.G.O.N.

Larsen, Mogens Trolle. 1976. *The Old Assyrian City-State and Its Colonies. Mesopotamia* 4. Copenhagen: Akademisk Forlag.

———. 1993. *The Conquest of Assyria*. London: Routledge.

Lawler, Andrew. 2003a. "Impending War Stokes Battle over Fate of Iraqi Antiquities." *Science* 299: 643.

————. 2003b. "Mayhem in Mesopotamia." *Science* 301: 582–9.

Layard, Austen H. 1853. *Discoveries among the Ruins of Nineveh and Babylon*. New York: Harper & Brothers.

Le Brun, A. and F. Vallat. 1978. "L'Origine de l'écriture à Suse." *Cahiers de la Délégation archéologique française en Iran* 8: 11–59.

Leemans, W. F. 1960. *Foreign Trade in the Old Babylonian Period. Studia et Documenta* 3. Leiden: E. J. Brill.

Lévy, Edmond, ed. 2000. *La codification des lois dans l'Antiquité: Actes du Colloque de Strasbourg 27–29 novembre 1997*. Université Marc Bloch de Strasbourg. *Travaux du Centre de Recherche sur le Proche-Orient et la Grèce Antiques* 16. Leiden: E. J. Brill.

Lewis, Brian. 1980. *The Sargon Legend: A Study of the Akkadian Text and the Tale of the Hero Who Was Exposed at Birth. American Schools of Oriental Research Dissertation Series* 4. Cambridge, Mass.: American Schools of Oriental Research.

Lieu, Samuel N. C. 1992. *Manichaeism in the Later Roman Empire and Medieval China: A Historical Survey*. Dover, N.H.: Manchester University Press.

————. 1994. *Manichaeism in Mesopotamia and the Roman East*. Leiden: E. J. Brill.

Limet, H. 1971. *Les légendes des sceaux cassites*. Académie royale de Belgique, Classe des Lettres et des Sciences morales et politiques, *Mémoires* 60/2. Brussels: Académie royale.

————. 1986. "Les guerres à l'époque sumérienne." *Acta Orientalia Belgica* 9: 27–41.

Lion, Brigitte and Cécile Michel, eds. 2006. *De la domestication au tabou: Le cas des suidés au Proche-Orient ancien. Travaux de la Maison René-Ginouvès* 1. Paris: De Boccard.

Lipin, L. A. 1960/1. "The Assyrian Family in the Second Half of the Second Millennium BC." *Cahiers d'Histoire Mondiale* 6: 628–43.

Littauer, Mary A. and Joost H. Crouwel. 1979. *Wheeled Vehicles and Ridden Animals in the Ancient Near East*. Leiden: E. J. Brill.

————. 2002. *Selected Writings on Chariots, Other Early Vehicles, Riding and Harness*. Edited by Peter Raulwing. *Culture and History of the Ancient Near East* 6. Leiden: E. J. Brill.

Liverani, Mario. 1976. "La concezione dell'universo." In: Sabatino Moscati, ed., *L'Alba della Civiltà*, 3: 439–521. Torino: UTET.

————. 1986. *L'Origine delle città: Le prime communità urbane del Vicino Oriente*. Rome: Riuniti.

————. 1988a. *Antico Oriente: Storia, Società, Economia*. Rome: Laterza.

Liverani, Mario. 1988b. "The Growth of the Assyrian Empire in the Habur/Middle Euphrates Area: A New Paradigm." *State Archives of Assyria Bulletin* 2: 81–98.

———. 1998. *Le lettere di el-Amarna*. Brescia: Paideia.

———. 2001. *International Relations in the Ancient Near East, 1600–1100 BC*. Basingstoke, UK: Palgrave.

———. 2003. "The Rise and Fall of Media." In: Giovanni B. Lanfranchi, Michael Roaf, and Robert Rollinger, eds., *Continuity of Empire(?): Assyria, Media, Persia*, pp. 1–12. *History of the Ancient Near East/Monographs* 5. Padua: S.A.R.G.O.N.

———. 2004. "Assyria in the Ninth Century: Continuity or Change?" In: Grant Frame, ed., *From the Upper Sea to the Lower Sea: Studies in the History of Assyria in Honour of A. K. Grayson*, pp. 213–26. Leiden: Nederlands Instituut voor het Nabije Oosten.

———. 2006. *Uruk, the First City*. Edited and translated by Zainab Bahrani and Marc Van De Mieroop. London: Equinox.

Livingstone, Alasdair. 2007. "Assurbanipal: Literate or Not?" *Zeitschrift für Assyriologie* 97: 98–118.

Lloyd, Seton. 1978. *The Archaeology of Mesopotamia from the Old Stone Age to the Persian Conquest*. New York: Thames and Hudson.

———. 1980. *Foundations in the Dust: The Story of Mesopotamian Exploration*. New York: Thames and Hudson.

Luckenbill, Daniel David. 1924. *The Annals of Sennacherib*. Oriental Institute Publications 2. Chicago: The Oriental Institute of the University of Chicago.

———. 1927. *Ancient Records of Assyria and Babylonia*. Chicago: University of Chicago Press.

Lukonin, V. G. 1983. "Political, Social and Administrative Institutions: Taxes and Trade." In: Ehsan Yarshater, ed., *The Cambridge History of Iran*, 3(2): 681–746. Cambridge, UK: Cambridge University Press.

MacMullen, Ramsay. 1997. *Christianity and Paganism in the Fourth to Eighth Centuries*. New Haven: Yale University Press.

Maeda, T. 1992. "The Defense Zone during the Rule of the Ur III Dynasty." *Acta Sumerologica* 14: 135–72.

Maekawa, Kazuya. 1973/4. "The Development of the É.MÍ in Lagash during Early Dynastic III." *Mesopotamia* 8/9: 77–144.

———. 1981. "The Agricultural Texts of Ur III Lagash of the British Museum." *Acta Sumerologica* 3: 37–61.

———. 1984. "Cereal Cultivation in the Ur III Period." *Bulletin on Sumerian Agriculture* 1: 73–96.

————. 1987. "The Agricultural Texts of Ur III Lagash of the British Museum V." *Acta Sumerologica* 9: 89–129.

Maidman, Maynard. 1995. "Nuzi: Portrait of an Ancient Mesopotamian Provincial Town." In: Jack M. Sasson, ed., *Civilizations of the Ancient Near East*, 2: 931–47. New York: Scribner's.

Maisels, Charles Keith. 1993. *The Near East: Archaeology in the "Cradle of Civilization."* London: Routledge.

Mallowan, Max. 1978. *The Nimrud Ivories.* London: British Museum Publications.

Mander, Pietro. 1984. "I Colofoni di Fara, Abu-Salabikh ed Ebla: Approccio Prosopografico." In: Luigi Cagni, ed., *Il Bilinguismo a Ebla: Atti del Convegno Internazionale (Napoli, 19–22 aprile 1982),* pp. 337–65. Seminario di Studi Asiatici, *Series Minor* 22. Naples: Istituto Universitario Orientale.

Marchesi, Gianni. 2004. "Who Was Buried in the Royal Tombs of Ur? The Epigraphic and Textual Data." *Orientalia* 73: 153–97.

Margueron, J.-C. 1982. *Recherches sur les palais mésopotamiens de l'âge du bronze.* Paris: Paul Geuthner.

————. 1995. "Mari: A Portrait in Art of a Mesopotamian City-State." In: Jack M. Sasson, ed., *Civilizations of the Ancient Near East*, 2: 885–900. New York: Scribner's.

Maricq, A. 1957. "Les dernières années de Hatra: L'alliance romaine." *Syria* 34: 288–96.

Marsden, Eric W. 1964. *The Campaign of Gaugamela.* Liverpool: Liverpool University Press.

Matthews, Roger J. 1991. "Fragments of Officialdom from Fara." *Iraq* 53: 1–15.

————. 1993. *Cities, Seals and Writing: Archaic Seal Impressions from Jemdet Nasr and Ur. Materialien zu den frühen Schriftzeugnissen des Vorderen Orients* 2. Berlin: Gebr. Mann Verlag.

————. 2003. *The Archaeology of Mesopotamia: Theories and Approaches.* London: Routledge.

Matthiae, Paolo. 1996. *La storia dell'arte dell'Oriente Antico: I grandi imperi.* Milan: Electa.

————. 1997. *La storia dell'arte dell'Oriente Antico: I primi imperi e i principati del ferro.* Milan: Electa.

Maul, Stefan M. 2003. "Die Reste einer mittelassyrischen Beschwörerbibliothek aus dem Königspalast zu Assur." In: Walther Sallaberger, Konrad Volk, and Annette Zgoll, eds., *Literatur, Politik und Recht: Festschrift für Claus Wilcke,* pp. 181–94. Wiesbaden: Harrassowitz.

Maul, Stefan M. 2005. *Das Gilgamesch-Epos: Neu übersetzt und kommentiert*. Munich: C. H. Beck.

McDonald, Diana. 2005. "From the Kassite Temple of Karaindash." In: Milbry Polk and Angela M. H. Schuster, eds. *The Looting of the Iraq Museum, Baghdad: The Lost Legacy of Ancient Mesopotamia*, pp. 144–5. New York: Abrams.

McGovern, Patrick E. 2003. *Ancient Wine: The Search for the Origins of Viniculture*. Princeton: Princeton University Press.

Meadow, Richard H. 1986. *Equids in the Ancient World*. Wiesbaden: Reichert Verlag.

Mellaart, James. 1967. *Çatal Hüyük: A Neolithic Town in Anatolia*. New York: McGraw Hill.

———. 1975. *The Neolithic of the Near East*. New York: Scribner's.

Melville, Sarah C. 1999. *The Role of Naqia/Zakutu in Sargonid Politics. State Archives of Assyria, Studies* 10. Helsinki: Neo-Assyrian Text Corpus Project.

Meyendorff, John. 1964. "Byzantine Views of Islam," *Dumbarton Oaks Papers* 18: 115–32.

Meyer, Jan-Waalke. 1999. "Der Palast von Aqar Quf: Stammestrukturen in der kassitischen Gesellschaft." In: Barbara Böck, Eva Cancik-Kirschbaum, and Thomas Richter, eds., *Munuscula Mesopotamica: Festschrift für Johannes Renger*, pp. 317–26. *Alter Orient und Altes Testament* 267. Münster: Ugarit-Verlag.

Michalowski, Piotr. 1984. "History as Charter: Some Observations on the Sumerian King List." In: Jack M. Sasson, ed., *Studies in Literature from the Ancient Near East by Members of the American Oriental Society. American Oriental Series* 65 = *Journal of the American Oriental Society* 103: 237–48.

———. 1987. "Charisma and Control: On Continuity and Change in Early Mesopotamian Bureaucratic Systems." In: McGuire Gibson and Robert D. Biggs, eds., *Aspects of Bureaucracy in the Ancient Near East*, pp. 55–68. *Studies in Ancient Oriental Civilization* 46. Chicago: Oriental Institute of the University of Chicago.

———. 1989. *The Lamentation over the Destruction of Sumer and Ur. Mesopotamian Civilizations* 1. Winona Lake, Ind.: Eisenbrauns.

———. 1990. "Early Mesopotamian Communicative Systems." In: Ann C. Gunter, ed., *Investigating Artistic Environments in the Ancient Near East*, pp. 53–69. Washington, D.C.: Smithsonian Institution.

———. 1994. "Writing and Literacy in Early States: A Mesopotamian Perspective." In: D. Keller-Cohen, ed., *Literacy: Interdisciplinary Conversations*, pp. 49–70. Cresskill, N.J.: Hampton Press.

————. 1996. "Mesopotamian Cuneiform, Origins." In: William Bright, ed., *The World's Writing Systems*, pp. 33–6. Oxford: Oxford University Press.

————. 1999. "Sumer Dreams of Subartu: Politics and the Geographical Imagination." In: K. Van Lerberghe and G. Voet, eds., *Languages and Cultures in Contact: At the Crossroads of Civilizations in the Syro-Mesopotamian Realm: Proceedings of the 42th RAI*, pp. 305–15. Leuven: Peeters.

Michel, Cécile. 2001. *Correspondance des marchands de Kanish au début du IIᵉ millénaire avant J.-C. Littératures anciennes du Proche-Orient* 19. Paris: Les Editions du Cerf.

Milano, Lucio, ed. 1994. *Drinking in Ancient Societies: History and Culture of Drinks in the Ancient Near East: Papers of a Symposium Held in Rome, May 17–19, 1990. History of the Ancient Near East/Studies* 6. Padua: Sargon srl.

Millar, Fergus. 1993. *The Roman Near East, 31 BC–AD 337.* Cambridge, Mass.: Harvard University Press.

————. 1998a. "Caravan Cities: The Roman Near East and Long-Distance Trade by Land." In: Hannah M. Cotton and Guy M. Rogers, eds., *The Greek World, the Jews, & the East*, pp. 275–99. Chapel Hill: University of North Carolina Press.

————. 1998b. "Looking East from the Classical World: Colonialism, Culture, and Trade from Alexander the Great to Shapur I." In: Hannah M. Cotton and Guy M. Rogers, eds., *The Greek World, the Jews, & the East*, pp. 300–27. Chapel Hill: University of North Carolina Press.

————. 1998c. "Ethnic Identity in the Roman Near East, A.D. 325–450: Language, Religion, and Culture." In: Hannah M. Cotton and Guy M. Rogers, eds., *The Greek World, the Jews, & the East*, pp. 378–405. Chapel Hill: University of North Carolina Press.

Minorsky, V. 1944. "Vīs o Rāmīn, a Parthian Romance." *Bulletin of the School of Oriental and African Studies, University of London* 11: 741–63.

Miquel, A. 1986. "'Irāq." *Encyclopedia of Islam*, second edition, 4: 1250–3.

Momigliano, Arnaldo. 1975. *Alien Wisdom: The Limits of Hellenization.* Cambridge, UK: Cambridge University Press.

Moorey, P.R.S. 1970. "Pictorial Evidence for the History of Horse-riding in Iraq before the Kassite Period." *Iraq* 32: 36–50.

————. 1982. *Ur "of the Chaldees": A Revised and Updated Edition of Sir Leonard Woolley's Excavations at Ur.* Ithaca: Cornell University Press.

Moorey, P.R.S. 1994. *Ancient Mesopotamian Materials and Industries: The Archaeological Evidence.* Oxford: Clarendon Press.

Moortgat, Anton. 1967. *The Art of Ancient Mesopotamia: The Classical Art of the Near East.* Translated by Judith Filson. London: Phaidon.

Moran, William L. 1992. *The Amarna Letters.* Baltimore: The Johns Hopkins University Press.

Müller-Kessler, Christa. 2004. "The Question of the Origin of the Mandaeans." *Aram* 16: 47–60.

Musche, Brigitte. 1999. *Die Liebe in der altorientalischen Dichtung. Studies in the History and Culture of the Ancient Near East* 15. Leiden: E. J. Brill.

Muses. See Foster, B. 2005b.

Nashef, Khalid. 2004. *Tadmīr al-Turāth al-Hiḍārī al-ʿIrāqī, Fuṣūl al-Kārithah.* Beirut: Dar al-Muraʾi.

Naveh, Joseph and Shaul Shaked. 1985. *Amulets and Magic Bowls: Aramaic Incantations of Late Antiquity.* Jerusalem: Magnes Press.

Nesselrath, H.-G. 1999. "Herodot und Babylon: Der Hauptort Mesopotamiens in den Augen eines Griechen des 5. Jh.s v. Chr." In: Johannes Renger, ed., *Babylon: Focus mesopotamischer Geschichte, Wiege früher Gelehrsamkeit, Mythos in der Moderne: 2. Internationales Colloquium der Deutschen Orient-Gesellschaft 24.–26. März in Berlin*, pp. 189–206. Saarbrücken: Saarbrückener Druckerei und Verlag.

Neumann, Hans. 1987. *Handwerk in Mesopotamien: Untersuchungen zu seiner Organisation in der Zeit der III. Dynastie von Ur. Schriften zur Geschichte und Kultur des Alten Orients* 19. Berlin: Akademie Verlag.

———. 1992. "Nochmals zum Kaufmann in neusumerischer Zeit: Die Geschäfte des Ur-dun und anderer Kaufleute aus Nippur." In: Dominique Charpin and Francis Joannès, eds., *La circulation des biens, des personnes et des idées dans le Proche-Orient ancien: Actes de la XXXVIIIᵉ Rencontre Assyriologique Internationale (Paris, 8–10 juillet 1991)*, pp. 83–94. Paris: Editions Recherche sur les Civilisations.

Neusner, Jacob. 1966. *A History of the Jews in Babylonia, II: The Early Sassanian Period. Studia Post-Biblica* 11. Leiden: E. J. Brill.

———. 1968. *A History of the Jews in Babylonia, III: From Shapur I to Shapur II. Studia Post-Biblica* 12. Leiden: E. J. Brill.

———. 1969a. *A History of the Jews in Babylonia, I: The Parthian Period. Studia Post-Biblica* 9. Leiden: E. J. Brill.

————. 1969b. *A History of the Jews in Babylonia, IV: The Age of Shapur II. Studia Post-Biblica* 14. Leiden: E. J. Brill.

————. 1970. *A History of the Jews in Babylonia, V: Later Sassanian Times. Studia Post-Biblica* 15. Leiden: E. J. Brill.

Newman, J. 1932. *The Agricultural Life of the Jews in Babylonia between the Years 200 C.E. and 500 C.E.* Oxford: Oxford University Press.

Nicholson, R. A. 1907. *A Literary History of the Arabs.* Cambridge, UK: Cambridge University Press.

Nissen, Hans J. 1971. "Südbabylonien in parthischer und sassanidischer Zeit." *Baghdader Mitteilungen* 6: 79–86.

————. 1986. "The Archaic Texts from Uruk." *World Archaeology* 17/3: 317–34.

————. 1988. *The Early History of the Ancient Near East, 9000–2000 B.C.* Translated by Elizabeth Lutzeier, with Kenneth J. Northcott. Chicago: University of Chicago Press.

Nissen, Hans J., Peter Damerow, and Robert Englund. 1993. *Early Writing and Techniques of Economic Administration in the Ancient Near East.* Chicago: University of Chicago Press.

Nodelman, S. 1960. "A Preliminary History of Characene." *Berytus* 13: 83–121.

Nougayrol, Jean. 1955. "Les rapports des haruspicines étrusques et assyro-babyloniens et le foie d'argile de Falerii Veteres (Villa Giulia 3786)." *Académie des Inscriptions et Belles-lettres: Comptes rendus des séances de l'année 1955*, pp. 509–15. Paris: Editions Klincksieck.

————. 1957/8. "Les fragments en pierre du Code Hammourabien (I)." *Journal Asiatique* 245: 339–66, (II) 246: 143–55.

Nylander, Carl. 1980. "Earless in Nineveh: Who Mutilated Sargon's Head?" *American Journal of Archaeology* 84: 329–33.

Oates, David. 1968. *Studies in the Ancient History of Northern Iraq.* London: The British Academy.

————. 1973. "Early Vaulting in Mesopotamia." In: D. E. Strong, ed., *Archaeological Theory and Practice*, pp. 183–91. London: Seminar Press.

Oates, David and Joan Oates. 1976. *The Rise of Civilization.* London: Phaidon.

————. 1989. "Akkadian Buildings at Tell Brak." *Iraq* 51: 193–211.

————. 2001. *Nimrud: An Assyrian Imperial City Revealed.* London: British School of Archaeology in Iraq.

Oates, Joan. 1973. "The Background and Development of Early Farming Communities in Mesopotamia and the Zagros." *Proceedings of the Prehistoric Society* 1973: 147–81.

Oates, Joan. 1979. *Babylon*. London: Thames and Hudson.

Oded, Bustany. 1979. *Mass Deportations and Deportees in the Assyrian Empire*. Wiesbaden: Harrassowitz.

Oelsner, Joachim. 1982. "Landvergabe im kassitischen Babylonien." In: *Societies and Languages of the Ancient Near East: Studies in Honour of I. M. Diakonoff*, pp. 279–84. Warminster, UK: Aris & Phillips.

Olbrys, Miroslav, Agnieszka Dolatowska, and Tomasz Burda. 2004. *Report on the Current Condition of Babylon Archaeological Site (The Military Camp Alpha Site)*. Warsaw: Ministry of Culture.

Olmstead, A. T. 1918. "The Calculated Frightfulness of Ashur Nasir Apal." *Journal of the American Oriental Society* 38: 209–63.

Oppenheim, A. Leo. 1954. "The Seafaring Merchants of Ur." *Journal of the American Oriental Society* 74: 6–17.

———. 1959. "On an Operational Device in Mesopotamian Bureaucracy." *Journal of Near Eastern Studies* 18: 121–8.

———. 1961. "The Mesopotamian Temple." In: G. Ernest Wright and David Noel Freedman, eds., *The Biblical Archaeologist Reader*, 1: 158–69. Garden City, N.Y.: Anchor Books.

———. 1977. *Ancient Mesopotamia: Portrait of a Dead Civilization*. Revised edition completed by Erica Reiner. Chicago: University of Chicago Press.

———. 1978. "Man and Nature in Mesopotamian Civilization." In: Charles Coulston Gillispie, ed., *Dictionary of Scientific Biography*, 15 (*Supplement* 1): 634–66. New York: Charles Scribner's Sons.

Ostrogorsky, George. 1957. *History of the Byzantine State*. Translated by Joan Hussey. New Brunswick, N.J.: Rutgers University Press.

Pallis, Sven A. 1956. *The Antiquity of Iraq: A Handbook of Assyriology*. Copenhagen: Ejnar Munksgaard.

Parker, Grant. 2000. "'Ex Oriente Luxuria': Indian Commodities and Roman Experience." *Journal of the Economic and Social History of the Orient* 45: 40–95.

Parpola, Simo and Kazuko Watanabe. 1988. *Neo-Assyrian Treaties and Loyalty Oaths. State Archives of Assyria* 2. Helsinki: Helsinki University Press.

Parrot, André. 1974. *Mari, capitale fabuleuse*. Paris: Payot.

Paynter, Sarah and Michael Tite. 2001. "The Evolution of Glazing Technologies in the Ancient Near East and Egypt." In: Andrew J. Shortland, ed., *The Social Context of Technological Change: Egypt and the Near East, 1650–1550 BC*, pp. 239–54. Oxford: Oxbow Books.

Pedersén, Olof. 1998. *Archives and Libraries in the Ancient Near East 1500–300 B.C.* Bethesda, Md.: CDL Press.

Peters, Frank E. 1970. *The Harvest of Hellenism: A History of the Near East from Alexander the Great to the Triumph of Christianity.* New York: Simon and Schuster.

Pickworth, Diana. 2005. "Excavations at Nineveh: The Halzi Gate." *Iraq* 57: 295–316.

Pientka, R. 1998. *Die spätaltbabylonische Zeit: Abiešuḫ bis Samsuiluna: Quellen, Jahresdaten, Geschichte.* Imgula 2. Münster: Rhema.

Pingree, David. 1998. "Legacies in Astronomy and Celestial Omens." In: Stephanie Dalley, ed., *The Legacy of Mesopotamia,* pp. 125–37. Oxford: Oxford University Press.

Pittman, Holly. 1996. "Constructing Context: The Gebel el Arak Knife: Greater Mesopotamia and Egyptian Interaction in the Late Fourth Millennium." In: Jerrold S. Cooper and Glenn M. Schwartz, eds., *The Study of the Ancient Near East in the Twenty-first Century,* pp. 1–29. Baltimore: The Johns Hopkins University Press.

Polk, Milbry and Angela M. H. Schuster, eds. 2005. *The Looting of the Iraq Museum, Baghdad: The Lost Legacy of Ancient Mesopotamia.* New York: Abrams.

Pollock, Susan. 1999. *Ancient Mesopotamia, the Eden That Never Was.* Cambridge, UK: Cambridge University Press.

Pomponio, Francesco and Giuseppi Visicato. 1994. *Early Dynastic Administrative Tablets of Šuruppak.* Dipartimento di Studi Asiatici, Series Maior 6. Naples: Istituto Universitario Orientale.

Pongratz-Leisten, Beate. 1994. *Ina šulmi īrub. Die kulttopographische und ideologische Programmatik der akītu-Prozession in Babylonien und Assyrien im 1. Jahrtausend v. Chr. Baghdader Forschungen* 16. Mainz: von Zabern.

Porada, Edith. 1989. "Problems of Late Assyrian Reliefs." In: A. Leonard and B. B. Williams, eds., *Essays in Ancient Civilization Presented to Helene J. Kantor,* pp. 243–8. *Studies in Ancient Oriental Civilization* 47. Chicago: Oriental Institute of the University of Chicago.

Porter, Barbara Nevling. 1993. *Images, Power, and Politics: Figurative Aspects of Esarhaddon's Babylonian Policy. Memoirs of the American Philosophical Society* 208. Philadelphia: American Philosophical Society.

Postgate, Nicholas. 1977. *The First Empires.* Oxford: Elsevier-Phaidon.

———. 1982. "Ilku and Land Tenure in the Middle Assyrian Kingdom: A Second Attempt." In: *Societies and Languages of the Ancient Near East: Studies in Honour of I. M. Diakonoff,* pp. 301–13. Warminster, UK: Aris & Phillips. [Also in Postgate 2007: 112–21.]

Postgate, Nicholas. 1989. "Ownership and Exploitation of Land in Assyria in the 1st Millennium B.C." In: Marc Lebeau and Philippe Talon, eds., *Reflets des deux fleuves: Volume de mélanges offerts à André Finet*, pp. 141–52. Leuven: Peeters. [Also in Postgate 2007: 181–92.]

———. 1992. *Early Mesopotamia: Society and Economy at the Dawn of History*. London: Routledge.

———. 2007. *The Land of Assur & the Yoke of Assyria: Studies on Assyria 1971–2005*. Oxford: Oxbow Books.

Potts, Daniel T. 1997. *Mesopotamian Civilization: The Material Foundations*. Ithaca: Cornell University Press.

———. 2000. "Before Alexandria: Libraries in the Ancient Near East." In: Roy Macleod, ed., *The Library of Alexandria: Centre of Learning in the Ancient World*, pp. 19–33. London: I. B. Tauris.

———, ed. 1983. *Dilmun: New Studies in the Archaeology and Early History of Bahrein. Berliner Beiträge zum Vorderen Orient* 2. Berlin: Dietrich Reimer Verlag.

Price, T. Douglas and Anne Brigitte Gebauer, eds. 2003. *Last Hunters—First Farmers: New Perspectives on the Prehistoric Transition to Agriculture*. Santa Fe: School of American Research.

Radner, Karen. 2005. *Die Macht des Namens: Altorientalische Strategien zur Selbsterhaltung. Santag* 8. Wiesbaden: Harrassowitz.

Reade, Julian E. 1980. "Space, Scale, and Significance in Assyrian Art." *Baghdader Mitteilungen* 11: 71–4.

———. 1986. "Archaeology and the Kuyunjik Archives." In: Klaas Veenhof, ed., *Cuneiform Archives and Libraries: Papers Read at the 30ᵉ Rencontre Assyriologique Internationale, Leiden, 4–8 July 1983*, pp. 213–22. Leiden: Nederlands Historisch-Archaeologisch Instituut te Istanbul.

———. 1998. *Assyrian Scuplture*. Cambridge, Mass.: Harvard University Press.

———. 2003. "The Royal Tombs of Ur." In: Joan Aruz, ed., *Art of the First Cities: The Third Millennium B.C. from the Mediterranean to the Indus*, pp. 93–132 (with catalogue entries by others). New York: Metropolitan Museum of Art.

Reiner, Erica. 1961. "The Aetiological Myth of the Seven Sages." *Orientalia* 30: 1–11.

Renfrew, Colin, J. E. Dixon, and J. R. Cann. 1966. "Obsidian and Early Cultural Contacts in the Near East." *Proceedings of the Prehistoric Society* 32: 30–72.

Renger, Johannes M. 1995. "Institutional, Communal, and Individual Ownership or Possession of Arable Land in Ancient Mesopotamia from the End of the Fourth to the End of the First Millennium B.C." *Chicago-Kent Law Review* 71/1: 269–319.

Richardson, Seth. 2007. "The World of Mesopotamian Countrysides." In: Gwendolyn Leick, ed., *The Babylonian World*, pp. 12–38. London: Routledge.

Roaf, Michael. 1990. *Cultural Atlas of Mesopotamia and the Ancient Near East*. Oxford: Facts on File.

Robinson, Andrew. 1995. *The Story of Writing: Alphabets, Hieroglyphs and Pictographs*. London: Thames and Hudson.

Robinson, B. W. 2002. *The Persian Book of Kings: An Epitome of the Shahnama of Firdawsi*. New York: Routledge Curzon.

Robson, Eleanor. 1999. *Mesopotamian Mathematics, 2100–1600 BC: Technical Constants in Bureaucracy and Education*. Oxford Editions of Cuneiform Texts 14. Oxford: Clarendon Press.

———. 2001. "Technology in Society: Three Textual Case Studies from Late Bronze Age Mesopotamia." In: Andrew J. Shortland, ed., *The Social Context of Technological Change: Egypt and the Near East, 1650–1550 BC*, pp. 39–57. Oxford: Oxbow Books.

Robson, Eleanor, Luke Treadwell, and Chris Gosden, eds. 2006. *Who Owns Objects? The Ethics and Politics of Collecting Cultural Artefacts*. Oxford: Oxbow Books.

Rochberg, Francesca. 1998. *Babylonian Horoscopes*. Transactions of the American Philosophical Society 88/1. Philadelphia: American Philosophical Society.

Rollinger, Robert. 1993. *Herodots babylonischer Logos: eine kritische Untersuchung*. Innsbruck: Verlag des Instituts für Sprachwissenschaft der Universität Innsbruck.

Romer, John and Elizabeth Romer. 1995. *The Seven Wonders of the World: A History of the Modern Imagination*. New York: Henry Holt.

Römer, W. P. 1969. "Religion of Ancient Mesopotamia." In: George Widengren, ed., *Historia Religionum: Handbook for the History of Religions, 1: Religions of the Past*, pp. 115–94. Leiden: E. J. Brill.

Root, Margaret Cool. 1979. *The King and Kingship in Achaemenid Art*. Leiden: E. J. Brill.

Rosenthal, Franz. 1987. "Aramaic." *Encyclopedia Iranica*, 2: 251–6. New York: Encyclopedia Iranica Foundation.

Rostovtzeff, Michael. 1943. "The Parthian Shot." *American Journal of Archaeology* 47: 174–87.

Roth, Martha. 1989. *Babylonian Marriage 7th–3rd Centuries B.C. Alter Orient und Altes Testament* 222. Neukirchen-Vluyn: Kevelaer.

———. 1989/90. "The Material Composition of the Neo-Babylonian Dowry." *Archiv für Orientforschung* 36/37: 1–55.

———. 1995. "Mesopotamian Legal Traditions and the Laws of Hammurabi." *Chicago-Kent Law Review* 71/1: 13–39.

———. 1997. *Law Collections from Mesopotamia and Asia Minor*, second edition. *SBL Writings from the Ancient World Series* 6. Atlanta: Scholars Press.

Rothfield, Lawrence, ed. 2008. *Antiquities under Siege: Cultural Heritage Protection after the Iraq War.* London: Altamira Press.

Rubio, Gonzalo. 2005. "On the Linguistic Landscape of Early Mesopotamia." In: W. H. van Soldt, ed., *Ethnicity in Ancient Mesopotamia: Papers Read at the 48th Rencontre Assyriologique Internationale, Leiden, 1–4 July 2002*, pp. 316–32. Leiden: Nederlands Instituut voor het Nabije Oosten.

Russell, John Malcolm. 1991. *Sennacherib's Palace without Rival at Nineveh.* Chicago: University of Chicago Press.

———. 1997. *From Nineveh to New York.* New Haven: Yale University Press.

———. 1999. *The Writing on the Wall: Studies in the Architectural Context of Late Assyrian Palace Inscriptions.* Winona Lake, Ind.: Eisenbrauns.

Sachs, Abraham. 1976. "The Latest Datable Cuneiform Texts." In: Barry Eichler, ed., *Kramer Anniversary Volume: Cuneiform Studies in Honor of Samuel Noah Kramer*, pp. 379–98. *Alter Orient und Altes Testament* 25. Neukirchen-Vluyn: Butzon & Bercker Kevelaer.

Sack, Ronald. 1972. *Amēl-Marduk 562–560 B.C. Alter Orient und Altes Testament*, Sonderreihe 4. Neukirchen-Vluyn: Butzon & Bercker Kevelaer.

———. 1978. "Nebuchadnezzar and Nabonidus in Folklore and History." *Mesopotamia* 17: 67–131.

Sader, Hélène. 1989. "The 12th Century B.C. in Syria: The Problem of the Rise of the Arameans." In: William A. Ward and Martha Sharpe Joukowsky, eds., *The Crisis Years: The Twelfth Century B.C., from beyond the Danube to the Tigris*, pp. 157–63. Dubuque, Iowa: Kendall/Hunt.

Sallaberger, Walther. 1999. "Ur III-Zeit." In: Pascal Attinger and Markus Wäfler, eds., *Mesopotamien, Akkade-Zeit und Ur III-Zeit*, pp. 121–390. *Orbis Biblicus et Orientalis* 160/3. Göttingen: Vandenhoeck & Ruprecht.

Sancisi-Weerdenburg, H. 1993. "Alexander at Persepolis." In: Jesper Carlsen, ed., *Alexander the Great: Reality and Myth*, pp. 177–88. *Analecta Romana Istituti Danici Supplement* 21. Rome: L'Erma di Bretschneider.

Sandars, Nancy K. 1985. *The Sea Peoples, Warriors of the Mediterranean*. Revised edition. London: Thames and Hudson.

Sassmannshausen, Leonard. 1999. "The Adaptation of the Kassites to the Babylonian Civilization." In: K. Van Lerberghe and G. Voet, eds., *Languages and Cultures in Contact: At the Crossroads of Civilizations in the Syro-Mesopotamian Realm: Proceedings of the 42th Rencontre Assyriologique Internationale*, pp. 409–24. Leuven: Peeters.

Schaudig, H. 2001. *Die Inschriften Nabonids von Babylon und Kyros' des Großen samt den in ihrem Umfeld entstandenen Tendenzschriften, Textausgabe und Grammatik. Alter Orient und Altes Testament* 256. Münster: Ugarit-Verlag.

Schlesinger, Victoria. 2007. "Desert Solitaire." *Archaeology*, July/August: 9.

Schlumberger, Daniel. 1983. "Parthian Art." In: Ehsan Yarshater, ed., *The Cambridge History of Iran*, 3(2): 1027–54. Cambridge, UK: Cambridge University Press.

Schmandt-Besserat, Denise. 1996. *How Writing Came About*. Austin: University of Texas Press.

———. 2007. *When Writing Met Art: From Symbol to Story*. Austin: University of Texas Press.

Schneider, Rolf Michael. 2007. "Friend *and* Foe: The Orient in Rome." In: Vesta Sarkhosh Curtis and Sarah Stewart, eds., *The Age of the Parthians: The Idea of Iran*, 2: 50–86. London: I. B. Tauris.

Schwab, Raymond. 1984. *The Oriental Renaissance: Europe's Rediscovery of India and the East, 1680–1880*. Translated by Gene Patterson-Black and Victor Reinking. New York: Columbia University Press.

Scurlock, Joanne. 2005. *Diagnoses in Assyrian and Babylonian Medicine: Ancient Sources, Translations, and Modern Medical Analyses*. Urbana: University of Illinois Press.

Segal, J. B. 1955. "Mesopotamian Communities from Julian to the Rise of Islam." *Proceedings of the British Academy* 41: 109–39.

Seidl, Ursula. 1989. *Die babylonischen Kudurru-Reliefs: Symbole Mesopotamischer Gottheiten. Orbis Biblicus et Orientalis* 87. Göttingen: Vandenhoeck & Ruprecht.

Seminara, Stefano. 2001. *La versione accadica del* LUGAL-E: *La tecnica babilonese della traduzione dal sumerico e le sue "regole." Materiali per il Vocabolario Sumerico* 8. Rome: Università degli Studi di Roma "La Sapienza," Dipartimento di Studi Orientali.

Shahid, Irfan. 1965. "Ghassān." *Encyclopaedia of Islam*, second edition, 2: 1020-1. Leiden: E. J. Brill.

——. 1986. "al-Ḥīra." *Encyclopaedia of Islam*, second edition, 3: 462–3. Leiden: E. J. Brill.

Sharlach, Tonia M. 2004. *Provinicial Taxation and the Ur III State. Cuneiform Monographs* 26. Leiden: E. J. Brill.

Shaw, Wendy M. K. 2003. *Possessors and Possessed: Museums, Archaeology, and the Visualization of History in the Late Ottoman Empire*. Berkeley: University of California Press.

Shepherd, Dorothy. 1983. "Sassanian Art." In: Ehsan Yarshater, ed., *The Cambridge History of Iran*, 3(2): 1055–112. Cambridge, UK: Cambridge University Press.

Sherratt, Andrew. 1997. "Climatic Cycles and Behavioural Revolutions: The Emergence of Modern Humans and the Beginnings of Farming." *Antiquity* 71: 271–87.

Sherwin-White, Susan. 1987. "Seleucid Babylonia: A case study for the installation and development of Greek rule." In: Amélie Kuhrt and Susan Sherwin-White, eds., *Hellenism in the East: The Interaction of Greek and Non-Greek Civilizations from Syria to Central Asia after Alexander*, pp. 1–31. Berkeley: University of California Press.

Sieverstein, U. 1992. "Das Messer vom Gebel el-Arak." *Baghdader Mitteilungen* 23: 1–70.

Simpson, St. John. 1997. "Ctesiphon." In: Eric M. Meyers, ed., *The Oxford Encyclopedia of Archaeology in the Near East*, 2: 77–9. Oxford: Oxford University Press.

——. 2000. "Mesopotamia in the Sasanian Period: Settlement Patterns, Arts and Crafts." In: John Curtis, ed., *Mesopotamia and Iran in the Parthian and Sasanian Periods: Rejection and Revival c. 238 BC–AD 642*, pp. 57–66. London: British Museum Press.

Sitzler, D. 1995. *"Vorwurf gegen Gott": Ein religiöses Motiv im alten Orient (Ægypten und Mesopotamien)*. Wiesbaden: Harrassowitz.

Sjöberg, Åke. 1960. *Der Mondgott Nanna-Suen in der sumerischen Überlieferung*. Stockholm: Almqvist & Wiksell.

——. 1969. *The Collection of Sumerian Temple Hymns*, with E. J. Bergmann S. J. *Texts from Cuneiform Sources* 3. Locust Valley, N.Y.: J. J. Augustin.

Slanski, Kathryn. 2003. *The Babylonian Entitlement* narûs (kudurrus): *A Study in Their Form and Function. ASOR Books* 9. Boston: American Schools of Oriental Research.

Slotsky, Alice. 1997. *The Bourse of Babylon: Market Quotations in the Astronomical Diaries of Babylonia*. Bethesda, Md.: CDL Press.

Smith, B. D. 1995. *The Emergence of Agriculture*. New York: Scientific American Library.

Snell, Daniel C. 1982. *Ledgers and Prices: Early Mesopotamian Merchant Accounts. Yale Near Eastern Researches* 8. New Haven: Yale University Press.

Sollberger, Edmond. 1951. "Un 'état néant' sous la IIIᵉ Dynastie d'Ur." *Revue d'Assyriologie* 45: 116.

———. 1976/80. "Ibbī-Sin." *Reallexikon der Assyriologie,* 5: 1–8. Berlin: De Gruyter.

Sommer, Michael. 2005. *Roms Orientalischer Steppengrenze: Palmyra— Edessa—Dura Europos—Hatra: Eine Kulturgeschichte von Pompeius bis Diocletian. Oriens und Occidens* 9. Stuttgart: Franz Steiner Verlag.

Sommerfeld, Walter. 1995. "The Kassites of Ancient Mesopotamia: Origins, Politics and Culture." In: Jack M. Sasson, ed., *Civilizations of the Ancient Near East,* 2: 917–30. New York: Scribner's.

Sprengling, Martin. 1953. *Third Century Iran: Sapor and Kartir.* Chicago: University of Chicago Press.

Stauder, W. 1972/5. "Harfe." *Reallexikon der Assyriologie,* 4: 114–20. Berlin: De Gruyter.

Stein, Gil. 1994. "Economy, Ritual, and Power in 'Ubaid Mesopotamia." In: Gil Stein and Mitchell S. Rothman, eds., *Chiefdoms and Early States in the Near East: The Organizational Dynamics of Complexity. Monographs in World Archaeology* 18, pp. 35–46. Madison: Prehistory Press.

Steinkeller, Piotr. 1981. "The Renting of Fields in Early Mesopotamia and the Development of the Concept of Interest in Sumerian." *Journal of the Economic and Social History of the Orient* 24: 113–45.

———. 1987. "The Administrative and Economic Organization of the Ur III State: The Core and the Periphery." In: McGuire Gibson and Robert D. Biggs, eds., *Aspects of Bureaucracy in the Ancient Near East,* pp. 19–41. *Studies in Ancient Oriental Civilization* 46. Chicago: Oriental Institute of the University of Chicago.

———. 1988. "Grundeigentum in Babylonien von Uruk IV bis zur frühdynastischen Periode II." In: *Das Grundeigentum in Mesopotamien. Jahrbuch für Wirtschaftsgeschichte, Sonderband,* pp. 11–27.

———. 1993. "Early Political Development in Mesopotamia and the Origins of the Sargonic Empire." In: Mario Liverani, ed., *Akkad, the First World Empire: Structure, Ideology, Traditions*, pp. 107–29. *History of the Ancient Near East, Studies* 5. Padua: Sargon.

————. 1999. "On Rulers, Priests and Sacred Marriage: Tracing the Evolution of Early Sumerian Kingship." In: Kazuko Watanabe, ed., *Priests and Officials in the Ancient Near East: Papers of the Second Colloquium on the Ancient Near East—The City and Its Life, Held at the Middle Eastern Culture Center in Japan (Mitaka, Tokyo), March 22–24, 1996*, pp. 103–37. Heidelberg: Universitätsverlag C. Winter.

————. 2002. "Archaic City Seals and the Question of Mesopotamian Unity." In: Tzvi Abusch, ed., *Riches Hidden in Secret Places: Ancient Near Eastern Studies in Memory of Thorkild Jacobsen*, pp. 249–57. Winona Lake, Ind.: Eisenbrauns.

Stol, Marten. 2004. "Wirtschaft und Gesellschaft in altbabylonischer Zeit." In: Pascal Attinger, Walther Sallaberger, and Markus Wäfler, eds., *Mesopotamien: Die altbabylonische Zeit*, pp. 643–975. *Orbis Biblicus et Orientalis* 160/4. Göttingen: Vandenhoeck & Ruprecht.

Stolper, Matthew W. 1985. *Entrepreneurs and Empire: The Murašû Archive, the Murašû Firm, and Persian Rule in Babylonia*. Leiden: Nederlands Instituut voor het Nabije Oosten.

————. 2004. "The Kasr Texts, the Rich Collection, the Bellino Copies and the Grotefend Nachlass." In: J. G. Dercksen, ed., *Assyria and Beyond: Studies Presented to Mogens Trolle Larsen*, pp. 511–49. Leiden: Nederlands Instituut voor het Nabije Oosten.

Stone, Elizabeth C. 1987. *Nippur Neighborhoods. Studies in Ancient Oriental Civilization* 44. Chicago: Oriental Institute of the University of Chicago.

Stratos, Andreas N. 1972. *Byzantium in the Seventh Century*. Translated by Harry T. Hionides. Amsterdam: Adolf M. Hakkert.

Streuver, Stuart, ed. 1971. *Prehistoric Agriculture*. Garden City, N.Y.: The Natural History Press.

Strommenger, Eva. 1962. *Fünf Jahrtausende Mesopotamien*. Munich: Hirmer.

————. 1963. "Das Felsrelief von Darband-i-Gaur." *Baghdader Mitteilungen* 2: 83–8.

Stronach, David. 1978. *Pasargadae*. Oxford: Oxford University Press.

Studevent-Hickman, Benjamin. 2007. "The Ninety-Degree Rotation of the Cuneiform Script." In: Jack Cheng and Marian Feldman, eds., *Ancient Near Eastern Art in Context: Studies in Honor of Irene J. Winter by Her Students*, pp. 485–513. Leiden: E. J. Brill.

Swartz, Michael D. 2006. "Jewish Magic in Late Antiquity." In: Steven T. Katz, ed., *The Cambridge History of Judaism*, 4: 699–720. Cambridge, UK: Cambridge University Press.

Tadmor, Hayyim. 1982. "The Aramaization of the Assyrian Empire: Aspects of Western Impact." In: Hans-Jörg Nissen and Johannes Renger, eds., *Mesopotamien und seine Nachbarn: Politische and kulturelle Wechselbeziehungen im Alten Vorderasien vom 4. bis 1. Jahrtausend v. Chr: XXV. Rencontre Assyriologique Internationale Berlin 3. bis 7. Juli 1978*, 2: 449–70. *Berliner Beiträge zum Vorderen Orient* 1. Berlin: Dietrich Reimer Verlag.

———. 1999. "World Dominion: The Expanding Horizon of the Assyrian Empire." In: L. Milano, S. de Martino, F. M. Fales, and G. B. Lanfranchi, eds., *Landscapes, Territories, Frontiers and Horizons in the Ancient Near East: Papers Presented to the XLIV Rencontre Assyriologique Internationale Venezia, 7–11 July 1997*, 1: 55–72. Padua: Sargon srl.

Tafazzoli, Ahmad. 2000. *Sassanian Society*. New York: Bibliotheca Persica Press.

Talon, Philippe. 2001. "*Enuma eliš* and the Transmission of Babylonian Cosmology to the West." In: Robert M. Whiting, ed., *Mythology and Mythologies: Methodological Approaches to Intercultural Influences*, pp. 265–77. *Melammu Symposia* 2. Helsinki: Neo-Assyrian Text Corpus Project.

Tao, Wang. 2007. "Parthia in China: A Re-examination of the Historical Records." In: Vesta Sarkhosh Curtis and Sarah Stewart, eds., *The Age of the Parthians: The Idea of Iran*, 2: 87–104. London: I. B. Tauris.

Temple, Robert K. G. 1999. *The Crystal Sun: Rediscovering a Lost Technology of the Ancient World*. London: Arrow.

Thomason, Alison Karmel. 2005. *Luxury and Legitimation: Royal Collecting in Ancient Mesopotamia*. London: Ashgate Publishing.

Tisserant, E. 1931. "Eglise Nestorienne." *Dictionnaire de Théologie Catholique*, 11: 157–323. Paris: Letouzay.

Tomabechi, Y. 1983. "Wall Paintings from Dur-Kurigalzu." *Journal of Near Eastern Studies* 42: 123–31.

Tomber, Roberta. 2007. "Rome and Mesopotamia—Importers into India in the First Millennium A.D." *Antiquity* 81: 972–88.

Treadgold, Warren. 1997. *A History of the Byzantine State and Society*. Stanford: Stanford University Press.

Tubb, Kathryn W., ed. 1995. *Antiquities Trade and Betrayed: Legal, Ethical and Conservation Issues*. London: Archetype Press.

Turcan, Robert. 1993. *Mithra et le Mithraicisme*. Paris: Les Belles Lettres.

Ucko, Peter J. and G. W. Dimbleby, eds. 1969. *The Domestication and Exploitation of Plants and Animals*. London: Duckworth.

Van De Mieroop, Marc. 1987. "The Archive of Balmunamhe." *Archiv für Orientforschung* 34: 1–29.

————. 1992. *Society and Enterprise at Old Babylonian Ur*. Berliner Beiträge zum Vorderen Orient 12. Berlin: Dietrich Reimer Verlag.

————. 1993. "The Reign of Rim-Sin." *Revue d'Assyriologie* 87: 47–69.

————. 1999. "Literature and Political Discourse in Ancient Mesopotamia: Sargon II of Assyria and Sargon of Agade." In: Barbara Böck, Evan Cancik-Kirschbaum, and Thomas Richter, eds., *Munuscula Mesopotamica: Festschrift für Johannes Renger*, pp. 327–39. Alter Orient und Altes Testament 267. Münster: Ugarit-Verlag.

————. 2002. "In Search of Prestige: Foreign Contacts and the Rise of an Elite in Early Dynastic Babylonia." In: E. Ehrenberg, ed., *Leaving No Stones Unturned: Essays on the Ancient Near East and Egypt in Honor of Donald P. Hansen*, pp. 125–37. Winona Lake, Ind.: Eisenbrauns.

————. 2005. *King Hammurabi*. Malden, Mass.: Blackwell.

————. 2007. *The Eastern Mediterranean in the Age of Ramesses II*. Malden, Mass.: Blackwell.

Van der Spek, Robartus J. 1986. *Grondbezit in het Seleucidische Rijk*. Amsterdam: Vrije Universiteit.

————. 1993. "New Evidence on Seleucid Land Policy." In: H. Sancisi-Weerdenburg, R. J. Van der Spek, H. Teitler, and H. Wallinga, eds., *De Agricultura: In Memoriam Pieter Willem de Neeve (1945–1990)*, pp. 61–77. Amsterdam: J. C. Gieben.

————. 2000. "The Effect of War on the Prices of Barley and Agricultural Land in Hellenistic Babylonia." In: J. Andreau, P. Briant, and R. Descati, eds., *Economie antique: La guerre dans les économies antiques*, pp. 293–313. Entretiens d'archéologie et d'histoire de Saint-Bertrand-de-Commingues 5. Saint-Bertrand-de-Commingues: Musée archéologique départementale.

————. 2001. "The Theatre of Babylon in Cuneiform." In: W. H. Van Soldt, J. G. Dercksen, N. J. C. Kouwenberg, and T. J. H. Krispijn, eds., *Veenhof Anniversary Volume: Studies Presented to Klaas R. Veenhof on the Occasion of His Sixty-Fifth Birthday*, pp. 445–56. Leiden: Nederlands Instituut voor het Nabije Oosten.

————. 2005. "Ethnic Segregation in Hellenistic Babylonia." In: W. H. Van Soldt, ed., *Ethnicity in Ancient Mesopotamia: Papers*

Read at the 48th Rencontre Assyriologique Internationale, Leiden, 1–4 July 2002, pp. 393–408. Leiden: Nederlands Instituut voor het Nabije Oosten.

Van Dijk, J.J.A. 1971. "Sumerische Religion." In: J. Asmussen and J. Laessøe, eds., *Handbuch der Religionsgeschichte*, 1: 431–96. Göttingen: Vandenhoeck & Ruprecht.

Van Driel, G. 1987. "Continuity or Decay in the Late Achaemenid Period: Evidence from Southern Mesopotamia." *Achaemenid History* 1: 159–81.

Van Lerberghe, K. 1995. "Kassites and Old Babylonian Society: A Reappraisal." In: K. Van Lerberghe and A. Schoors, eds., *Immigration and Emigration within the Ancient Near East: Festschrift E. Lipiński*, pp. 379–94. *Orientalia Lovaniensia Analecta* 65. Louvain: Peeters.

Vanstiphout, Herman. 1990/2. "The Mesopotamian Debate Poems: A General Presentation." *Acta Sumerologica* 12: 271–318; 14: 339–67.

———. 2003. *Epics of Sumerian Kings: The Matter of Aratta*. SBL Writings from the Ancient World Series 20. Atlanta: Scholars Press.

Vargyas, P. 1997. "Les prix des denrées alimentaires de première nécessité en Babylonie à l'époque achéménide et hellénistique." In: J. Andreau, P. Briant, and R. Descat, eds., *Economie antique: Prix et formation des prix dans les économies antiques*, pp. 335–54. Saint-Bertrand-de-Commingues: Musée archéologique départementale.

Veenhof, Klaas, ed. 1986. *Cuneiform Archives and Libraries: Papers read at the 30ᵉ Rencontre Assyriologique Internationale, Leiden, 4–8 July 1983*. Leiden: Nederlands Historisch-Archaeologisch Instituut te Istanbul.

Veldhuis, Niek. 2004. *Religion, Literature, and Scholarship: The Sumerian Composition "Nanše and the Birds"*. Cuneiform Monographs 22. Leiden: E. J. Brill.

Verbrugghe, Gerald P. and John M. Wickersham. 2001. *Berossus and Manetho, Introduced and Translated: Native Traditions in Ancient Mesopotamia and Egypt*. Ann Arbor: University of Michigan Press.

Verstandig, André. 2001. *Histoire de l'Empire Parthe (−250–227)*. Brussels: Le Cri.

Villard, Pierre. 1997. "L'Education d'Assurbanipal." *Ktema* 22: 135–49.

Visicato, Giuseppe and Aage Westenholz. 2005. "An Early Dynastic Archive from Ur Involving the Lugal." *Kaskal* 2: 55–78.

Vogel, Carol. 2007. "Tiny Lioness Commands Many Millions." *The New York Times*, 6 December: E2.

Vööbus, Arthur. 1987. *Studies in the History of the Gospel Text in Syriac: New Contributions to the Sources Elucidating the History of the Traditions. Corpus Scriptorum Christianorum Orientalium subsidia* 79. Louvain: Peeters.

Waldbaum, Jane C. 2005. "Tell it to the Marines. . . ". *Archaeology*, November/December: 6.

Walker, Christopher B. F., ed. 1996. *Astronomy Before the Telescope*. London: British Museum Press.

Wallach, Janet. 1996. *Desert Queen*. New York: Doubleday.

Wapnish, Paula. 1995. "Towards Establishing a Conceptual Basis for Animal Categories in Archaeology." In: David B. Small, ed., *Methods in the Mediterranean: Historical and Archaeological Views on Texts and Archaeology*. Leiden: E. J. Brill.

Waschow, Heinz. 1936. *Babylonische Briefen aus der Kassitenzeit. Mitteilungen der Deutschen Orient-Gesellschaft* 10/I. Leipzig: Hinrichs.

Weidner, Ernst. 1939. "Jojachin, König von Juda, in babylonischen Keilschrifttexten." In: *Mélanges Syriens offerts à Monsieur René Dussaud*, 2: 923–35. Paris: Geuthner.

———. 1952/3. "Die Bibliothek Tiglatpilesers I." *Archiv für Orientforschung* 16: 197–213.

Weiss, Harvey. 1986. "The Origins of Cities in Dry-Farming Syria and Mesopotamia in the Third Millennium B.C." In: H. Weiss, ed., *The Origins of Cities in Dry-Farming Syria and Mesopotamia in the Third Millennium B.C.*, pp. 1–6. Guilford, Conn.: Four Quarters.

———. 1997. "Late Third Millennium Abrupt Climate Change and Social Collapse in West Asia and Egypt." In: H. N. Dalfes, George Kukla, and Harvey Weiss, eds., *Third Millennium BC Climate Change and Old World Collapse*, pp. 711–23. Berlin: Springer Verlag.

Weiss, Harvey and Marie-Agnès Courty. 1993. "The Genesis and Collapse of the Akkadian Empire: The Accidental Refraction of Historical Law." In: Mario Liverani, ed., *Akkad, The First Universal Empire: Structure, Ideology, Traditions*, pp. 131–55. Padua: Sargon.

Wensinck, A. J. 1927. "al-ʿIrāḳ." *Encyclopedia of Islam*, 4: 513–9.

Westbrook, Raymond, ed. 2003. *A History of Ancient Near Eastern Law. Handbuch der Orientalistik, Erste Abt., Nahe und Mittlere Osten*, 72 Bd. Leiden: E. J. Brill.

Westenholz, Aage. 1979. "The Old Akkadian Empire in Contemporary Opinion." In: Mogens T. Larsen, ed., *Power and Propaganda: A Symposium on Ancient Empires*, pp. 107–23. *Mesopotamia* 7. Copenhagen: Akademisk Forlag.

————. 1987. *Old Sumerian and Old Akkadian Texts in Philadelphia, Part Two: The "Akkadian" Texts, the Enlilemaba Texts, and the Onion Archive*. Copenhagen: Museum Tusculanum Press.

————. 1999. "The Old Akkadian Period: History and Culture." In: Pascal Attinger and Markus Wäfler, eds., *Mesopotamien: Akkade-Zeit und Ur III-Zeit*, pp. 17–117. *Orbis Biblicus et Orientalis* 160/3. Göttingen: Vandenhoeck & Ruprecht.

Westenholz, Joan Goodnick. 1983. "Heroes of Akkad." In: Jack M. Sasson, ed., *Studies in Literature from the Ancient Near East by Members of the American Oriental Society. American Oriental Series* 65 = *Journal of the American Oriental Society* 103: 327–36.

————. 1992. "Enheduanna, En-Priestess, Hen of Nanna, Spouse of Nanna." In: Hermann Behrens, Darlene Loding, and Martha T. Roth, eds., *DUMU-E$_2$-DUB-BA-A: Studies in Honor of Åke W. Sjöberg*, pp. 539–56. *Occasional Publications of the Samuel Noah Kramer Fund* 11. Philadelphia: University Museum of Archaeology and Anthropology.

————. 1997. *Legends of the Kings of Akkade. Mesopotamian Civilizations* 7. Winona Lake, Ind.: Eisenbrauns.

Whitehouse, David. 1996. "Sasanian Maritime Activity." In: Julian Reade, ed., *The Indian Ocean in Antiquity*, pp. 339–49. London: Kegan Paul.

Widengren, George. 1956. "Recherches sur le féodalisme iranien." *Orientalia Suecana* 5: 79–182.

————. 1983. "Manichaeism and Its Iranian Background." In: Ehsan Yarshater, ed., *The Cambridge History of Iran*, 3(2): 965–90. Cambridge, UK: Cambridge University Press.

Wiesehöfer, Josef. 2001. *Ancient Persia from 550 BC to 650 AD*. Translated by Azizeh Azodi. London: I. B. Tauris.

————. 2007. "From Achaemenid Imperial Order to Sasanian Diplomacy: War, Peace, and Reconciliation in Pre-Islamic Iran." In: Kurt Raaflaub, ed., *War and Peace in the Ancient World*, pp. 121–40. Malden, Mass.: Blackwell.

Wiessner, Gernot. 1967. *Zur Martyrerüberlieferung aus der Christenverfolgung Schapurs II*. Göttingen: Vandenhoeck & Ruprecht.

Wigram, Arthur. 1910. *An Introduction to the History of the Assyrian Church, or the Church of the Sassanid Persian Empire 100–640 A.D.* London: Society for Promoting Christian Knowledge.

————. 1929. *The Assyrians and Their Neighbours*. London: G. Bell & Sons.

Wilcke, Claus. 1970. "Drei Phasen des Niedergangs des Reiches von Ur III." *Zeitschrift für Assyriologie* 60: 54–69.

———. 1972. "Der aktuelle Bezug der Sammlung der sumerischen Tempelhymnen und ein Fragment eines Klageliedes." *Zeitschrift für Assyriologie* 62: 35–62.

Wilcken, Ulrich. 1967. *Alexander the Great.* Translated by G. C. Richards. New York: W. W. Norton & Company.

Wilhelm, Gernot. 1989. *The Hurrians.* Translated by Jennifer Barnes. Warminster, UK: Aris & Phillips.

Winter, Irene J. 1985. "After the Battle Is Over: The Stele of the Vultures and the Beginning of Historical Narrative in the Art of the Ancient Near East." In: H. L. Kessler and M. S. Simpson, eds., *Pictorial Narrative in Antiquity and the Middle Ages,* pp. 11–32. Washington, D.C.: National Gallery of Art.

———. 1987. "Women in Public: The Disk of Enheduanna, the Beginning of the Office of *EN*-Priestess and the Weight of Visual Evidence." In: Jean-Marie Durand, ed., *La Femme dans le Proche-Orient antique: Compte Rendu de la XXXIIIᵉ Rencontre Assyriologique Internationale (Paris, 7–10 juillet 1986),* pp. 189–201. Paris: Editions Recherche sur les Civilisations.

———. 1989. "The Body of the Able Ruler: Towards an Understanding of the Statues of Gudea." In: Hermann Behrens, Darlene Loding, and Martha T. Roth, eds., *DUMU-E₂-DUB-BA-A, Studies in Honor of Åke W. Sjöberg,* pp. 573–83. *Occasional Publications of the Samuel Noah Kramer Fund* 11. Philadelphia: University Museum of Archaeology and Anthropology.

———. 1999. "Tree(s) on the Mountain: Landscape and Territory on the Victory Stele of Naram-Sin." In: L. Milano, S. de Martino, F. M. Fales, and G. B. Lanfranchi, eds., *Landscapes, Territories, Frontiers and Horizons in the Ancient Near East: Papers presented to the XLIV Rencontre Assyriologique Internationale, Venezia, 7–11 July 1997,* 1: 63–72. Padua: Sargon srl.

Wiseman, Donald J. 1985. *Nebuchadrezzar and Babylon: The Schweich Lectures 1983.* Oxford: Oxford University Press.

Wissemann, M. 1982. *Die Parther in der augusteischer Dichtung.* Frankfurt: P. Lang.

Wolski, J. 1956/8. "The Decay of the Iranian Empire of the Seleucids and the Chronology of the Parthian Beginnings." *Berytus* 12: 35–52.

Woods, Christopher E. 2004. "The Sun-God Tablet of Nabû-apla-iddina Revisited." *Journal of Cuneiform Studies* 56: 23–103.

Woolley, C. Leonard. 1934. *Ur Excavations: The Royal Cemetery*. Oxford: Oxford University Press.

Wright, G. A. 1969. *Obsidian Analysis and Prehistoric Near Eastern Trade: 7500 to 3500 B.C.* Anthropological Papers, Museum of Anthropology, University of Michigan, No. 37. Ann Arbor: The University of Michigan.

Wright, Henry T. 1969. *The Administration of Rural Production in an Early Mesopotamian Town*. Anthropological Papers, Museum of Anthropology, University of Michigan, No. 38. Ann Arbor: The University of Michigan.

————. 2001. "Cultural Action in the Uruk World." In: M. S. Rothman, ed., *Uruk Mesopotamia and Its Neighbors: Cross-cultural Interactions and Their Consequences in the Era of State Formation*, pp. 123–48. Santa Fe: School of American Research.

Wunsch, Cornelia. 1993. *Die Urkunden des babylonischen Geschäftsmannes Iddin-Marduk: Zum Handel mit Naturalien im 6. Jahrhundert v. Chr.* Groningen: Styx.

————. 1999. "Neubabylonische Urkunden: Die Geschäftsurkunden der Familie Egibi." In: Johannes Renger, ed., *Babylon: Focus mesopotamischer Geschichte, Wiege früher Gelehrsamkeit, Mythos in der Moderne*, pp. 343–64. *2. Internationales Colloquium der Deutschen Orient-Gesellschaft 24.–26. März in Berlin.* Saarbrücken: Saarbrückener Druckerei und Verlag.

————. 2000. "Neubabylonische Geschäftsleute und ihre Beziehungen zu Palast- und Tempelverwaltungen: Das Beispiel der Familie Egibi." In: A. C. V. M. Bongenaar, ed., *Interdependency of Institutions and Private Entrepreneurs*, pp. 95–118. *MOS Studies 2: Proceedings of the Second MOS Symposium (Leiden, 1998)*. Leiden: Nederlands Instituut voor het Nabije Oosten.

Yadin, Yigael. 1963. *The Art of Warfare in Biblical Lands in the Light of Archaeological Study*. Translated by M. Pearlman. New York: McGraw-Hill.

Yarshater, Ehsan. 1971. "Were the Sassanians Heirs to the Achemenids?" In: *Atti del convegno internazionale sul tema la Persia nel Medioevo, (Roma, 31 marzo–5 aprile 1970)*, pp. 517–31. Rome: Accademia Nazionale dei Lincei.

————. 1983. "Iranian National History." In: Ehsan Yarshater, ed., *The Cambridge History of Iran*, 3(1): 319–477. Cambridge, UK: Cambridge University Press.

Yoffee, Norman. 1988. "The Collapse of Ancient Mesopotamian States and Civilizations." In: Norman Yoffee and G. L. Cowgill, eds.,

The Collapse of Ancient States and Civilizations, pp. 44–68. Tucson: University of Arizona Press.

Young, T. Cuyler, P. E. L. Smith, and P. Mortensen, eds. 1983. *The Hilly Flanks and Beyond: Essays on the Prehistory of Southwestern Asia Presented to Robert J. Braidwood, November 15, 1982. Studies in Ancient Oriental Civilization* 36. Chicago: Oriental Institute of the University of Chicago.

Zaccagnini, Carlo. 1973. *Lo scambio dei doni nel Vicino Oriente durante i secoli xv–xiii. Orientis Antiqui Collectio* 11. Rome: Centro per le Antichità e la Storia dell'Arte del Vicino Oriente.

Zarins, Juris. 1990. "Early Pastoral Nomadism and the Settlement of Lower Mesopotamia." *Bulletin of the American Schools of Oriental Research* 280: 31–65.

Zervos, Christian. 1935. *L'Art de la Mésopotamie*. Paris: Cahiers d'Art.

Zettler, Richard L. 1989. "12th Century B.C. Babylonia: Continuity and Change." In: William A. Ward and Martha Sharpe Joukowsky, eds., *The Crisis Years: The Twelfth Century B.C., from beyond the Danube to the Tigris*, pp. 174–81. Dubuque, Iowa: Kendall/Hunt.

Zettler, Richard L. and Lee Horne, eds. 1998. *Treasures from the Royal Tombs of Ur*. Philadelphia: University Museum of Archaeology and Anthropology.

Zimansky, Paul. 1985. *Ecology and Empire: The Structure of the Urartian State. Studies in Ancient Oriental Civilization* 41. Chicago: Oriental Institute of the University of Chicago.

INDEX

accounting, 28, 32, 33; reform of, 56
Adab, 41
Adad, 95, 171
Adad-nadin-ahe, 155
Adi ibn Zaid, 181–2
Aegyptiaca, 152
Afghanistan, 160, 161, 163, 170,
210; as source of lapis lazuli, 38;
as source of tin, 106
Agade, 53, 55, 58–61; ancient excavations of, 135; in Neo-Babylonian
period, 135; in Old Babylonian
period, 74; omen about, 96
agriculture: accounting for, 67; field
shape in, 27; at Jemdet Nasr, 35;
Kassite, 92; labor for, 81; in law,
92; management of, 52–3, 68–9,
72, 77; and military colonies, 109;
origins of, 8, 12; productivity of,
13, 69; regional differences in, 13,
36, 105–6; seasonal tasks of, 9;
and seeder plow, 43, 66. *See also*
land
Ahiqar, 137
Ahriman, 170
Ahura-Mazda, 170
Akhenaten, 93, 109
Akkad, region of, 5; in Sumerian
King List, 62. *See also* Agade
Akkadian dynasty, 51–61, 106, 134;
memory of, 74. *See also* art, Akkadian; Naram-Sin, of Akkad; Sargon, of Akkad
Akkadian language, 52, 72, 124; in
accounting, 56; and Aramaic, 137;
in inscriptions, 58; as international
language, 93; in name-giving, 65;
as Semitic language, 40

Akkadian literature, 124, 131, 137;
in Assyria, 109–11; in Kassite pe-
riod, 88; in Late period, 138–40;
quoted, 1, 19, 20, 28–9, 48, 51,
61, 98, 132, 134, 139, 140. See
also *Atrahasis*; *Creation Epic*; *Epic
of Gilgamesh*; *Erra Epic*; *Poem of
the Righteous Sufferer*
Alashiya, 93
Aleppo, 76, 95
Alexander IV, 148
Alexander the Great, 147, 149, 153,
157, 159, 165
Alexandria, 188
Allah/Allat, 171
Amarna, 93, 109
Amarna letters, 93–4, 99, 114
Amenhotep III, 93
American Council for Cultural
Policy, 207
American Schools of Oriental
Research, 203
Amil-Marduk, 132
Amorites, 71–3, 87; in Akkadian pe-
riod, 60; arrival of, 69, 71–3;
compared to Arameans, 103, 112
Amu Darya River, 157
An, 17, 18
Anatolia: Assyrian colonies in, 106–
8; Hellenistic, 149; Hurrians in,
99; as river source, 1; as source of
obsidian, 9; as source of silver, 53;
Uruk colonies in, 30
Andrae, Walter, 200
animals, fantastic, 116, 131, 145,
151–2, 182–3. *See also* dragons
Annunitum, 95
Antigonus, 148, 153

Antioch, 152, 170, 184, 187, 188;
    Christian church of, 176, 178
Antiochus I Soter, 149, 151, 156,
    197
Antiochus III the Great, 164–5
Antiochus IV Epiphanes, 158–9
antiquarianism, 135, 185
antiquities, and war, 63, 78, 89, 101.
    See also antiquities law; antiquities
    trade; Iraq Museum
antiquities law, 20; in Iraq, 202, 204;
    in Ottoman Empire, 196
antiquities trade, 150, 162, 196,
    197, 204–6
Apamea, 152
Apollo, 156
aqueducts, 121
Arabia, 133, 142, 179–80
Arabic language, 40, 113, 180, 190;
    and meaning of Iraq, 5
Arabic literature: geographical, 5,
    192; poetry in, 181; quoted, 169,
    182
Arabic script, origins of, 182
Arabs: and Assyria, 130; Christian,
    176, 181; conquests of, 5, 6, 183,
    190; in Jordan Valley, 181; and
    Sassanians, 171, 186, 188, 189; as
    Semites, 194
Aramaic language: and Akkadian,
    137; and Arabs, 182; and astron-
    omy, 156; inscribed on bricks,
    155; as language of Christianity,
    115, 176; as language of Judaism,
    115, 175; as language of Persian
    Empire, 131, 143
Aramaic literature, 137, 142, 174
Aramaic script: used for Arabic, 182;
    used for Parthian, 159
Arameans, 116; in Babylonia, 114,
    130; compared to Amorites, 103,
    112; kingdoms of, 113; and pro-
    hibition of pork, 116
Aratta, 65
Arbela, 105, 176
archaeology: ancient, 135, 155; and
    archival reconstruction, 41–2,
    107; and context, 41, 198–9;

method and theory of, 5, 7, 16,
    20, 37, 117, 128, 195, 198–201;
    pottery in, 11; surveys in, 21, 29,
    209
Archimedes screw, 121
architecture: in art, 37; Assyrian re-
    vival, 203; columns in, 88, 131,
    135, 184; domestic, 10, 16;
    Islamic, 163; iwan in, 162, 169;
    Kassite, 88; Parthian, 90, 159,
    161–2; Roman, 170; Seleucid,
    152; temple, 14, 17, 21; vault in,
    162–3. See also bricks
archives. See tablets, cuneiform
Ardashir, 52, 167, 169, 184
Aristotle, 172
Armenia: Christianization of, 177;
    contested by Parthian and Roman
    Empires, 180, 184, 186, 188,
    189; terrain of, 119. See also
    Urartu
Arpachiya, 11
Arrapha, 99
Arsaces, 149, 156–7
art: Akkadian, 27, 56–8, 67, 79,
    126; Aramean, 116; Assyrian,
    110, 127, 157, 191, 203, 210;
    Babylonian, 130–1, 135; Byzan-
    tine, 163; Christian, 163, 170; on
    cylinder seals, 25–7; frontality in,
    163, 184; geometric patterns in,
    10, 20, 25; Kassite, 88–90; land-
    scape in, 56, 123; naturalistic, 25;
    Parthian, 162–3; perspective in,
    123; representational, 21–2;
    Roman, 163; Sassanian, 182–4;
    self-reference in, 22, 110; Seleu-
    cid, 155–6; stylization in, 10; of
    Third Dynasty of Ur, 67; at Uruk,
    17, 21–2. See also ivories; mosaics;
    plaques; pottery; seals; statues; ste-
    lae; stucco work; wall painting
Arwad, 111
Arzawa, 93
Aspanabr, 179
Asqudum, 75, 95
assassination: of Julius Caesar,
    166; of Labashi-Marduk, 132;

of Manishtusu, 55; of Rimush, 54; of Seleucus I Nikator, 149; of Sennacherib, 123, 129; of Tukulti-Ninurta I, 111
Assur, city: Amorite, 74–5; antiquities from, 89; as Christian city, 176; and decipherment of cuneiform, 193; excavations of, 200; libraries at, 125; Persian and Parthian, 143, 159, 160; region of, 105–6; tablets from, 198. See also Assyria/Assyrians
Assur, god, 105–6, 110, 113
Assurbanipal, 113; accession and civil war of, 129–30; education of, 92; library of, 123–6, 193, 194; and Susa, 114
Assur-nadin-shumi, 123
Assurnasirpal II, 115–9
Assur-uballit I, 109
Assyria/Assyrians: in Amarna period, 93–4; and Arabia, 180; and Babylonia, 103, 104, 109, 113; Christian church of, 176–7; destruction of, 115; in Greek thought, 175; and Hurrians, 169; imperial limits of, 113; Persian, 143; region of, 5; Sassanian, 159. See also art, Assyrian; Assur, city; Assurbanipal; Assurnasirpal II; government, provincial; Sennacherib
Assyrian King List, 108
Assyriology, 197–8, 206
astrology, 138, 155, 186
astronomy, 148, 156, 167; and astrology, 155; and astronomical diaries, 138, 166–7
Athens, academy of, 172
Atrahasis, 48–50, 125
Augustus, 166
Avesta, 171

Babylon, city: and Alexander the Great, 148; Assyrian attacks on, 110–1, 113, 130; centrality of, 103, 115, 139, 141; coinage of, 153; destruction of, 123; Elamite attack on, 102; under Hammurabi, 77; Hittite attack on, 86; imagery of, 192; Ishtar Gate of, 89, 90, 131, 183; kingship of, 114, 149; under Nebuchadnezzar II, 130; Parthian, 159, 160; Persian, 142, 144, 145; Processional Way of, 90, 130, 131; Sassanian, 179; and Seleucia, 152; in Shah-namah, 169; Stoic academy at, 155; streets of, 98
Babylon, site, 200, 204; and antiquities in World War II, 89; military base at, 210; mined for bricks, 197
Babylonia: and Assyria, 103, 104, 109, 110–1, 113–4, 115, 120; Chinese visit to, 161; Christian church in, 176; connections to Syria-Palestine from, 133, 174; decline of, under Samsuiluna, 86; merchants from, 108; under Persians, 143–4; region of, 5; as regional state, 87; and Romans, 166
Babyloniaca, 151
Babylonian language, 145, 146. See also Akkadian language
Babylonian Talmud, 168, 175
The Babylonian Tree, 164
Bactria, 149, 158, 160, 184
Baghdad: in Iraq War, 207–8; translation movement at, 186
Bahram I, 172
Bahrein, 161. See also Dilmun
Balikh River, 4, 109
Baqir, Taha, 204
Bardaeus, Jacob, 177
barley, 13, 67. See also agriculture
basilicas, Roman, 170
Basra, 160
beer, 10, 116; and drinking straw, 37. See also food
Behistun, relief at, 146, 193. See also decipherment
Bel, temple of, 168. See also Marduk
Bell, Gertrude, 201–3
Bellino, Carl, 193

Belshazzer, 133
Berlin Museum, 20, 22, 89, 198
Berossus, 151, 154
bevel-rimmed bowls, 16, 28, 29
Bible: and ancient Near East, 132–3,
    174, 191–5; Greek, 152; Syriac,
    176
birds, 27, 39, 43, 49, 50, 116, 121,
    161, 175
boatmen, 45, 85
boats, 49, 67, 73, 134; in figurative
    language, 140; Noah's Ark, 192
Bogdanos, Matthew, 209
Borsippa, 144, 168, 179, 197
brewing, 13, 67
bricks: construction with, 10, 15, 62,
    85, 110, 130, 145, 152, 155, 159;
    as curiosity, 191; glazed, 110, 114,
    116, 131, 145; Kassite, 88;
    molded, 89–90, 145; of Uruk pe-
    riod, 27, 29. See also architecture
British Museum, 44, 117, 196–8,
    200
British School of Archaeology in
    Iraq, 210
bronze: in architecture, 114, 121,
    131; produced, 45, 106; for stat-
    ues, 114; for weapons, 7
Budge, E. Wallis, 197
bullae, Seleucid, 153
bull-men, 135–6
Burnaburiash II, 93–4
Byzantium, 188. See also
    Constantinople

Calah. See Nimrud
calendar, 138
caravanserais, 179
Carchemish, 109
Carthage, 164, 188
Cassius, 166
Çatal Hüyük, 10–1
Central Asia, 142, 149, 156, 163
ceramics. See pottery
Chaldea, 104, 114, 120, 130, 147;
    region of, 5
Chaldaean Catholics, 177

Charax, 160
chariots, 124, 126; as royal gift, 109.
    See also warfare
China, 156, 161
Chosroes I, 181, 182, 184, 187–8
Christianity, 115, 171–3, 176, 177–
    8, 189, 195; and church councils,
    176; on origins of writing, 31;
    persecution of, 186; and relics,
    188–9. See also Armenia; Con-
    stantinople; Jesus
Christie's, 206, 210
chronicles, 134, 168
Churchill, Winston, 201
Cilicia, 113
cities: earliest, 15; foundation of,
    110, 119; growth of, 40; league of,
    36
Clay, Albert T., 203
climate change, 4–5, 40
clothing, 45, 84, 156; Assyrian, 117;
    Parthian, 163; in Royal Graves,
    37. See also headgear; textiles
coinage, 150, 153, 156, 162
colonies: Akkadian, 58; Assyrian,
    106–8; Phoenician, 113; of Uruk,
    29–30
commentaries, 97
Constantine I, 170, 188
Constantinople, 170, 181, 188, 189,
    196; and Christianity, 176–8
Constantius, 186
copper: in Royal Graves, 37; for stat-
    ues, 22; trade in, 45
Crassus, 165–6
Creation Epic, 126, 173
crime, 79. See also law
Croesus, 153
crowns. See headgear
Ctesiphon, 159, 166, 169, 179–81,
    183–4, 186–7, 189–90; Christi-
    anity at, 176
cuneiform script, 30, 131, 137, 146;
    decipherment of, 193–4; end of,
    166; name of, 192; orientation
    of, 90
Cyaxares, 130
cylinder seals. See seals, cylinder

Cyprus, 93
Cyrus the Great, 142, 153, 159, 173; legend of, 52

Dagan, 171
Damascius, 173
Damascus, 113, 181
Darius I, 143, 144, 145–6, 193
Darius III, 147–8, 159
date palm, 13, 79, 118, 140, 141
debt, 80, 81, 92, 112, 144
decipherment, 97, 131, 146, 193; in antiquity, 134
Demetrius II Nikator, 160
deportation, 54, 114–5, 130, 173
de Sarzec, Ernest, 44, 197
Deutsche Orient-Gesellschaft, 20, 200
Dilmun, 43, 45, 73–4, 77, 123
diorite, 45, 55, 61
diplomacy, 68, 73, 93–4
divination, 94–6, 125, 154; in Akkadian period, 95; and Naram-Sin, 60; and prices, 138; in Roman Empire, 155; and Sargon II, 120; texts of, 125
Diyala River, 4, 77, 204
domestication, 8–9, 12, 91
dragons: in art, 131, 160, 183; in figurative language, 118
dreams, 125, 133. See also divination
Dura Europas, 174, 184
Dur-Kurigalzu, 88, 100, 103
Dur-Sharrukin, 117, 119–20; excavation of, 203; looting at, 122

Eanna, 15, 17, 20, 21, 89, 143. See also Inanna/Ishtar
Eannatum, 43
Ebla, 41
Ecbatana, 152, 159
eclipses, 138. See also astronomy
economy: of Akkad, 52–3; free, 47; Hellenistic, 153–4; at Nuzi, 99–100; and prices, 154; redistributive, 28; regulation of, 80;

Sassanian, 179–80; staple-based, 27–8; tribute-based, 52. See also coinage
Edessa, 177, 186
edicts. See law
education, 35, 66, 79, 123–4, 124–5, 134, 137
Egypt, 129, 149, 152, 159, 175, 191, 195, 196; in Amarna period, 93, 94, 99; and Assyria, 129–30; Christianity in, 177; Ptolemaic, 158; Sassanian invasion of, 188; Uruk culture in, 30
Ekallatum, 74, 95, 103
Ekur, 47, 48, 58, 60, 66
Elam: and Antiochus IV Epiphanes, 159; and Assyria, 113–4, 123; and Babylonia, 57–8, 94, 100–103, 130; destruction of, 114; and Gudea, 62; and Nebuchadnezzar I, 102–3; trade at, 43; and Ur, 70; ziggurat of, 64, 114. See also Susa
Elamite language, 146, 193
elephants, 156, 165, 182, 186, 187; in art, 183
Elgin marbles, 195
Enheduanna, 53–4, 98; quoted, 19
Enki, 18, 48–9
Enkidu, 84, 120. See also Epic of Gilgamesh
Enlil: in Assyria, 110; and Flood, 48–50; hymn to, 66. See also Ekur
Enmerkar, 15, 65
Enmetena, 45–7, 202
Epic of Gilgamesh, 49, 83–5, 120, 125, 138, 154, 161, 194, 198, 199; quoted, 17, 84, 85; and Sargon II, 119–20
epics, 111, 125. See also Creation Epic; Epic of Gilgamesh; Erra Epic; Shah-namah
Eridu, 63
Erlenmeyer Collection, 206
Erra, 139–40
Erra Epic, 126, 139–40, 151
Esarhaddon, 105, 113, 124, 129, 137
Eshnunna, 74, 77, 80
Esther, 174

Etana, 39
eunuchs, 112
Euphrates River: and Amorites, 60, 71; and Arabs, 181; and Assyrian expansion, 109; battle near, 190; changing course of, 5–6, 86; creation of, 2; damming of, 161; flooding of, 4, 12; as route, 1, 5–6, 52–3; source of, 1; statue found near, 135; and Uruk culture, 29; and valley, desolation of, 180; and wall of Shu-Sin, 69
exilarch, 174
exotica, 5, 37, 55, 56, 118, 121, 161; trade in, 154, 181
extispicy, 96. See also divination
Ezida, 151

faience, 45, 100
Faisal I, 201, 202
families, 13, 20, 77, 140, 154, 157, 158, 172; and education, 137; Kassite, 87–8, 91; letters to, 108; at Nuzi, 100
famine, 70
feasting, 27, 39, 59, 60, 66, 98, 116, 133
fermentation. See beer
fertility, 14, 18; iconography of, 89. See also agriculture
Firdawsi, 168
fish, 13, 43, 75, 151–2
fishermen, 13, 35
fish-men, 152
flint, 28
Flood, 40, 84–5, 124, 194, 195
food, 18, 67, 70; cooking and storage of, 9, 10; recipes for, 81–2. See also feasting; rations
frankincense, 181
furniture, 37, 59, 66, 127–8, 141. See also gold; ivories

Garden of Eden, 192
gardens, 17, 68, 72, 121–3, 141, 145, 169, 173, 183, 192

Gaugamela, 147
German Oriental Society, 20, 200
Ghassanids, 181
Gilgamesh, 37, 65, 161. See also Epic of Gilgamesh
Girsu, 155
glass, 45; production of, 100–101; texts about, 153
glazing, 45. See also bricks
glyptic. See seals, cylinder
Gnosticism, 171–2
gods, in art, 17, 43, 56, 75, 110, 135. See also iconography; religion; seals, cylinder
gold: as basis for wealth, 42; for coins, 150, 153; from Egypt, 109; exchange of, 93; in furniture and jewelry, 36, 37, 38, 119, 127; for statues, 22, 114
Gordion III, 184
Goths, 187
government: city-state, 55; provincial, 55, 61, 90–1, 106, 115, 129, 143; Sassanian theory of, 178. See also kingship
grave goods, 98, 118
Greece, 164
Greek language, 155, 156, 175–6
Gregory the Illuminator, 177
Gudea, 61–2, 155. See also Lagash
Gula, 71
Gulf, 161, 180; geology of, 4–5; as limit, 5, 113, 130; sea battle in, 56; and trade, 43; as waterway, 30, 160
Gulf War, 101, 185, 204–5
Gutians, 60, 62

Hadad, 41, 171
Halaf ware, 10, 11, 14, 20
Hamath, 113
Hammurabi, 71, 73, 75, 76–7; death of, 85; period of, 27, 87, 93, 134, 137, 185. See also law
Hanging Gardens, 121–3, 192. See also gardens
Hannibal, 164

harps, 37–8, 83, 164. *See also* minstrels; music
Hassuna ware, 10
Hatra, 161–2, 163, 166, 184
Hatti. *See* Hittites
headgear, 56; as crown, 184; as royal cap, 22, 79, 119
Hebrew language, 40
Heraclius, 188–90
Herakles, 171
Herodotus, 131, 141, 143, 195
hieroglyphs, Egyptian, 192–3
Hira, 181–2, 188
Hittites, 86; end of empire of, 112; as great power, 93
Holy Land, 183, 191
Horace, 166
horoscopes, 138. *See also* astrology
horses, 103, 131, 157, 187, 190; as royal gift, 109; training of, 91–2
human sacrifice, 36–7
hunting, 8, 12; as royal activity, 92, 117, 118, 121, 183
Hurrians, 69, 99–100
husbandry, 9, 13, 43. *See also* agriculture; domestication
al-Husri, Sati', 203
Hussein, Saddam, 204
Hyde, Thomas, 192

Ibbi-Sin, 70
ice, storage of, 75
iconography, 18, 22, 26, 89, 118; of Assur, 105; at Kanesh, 106; at Uruk, 22
Inanna/Ishtar, 17, 18–9, 20, 135; and Agade, 53; in art, 75, 89; cult symbol of, 22, 26; and Enheduanna, 54; and Etana, 39; and Gilgamesh, 84; and Sargon, 51–2; and Ur-Nammu, 64
India, 156, 160, 176
Indo-European, 8, 194–5
Indus Valley, 148, 184
industry, and mass production, 28. *See also* glass; metallurgy; pottery
interest, 81. *See also* debt

Iran: and Akkadian kings, 53, 54, 56–7; and Antiochus I Soter, 150; Christian church in, 176; fortresses in, 126; geography of, 157; Hurrians in, 69; and Iraq, 4; *iwan* in, 163; as source of diorite, 45; as source of tin, 106; Uruk culture in, 16, 30. *See also* Elam; Susa
Iraq: geology of, 4; modern history of, 201–4; name of, 5; rivers of, 1–4
Iraq, Department of Antiquities, 202–5
Iraq Museum, 26, 38, 202–3, 205, 207–9; looting of, 11, 46, 101, 127, 207–9
Iraq War, 20, 162, 206–8, 210
iron, 141
irrigation, 12, 13, 27, 40; Hellenistic, 179; Kassite, 90–1; Sassanian, 179; of Third Dynasty of Ur, 67. *See also* agriculture
Ishbi-Erra, 72
Ishme-Dagan, 75
Ishtar. *See* Inanna/Ishtar
Isidore of Charax, 161
Isin, 71–2, 73
Islam, 190, 195
Israel, 113
ivories, 38, 117, 126–8
iwan, 162, 169

Jacobites, 177
Jemdet Nasr, 35–6, 55
Jeremiah, 173
Jerusalem, 113, 120, 130, 159, 170, 173, 174, 189
Jesus, 171; nature of, 176–7, 189
jewelry, 100, 141; Assyrian, 119; Parthian, 163
Jezira, 4, 180
Job, Book of, 99
John the Baptist, 171
Jordan River, 181; Arabs in valley of, 181–2
Joshua the Stylite, 180
Judah, 113, 130

Judaism, 115, 130, 168, 171, 173–5, 195; on origins of writing, 31; persecution of, 174–5
Julian, 187
Julius Caesar, 166
Justinian, 172, 179, 187, 188

Kabti-ilani-Marduk, 139
Kadashman-Enlil I, 93
Kalhu. *See* Nimrud
Kanesh, 106–8
Karaindash, 88
Kar-Tukulti-Ninurta, 110
Karun River, 103
Kashtiliash, 110–1
Kassites, 86, 87–92, 135; and Akkadian literature, 88; and Assyria, 94, 111; and Egypt, 93–4; language of, 87; religion of, 88
Kengir, 5
Kesh, 36
Khabur River, 4; Assyrian garrisons on, 109; colonization of, 58
Khorsabad. *See* Dur-Sharrukin
Khosr River, 121, 122
King of Agade, 59, 74
King of Kish, 59
King of Sumer and Akkad, 48, 73
King of the Four Quarters of the World, 62
kingship: and administration of temples, 48; agricultural policies of, 68; Amorite, 72–3; beginnings of, 39; dynastic principle of, 39; and gods, 43; Hellenistic, 149–50; at Lagash, 47; Parthian, 157; portrayal of, 118; Sassanian, 184; in Sumerian literature, 66, 70. *See also* rod and ring
Kish, 39–42, 86; and Akkadian kings, 52, 53, 59; Sassanian, 185; in Sumerian King List, 62
Koldewey, Robert, 200
Kudur-nahhunte, 102
kudurrus, 90, 137, 185
Kullab, 15, 31
Kuyunjik. *See* Nineveh

labor, 28, 67, 86, 90–1, 92
Lachish, 120, 194
Lagash: as Akkadian province, 55, 61; excavations at, 197; and Gudea, 61–2, 155; statue of Enmetena from, 45–7, 202; and Sumerian literature, 61–2; and trade with Dilmun, 44–5; and war with Umma, 42–4, 48
Lake Van, 111. *See also* Armenia; Urartu
Lakhmids, 181, 189
land: fiefs of, 144; grants of, 90, 91; management of, 140–1, 144, 153, 158, 160, 179; sale of, 42, 47, 68, 72, 73, 81, 100; and temples, 91, 140–1, 143; tenure and ownership of, 35, 88, 112, 178. *See also* agriculture
landscapes, 56, 123. *See also* art
lapis lazuli: and faience, 45; in figurative language, 53, 66; in Royal Graves, 36–8; source of, 38; in statuary, 22, 47
Larsa, 72, 77, 86. *See also* Rim-Sin
Latin language, 176
law: Amorite, 80; Assyrian, 112; capital cases in, 80, 134; codes of, 134; contracts in, 81; courts of, 81, 106, 134; decrees in, 80; documents of, 137; edicts in, 80, 112; of Eshnunna, 80; of Hammurabi, 77–81; handbooks of, 97, 124; judges in, 80; at Kanesh, 106; at Kassite Ur, 92; and king, 77–81, 134; and medicine, 97; oaths in, 81; ordeals in, 81, 134; Persian, 142–3; Sumerian phrases in, 72; of Ur-Nammu, 68
Lawrence, T. E., 201
Layard, Austen Henry, 117, 122, 193, 195, 196, 198; crystal lens of, 126; quoted, 6
Lebanon, cedars of, 145
lens, crystal, 126
Letter of Tansar, 169
Levant, and Egypt, 93

libraries, 111, 124–6, 152, 193, 199
Libya, 142
lions, 45, 65, 76, 116; in art, 131, 183
lists, lexical, 33, 41, 66, 97, 125
literacy, 106
literature. *See* Akkadian literature; Arabic literature; Aramaic literature; Parthian literature; Sassanian literature; Sumerian literature
Lloyd, Seton, 203
looting: ancient, 44, 118, 145, 148, 153, 159, 165; at Dur-Sharrukin, 122; at Lagash, 197; modern, 23, 25, 26, 38, 127, 136, 197, 205, 209; at Nineveh, 122; of tablets, 42, 107, 197. *See also* antiquities
Louvre Museum, 44, 57, 78
love: in art, 83; in literature, 54, 63, 82–3, 140
Lower Sea, 55. *See also* Gulf
Lugalzagesi, 48, 51
Lullubi, 56
Lydia, 153

Macedon, 147, 149, 164
Magan, 62
magi, 171
magic, 79, 83, 125, 154, 175; and magic bowls, 175
Magnesia, 164
Mandaeans, 171; language of, 175
Manetho, 152
Mani, 172
Manichaeism, 171, 186
Manishtusu, 54–5
maps, 141
Marcus Aurelius, 166
Marduk: and Assur, 113; and Babylon, 139; as creator, 1, 15, 103; Damascius on, 173; in dream, 133; in *Erra Epic*, 139, 151; and Jesus, 195; and Persians, 142; and *Poem of the Righteous Sufferer*, 98; prayer to, quoted, 129, 132; statue of, 103, 131; temple of, 64, 131, 153, 156, 192

Mari, 73, 75–6, 77, 95; commerce at, 43; as cultural intermediary, 41; destruction of, 75–6; divination at, 95; and Hammurabi, 75–7; and Sargon, 53
marriage, 79–80, 108, 112, 144, 147, 184; contracts for, 141; diplomatic, 94, 103; proposal of, 82
Mary, mother of Jesus, 176, 177
mathematics, 27, 124, 155, 167; texts about, 138
Mecca, 181
Medes, 126–8, 130, 133, 142, 143
Media, 121, 159, 160
medicine, 79, 154, 175, 181; and court physicians, 93; Kassite, 96, 97–8; texts about, 125
Mediterranean Sea: and Assyrians, 111, 113; and Ubaid culture, 14
Megiddo, 99
Meluhha, 62
Merodach-Baladan, 120
Merv, 158
Mesopotamia: legacy of, 167, 182; name of, 6
metallurgy, 45, 121. *See also* bronze; copper; gold; iron; silver; tin
Middle Assyrian empire, 109–12; cylinder seals of, 27
Middle Persian language, 175
minstrels, 37, 54, 65, 83, 163. *See also* music
Mitanni, 93, 99, 106
Mithra, cult of, 171–2
Mithridates I, 158–60
Moab, 113
monkeys, in art, 118
Monophysites, 177
moon god. *See* Nanna-Sin
mosaics, 20–1, 29, 30, 39, 89, 100, 183
Moses, 52
mountains: in art, 56, 79, 89; in literature, 5, 62, 182; and temple names, 48, 63
Muhammad, 190
Mursilis, 86

museums: ancient, 137; Imperial Ottoman, 196; Iraqi provincial, 101. *See also* Berlin Museum; British Museum; Iraq Museum; Louvre Museum
music, 37–8, 67, 83; and singing girls, 93, 112. *See also* harps; minstrels
myrrh, 181
mythology, 125, 194. *See also* religion

Elamite attack on, 102; Kassite, 90; and kingship, 73; Parthian, 100; translation activity at, 97; Sassanian, 179; ziggurat of, 63
Noah's Ark, 192
Numan, 182
number, concept of, 32. *See also* mathematics
Nusku, 110
Nuzi, 99–100

Nabonidus, 132–5, 140, 142, 180
Nabopolassar, 130, 135
Nabu, 151, 168
Nabu-apla-iddina, 135
Nabu-shuma-ukin, 131
Nanaya, 143, 151
Nanna-Sin, 36, 63, 74, 171; and Enheduanna, 53–4; and Nabonidus, 132–3
Nanshe, 42
Napoleon, 193
Naram-Sin, of Akkad, 55–60, 102, 135, 137; title of, 62
Naram-Sin, of Eshnunna, 74
Nebo, 151, 168
Nebuchadnezzar, name of, 145
Nebuchadnezzar I, 102–3
Nebuchadnezzar II, 102, 129–31, 133, 173, 185, 204; and Hanging Gardens, 121–2
Neo-Assyrian Empire, 113–28; seals of, 27
Neo-Hittites, kingdoms of, 113; reliefs of, 116
Nestorians/Nestorius, 177
Nimrud, 115–9, 197, 205; ivories from, 126–8
Nineveh, 105, 147, 160, 193–4, 197; gardens at, 121–2; library at, 124–6, 193, 194; looting at, 122; palace reliefs from, 110, 122–3, 194, 195; Sassanian, 189
Ningal, 19
Ningirsu, 42, 43, 61–2
Nippur, 40, 58, 60, 137; as cult center, 48, 64; destruction of, 86;

oaths: in law, 81; loyalty, 73, 129–30, 160
obsidian, 9, 22
Old Assyrian period, 108
Old Persian language, 193
Oman, 14, 45
omens. *See* divination
oracles, Assyrian, 125
ordeal, in law, 81, 134
Orodes II, 166
Orthodox Christianity, 177–8, 189
ostrich: bird, 27; eggs of, 161
Ostrogoths, 188
Ottoman Empire, 195–6; antiquities law of, 196; museum of, 196

paganism, 171–2
palaces: Assyrian, 112, 121–3, 183; Babylonian, 130; libraries of, 124–6; at Mari, 75; Neo-Hittite, 116; Northwest, 116–9; Parthian, 155; Persian, 145, 147, 183; Sassanian, 169, 179, 183
Palace without Rival, 121–3
Palestine, 130, 164, 173–4
Palmyra, 161
pantheon, 18
Parsua, 142
Parthian language, 159
Parthian literature, 163–4
Parthians, 149, 156–7, 158, 165, 168; archery of, 157; empire of, 159; memory of, 168–9
Pasagardae, 145
Pausanias, 147

Persepolis, 145, 147–8, 167, 192
Persian Empire, 131, 142, 148–9, 156, 167–8, 188; languages of, 115
Persian language, 143
Philip the Arab, 184
philology, Babylonian, 97
Phoenicians, 113; stylistic features of, 127
Pietro della Valle, 192
plaques, 39, 83, 116, 188; of Enheduanna, 53
Plato, 147, 172
Pliny the Elder, 152, 155
Plutarch, 158
Poem of the Righteous Sufferer, 98–9, 126
pollen, analysis of, 5
Polybius, 159
Pompey, 164
population, 30; control of, 50; decline of, 91; growth of, 9, 12; in Uruk period, 13
pork, prohibition of, 116
pottery: and chronology, 11; decoration of, 10, 11, 14, 20; glazed, 45, 100; Ubaid, 14; Uruk, 16, 28, 29; wheel-made, 16
prebends, 140, 153
Procopius, 179, 180
prophecy, at Mari, 95
Ptolemies, 152–3
Ptolemy I Soter, 149
Ptolemy II Philadelphus, 152
Ptolemy V, 193
Ptolemy Ceraunus, 149

queens, 95, 118–9, 121, 130, 151, 174, 180

rainfall, 4, 12, 13
Rassam, Hormuzd, 136, 196–7
rations, 28, 67. *See also* food
Rawlinson, Henry, 193, 195, 197, 198
Red Sea, 30, 180

reliefs: from Assyrian palaces, 110, 116–8, 126, 194, 210; rock, 56, 146, 183, 186, 193
religion: and archaeological periods, 7; in art, 22; and Assyrian rulers, 106; Islamic, 190, 195; Manichaean, 171, 186; Mesopotamian, 17–8; and mythology, 125, 194; pagan, 171–2; in Sassanian Empire, 170–1; and society, 28; Ubaid, 14; Zoroastrian, 170, 178. *See also* Christianity; Judaism; temples
Rich, Claudius, 193
Rim-Sin, of Larsa, 73–4, 76
Rim-Sin, pretender, 85
Rimush, 54–5
rod and ring, 75, 79, 135
Romans, 158, 159, 161, 170, 172; Christianization of, 172, 174, 176; and Parthians, 165, 166; and Sassanians, 168, 170, 180, 184, 186; and Seleucids, 158–9, 164; as sources for Mesopotamian history, 158, 163, 178, 187
Rosetta Stone, 193
Royal Graves. *See* Ur

"Sacred Tree," 117
Safar, Fuad, 204
sages, 102, 151
salinization, 40
Samaria, 113
Samarra ware, 10
Samsuiluna, 85–6, 185
Sanskrit language, 156, 192
Sardanapalus, 114, 130
Sargon, of Akkad, 51–5, 74; legend of, 119, 125; literature about, 65; memory of, 134; statue of, 135
Sargon II, 51, 113, 119–20
Sassan, 169
Sassanian literature, 169
Sassanians: art of, 182–4; and Byzantium, 187–9; as empire, 178–80; 185–7; society of, 178
satrapies, 156

scholarship, 97, 134–5, 151–2. *See also* education; libraries
schools. *See* education
science, Kassite, 94–6. *See also* astronomy; mathematics
scripts, decipherment of, 192
Scyths, 149, 157, 158, 160
Sealand, 5
seals, cylinder, 23–4, 26–7, 182, 191, 206, 209, 210; Akkadian, 36; glass, 100; iconography of, 39; at Jemdet Nasr, 36; at Kanesh, 106–8; Kassite, 88, 90; manufacture of, 67; Middle Assyrian, 110; at Shuruppak, 41–2; of Third Dynasty of Ur, 67; and writing, 56
seals, stamp, 23
Seleucia-on-the-Tigris, 152, 156, 159–60, 166, 179
Seleucid dynasty, 165
Seleucus I Nikator, 148, 149, 156
Semiramis, canal of, 161
Semites, 8, 40, 194; languages of, 71
senmurv, 182–3
Sennacherib, 113, 119–23, 129, 194
Septimus Severus, 161
Seven Wonders of the World, 131
sex, scandal about, 92. *See also* love
Shah-namah, 168–9
Shamash, 58, 79, 95, 111, 135, 171
Shamash-shum-ukin, 129–30
Shamshi-Adad, 73, 74–5, 76, 95, 106; and Assur, 108
Shapur I, 172, 184, 186
Shapur II, 181, 186; in art, 184
Sharkalisharri, 60, 137
Shehna, 74
shell, in art, 37–8
Shibtu, 95
Shinar, 5
Shubat-Enlil, 74
Shubshi-meshre-Shakkan, 98
Shulgi, 62, 64–7, 69, 137; omen of, 96
Shuruppak, 36, 40–2
Shu-Sin, 69
Shutruk-nahhunte, 100–102

Sidon, 113
siege craft, 126
silk, 161, 182
silver, 37, 38, 53, 114; as basis for wealth, 52; for coins, 150, 153; as medium of exchange, 45, 106
Silver Mountains, 53
Sin. *See* Nanna-Sin
Sippar, 58, 135–7, 198
slaves, 54, 81, 141, 144, 178
Smith, George, 194
snakes, 62, 85
society: Akkadian, 59; Amorite, 72, 79–82; Arab, 181; Assyrian, 108, 112, 115; Babylonian, 141–2, 144; Hellenistic, 153–4; Kassite, 87–8, 91; Parthian, 157–8; and royal dependents, 55; Sassanian, 178; stratification of, 27–8; Sumerian, 40, 42
Sotheby's, 210
Standard Inscription, 118
Standard of Ur, 39
statues: Akkadian, 55, 126, 135; cult, 75, 125; Elamite, 114; of Gudea, 61, 155; manufacture of, 67, 76; mutilation of, 126; styles of, 47; of Uruk period, 22; as war booty, 17, 103, 114
stelae: of Assurnasirpal II, 116; multiple copies of, 78; of Naram-Sin, 56–8, 102; of Ur-Nammu, 62; of the Vultures, 43–4, 53, 56
stucco work, 163, 183, 185
Subir, 5
subsistence, and archaeological periods, 9. *See also* food
Sumer: praises of, 66; region of, 5; unification of, 48
Sumer, periodical, 204
Sumerian King List, 39, 51, 61, 72, 108; satirized, 62; updated, 62
Sumerian language, 36, 40, 137, 154, 195; in accounting, 41, 56; at Assur, 111; in inscriptions, 58; in Kassite period, 88, 92, 97; in legal documents, 72; in name-giving, 72, 98

Sumerian literature: and Amorites, 71; authorship of, 54; genres of, 64–7; at Lagash, 61–2; at Larsa, 72; quoted, 10, 13, 19, 21, 31, 33, 43, 45, 54, 63–7, 87; study of, 124; translated into Akkadian, 97

sun god. *See* Shamash

surplus, 28

Suren, 158

Susa: and Alexander the Great, 147; colonization of, 58; destruction of, 114; early writing at, 32; excavations of, 57, 78; and laws of Hammurabi, 78; molded bricks at, 90; Persian, 114

Syr Darya River, 157, 170

Syria: and Amorites, 60; Arab settlement of, 182; Assyrian conquests of, 113; Christian church of, 176; and Euphrates Valley, 1, 4, 6, 166; Hurrians in, 99; merchants from, 108; and Naram-Sin, 55; and Parthians, 160, 163, 165, 166; Sassanian attack on, 184; stylistic features of, 127; Uruk colonization of, 16, 29; ziggurats of, 64

Syriac language, 175, 176

tablets, cuneiform: from Amarna, 93; in Assurbanipal's handwriting, 124; from Ebla, 41–2; excavation of, 197–9; and Herodotus, 131; invention of, 65; from Kanesh, 106; Kassite, 90; from Mari, 75–6; from Nippur, 48; from Nuzi, 99; sale of, 206, 209–10; shapes of, 56; from Shuruppak, 41–2; of Third Dynasty of Ur, 68; from Uruk, 33. *See also* libraries

Talmud, Babylonian, 168, 175

Tatian, 178

taxes, 68, 72, 106, 148, 153, 179

technology, and archaeological periods, 9. *See also* faience; glass; metallurgy

Teima, 133, 180

Tell al-Rimah, 101, 162

Tell Leilan, 74

Tell Razuk, 162

temples, 17–8; access to, 45, 47; of Anu and Adad, 110; archives of, 145; destruction of, in warfare, 42, 102, 139, 145; ideology of, 28; of Ishtar, at Assur, 110; of Ishtar, at Uruk, 88–9, 91; libraries of, 124; management of, 68; of Marduk, 148, 153; Ubaid, 14, 88; Uruk, 17. *See also* architecture; ziggurats

Tepe Gawra, 162

textiles, 123, 141, 154, 182; ceremonial, 117–8; knotted, 183; silk, 183; in trade, 45, 93, 106–8. *See also* clothing

Thaïs, 147

Third Dynasty of Ur, 62–70, 79; at Assur, 106; and literature, 65–6, 84; memory of, 74

Thomas, apostle, 176

Thutmosis III, 99

Tiamat, 103, 175

Tiglath-Pileser I, 103, 111, 125, 193

Tigris River: and Amorites, 71; at Assur, 105; changing course of, 6; creation of, 1, 4; damming of, 204; flooding of, 4, 12; as route, 4; source of, 1; tunnel of, 2, 55; and Upper Zab, 116; and wall of Shu-Sin, 69

tin: source of, 106; trade in, 45, 106

tokens, 32–3. *See also* writing

Tower of Babel, 64, 192

trade, 73–4, 154, 161; Assyrian, 106–8; and Babylon, 58, 77; control of, 72; and Dilmun, 43–4; Sassanian, 179; of Third Dynasty of Ur, 68

Trajan, 161, 166

translation: of astronomical texts, 156; from Greek, 186; Sassanian, 186; from Sumerian, 97

treaties, 99, 103, 104, 158

"Tree of Life," 117
Tukulti-Ninurta I, 109–11, 125;
    death of, 123
Turkey. See Anatolia
Turks, 87, 194
Tyre, 113

Ubaid culture, 13–5, 17, 185; tem-
    ples of, 63
Umma: looting of, 42; as member of
    league, 41; and war with Lagash,
    42, 48
Umm Dabaghiyah, 162
UNESCO Convention on Cultural
    Property, 206
University of Baghdad, 204
University of Chicago, 201
University of Pennsylvania Museum
    of Archaeology and Anthropology,
    200
Upper and Lower Seas, 5
Ur, 40, 137, 200, 202, 205; as cult
    center, 64; decline of, 77, 86; and
    Enheduanna, 53; Kassite, 92;
    kings of, 36–7; and Kish, 42; as
    member of league, 36; and
    Naram-Sin, 59; and Rim-Sin,
    73–4; Royal Graves of, 26, 36–9,
    45, 200; statues from, 46–7; in
    Sumerian King List, 62; ziggurat
    of, 63, 204–5. See also Third
    Dynasty of Ur
Urartu, 113, 119, 126
Urlumma, 42
Ur-Nammu, 62–4
Uruinimgina, 47–8
Uruk, city, 15–9, 20, 21, 28, 40,
    153, 154, 159, 160, 199, 203; and
    antiquities during World War II,
    89; colonization by, 29–30; de-
    cline of, 86; Elamite attack on,
    102; and Gilgamesh, 37, 84–5;
    and Gutians, 62; Kassite, 88;
    kingship of, 39; as member of
    league, 36; and Naram-Sin, 59;
    Sassanian, 179; and Shulgi, 65;
    temple of Ishtar of, 15, 17, 20,

21, 89, 140, 143; temple lands of,
    91; walls of, 21; ziggurat of, 63
Uruk, culture, 15–35; art of, 22–5,
    26, 43; colonies of, 29–30; histor-
    ical memory of, 52; metallurgy
    of, 45
Urukagina, 47–8
Uruk Head, 22–3
Uruk Vase, 22–5, 26, 43
Uta-napishtim, 84–5

Valerian, 186
Veh Ardashir, 179
Venus, planet, 138, 171
Victory Stele of Naram-Sin, 56–8,
    102
villages, earliest, 10–2
Vis and Ramin, 163–4
volcanoes, 4

wall painting, 75, 88, 110, 116
warfare, 39, 130, 144, 153, 157,
    160; archery in, 126; in art,
    118; and Assyrian army, 120,
    195; and booty, 17, 46, 52, 103,
    109, 111, 114, 127, 129, 133,
    148, 153, 159, 165, 166, 180,
    183, 188, 196, 197; chariotry in,
    91; first narrative of, 42; forti-
    fications of, 14, 35, 69; goddess
    of, 18; and Kassites, 86; and mili-
    tary fiefs, 179; professional sol-
    diers for, 91; standing army for,
    52–3
warfare strategy: Assyrian, 109, 113,
    116; Babylonian, 73, 77, 86; Byz-
    antine, 187, 189; Macedonian,
    148, 149; Median, 126; Neo-
    Babylonian, 133; Parthian, 157–8,
    160, 165; Sassanian, 179, 184,
    186, 187
Wari, 5
Washukanni, 99
Wasit, 204
wheat, 13. See also agriculture
winged bulls, 116, 183

winged genius, 27, 127
witchcraft. *See* magic
wool, 9, 13; trade in, 45. *See also*
  rations
Woolley, Leonard, 200–202
writing, invention of, 30–3
writing boards, 137

Xerxes, 147, 174

Yale Babylonian Collection, 107,
  199, 203
Yale University, 203
Yasmah-Adad, 75, 95

Yemen, 181
Yezdigird III, 190

Zab: rivers of, 4; Upper Zab, 116
Zachalias, 155
Zagros: early villages in, 8; Gutians
  in, 60; rock reliefs in, 56; wood-
  lands of, 5
Zakutu, 130
Zedekiah, 130
Zend Avestan, 192
ziggurats, 62–4, 88, 131, 192
Zimri-Lim, 75–6, 95
Zoroaster, 170–1
Zoroastrianism, 170, 178